Tajikistan

the Bradt Travel Guide

Sophie Ibbotson
Max Lovell-Hoare
with Ernest White II

edition
2

www.brad

Bradt T
The Glo

79 802 852 2

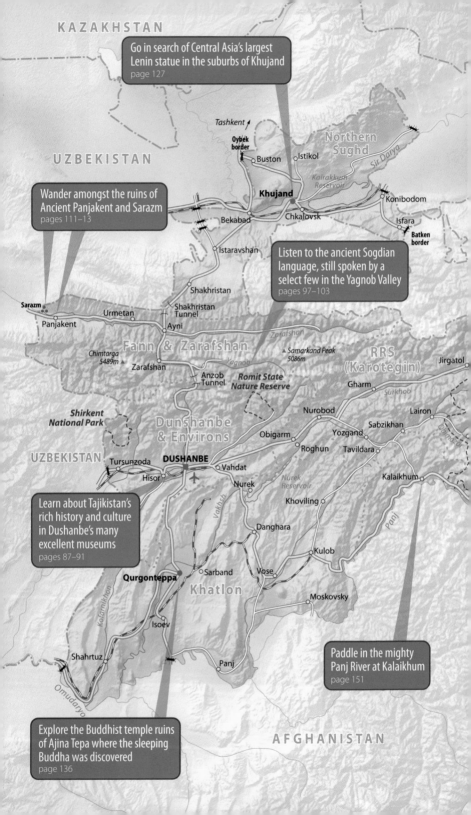

KAZAKHSTAN

Go in search of Central Asia's largest
Lenin statue in the suburbs of Khujand
page 127

UZBEKISTAN

Tashkent ↗

Oybek
border

Buston   Istikol

Northern
Sughd

Sir Darya

Wander amongst the ruins of
Ancient Panjakent and Sarazm
pages 111–13

Khujand

*Kairakkum
Reservoir*

Konibodom

Bekabad   Chkalovsk

Isfara

Batken
border

Istaravshan

Listen to the ancient Sogdian
language, still spoken by a
select few in the Yagnob Valley
pages 97–103

Shakhristan

Sarazm

Panjakent

Urmetan

Shakhristan
Tunnel

Ayni

Zarafshan

RRS
(Karotegin)

Jirgatol

Fann & Zarafshan

*Chimtarga
5489m*

Zarafshan

▲ Samarkand Peak
5086m

Yagnob

Anzob
Tunnel

*Romit State
Nature Reserve*

Gharm

Surkhob

Lairon

Nurobod

Yozgand

Sabzikhan

*Shirkent
National Park*

Dunshanbe
& Environs

Obigarm

Roghun

Tavildara

Panj

Kalaikhum

UZBEKISTAN

Tursunzoda

DUSHANBE

Vahdat

Hisor

Nurek

*Nurek
Reservoir*

Learn about Tajikistan's
rich history and culture
in Dushanbe's many
excellent museums
pages 87–91

Vakhsh

Khoviling

Danghara

Kulob

Qurgonteppa

Sarband

Khatlon

Vose

Moskovsky

Kofarnikhon

Isoev

Shahrtuz

Panj

Paddle in the mighty
Panj River at Kalaikhum
page 151

Omudaryo

Explore the Buddhist temple ruins
of Ajina Tepa where the sleeping
Buddha was discovered
page 136

AFGHANISTAN

KEY
■ Capital city
● Main town
○ Other town
✈ Airport
━━ Main road
━━━ Other road
━━━ Railway
━·━·━ International boundary
······ Regional boundary
- - - National park/reserve

UZBEKISTAN

Bradt

N

0   75km
0   50 miles

KYRGYZSTAN

CHINA

Karamyk
border

Kyzyl Art
Border

Lake
Karokul

Pamir Highway

Obikhingob

Peak Somoni
7495m

P

A

M

I

R

ngvor

Vanj Valley

Tajik National Park

Istiqlol Peak
6940m

Barchadif

Vanj

Bartang Valley

Bartang

Lake
Sarez

Rangkul

Murghab

Murghab

Oksu

Trek to the spectacular but
ultimately doomed Lake Sarez
pages 154–5

Rushon

Patkhor Peak
6083m

Lake
Yashikul

Murghab District

Pamir Highway

Pamir Highway

Bachchor

Alichur

Khorog

West-Central
GBAO

Zorkul
Lake

Pamir

Shaimak

Garm
Chashma

Karl Marx Peak
6723m

Kozidekh

Vrang

AFGHANISTAN

Drive the Pamir Highway across
the 'Roof of the World'
pages 171–4 & 179–83

Ishkashim

Panj

Cleanse your body and soul in the
natural hot springs of Garm Chashma
page 163

PAKISTAN

Tajikistan Don't miss...

Driving the Pamir Highway
Driving across the striking but largely empty Murghab Plateau is the highlight of the Pamir Highway, one of the world's best drives (MK/S) pages 171–83

Buz kashi
The traditional sport of *buz kashi*, also known as dead goat polo, is an adrenalin-fuelled rugby scrum on horseback played in mountain villages across Tajikistan (TK/A) page 178

Camping on the shore of Iskanderkul
This isolated lake, surrounded by the snow-capped peaks of the Fann Mountains, is a favourite among locals and visitors alike
(AP/S) pages 103–4

The ancient Panjakent ruins
This superb archaeological site has earned Panjakent the moniker 'the Pompeii of Central Asia'
(KT) pages 109–12

Trekking on the 'Roof of the World'
The Pamir Mountains offer trekkers a bewildering array of routes and the opportunity to escape all signs of habitation
(JC/DT) pages 180–1

Tajikistan in colour

left   In pride of place on Rudaki is the statue of Ismoili Somoni, the 10th-century emir now considered to be the father of the Tajik nation (T7113/S) page 90

below   The grand Palace of Nations boasts the second-tallest free-standing flagpole in the world at 165m (NN/DT) page 90

bottom   Whether you are looking for souvenirs or simply want to soak up the atmosphere, Dushanbe's Green Bazaar is well worth a visit (IT/A) page 83

above   The Firdausi National Library building incorporates aspects of both Stalinist and Islamic architecture. Since its foundation in 1933 it has expanded to house more than 2.5 million books (SD) page 88

right   Decorated with life-sized statues of Tajik poets and cultural heroes, the Writers' Union Building is one of Dushanbe's most striking constructions (MEP) page 91

below   Dushanbe's Central Park is a well-maintained space with numerous flower beds that come into bloom in early summer. Pictured here, the Arch of Rudaki (T7113/S) page 90

above The domes and minarets of Khujand are a reminder of the medieval influence of Islam in Tajikistan (MM/S) pages 118–27

below The 19th-century fortress of Hisor stands at a strategically important position in the mountains to the west of Dushanbe. As a result, the defences on this site have been razed 21 times since the settlement began (T7113/S) page 92

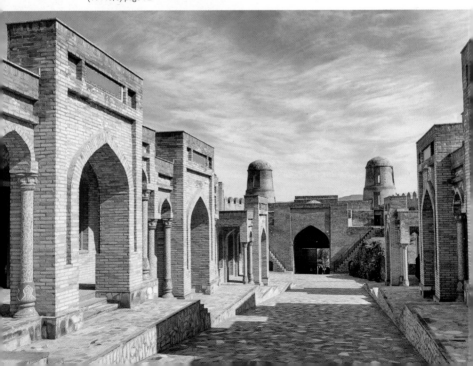

AUTHORS

Sophie Ibbotson and **Max Lovell-Hoare** moved to central Asia in 2008 and lived and worked in the 'Stans for the next five years, advising national governments and promoting investment. They developed the national tourism development strategy for the Kyrgyz Republic, have written and updated guidebooks to Tajikistan, Kyrgyzstan, Uzbekistan and Kazakhstan, and have led numerous expeditions in the region. As lecturers, they have addressed organisations including the Royal Geographical Society, the Royal Asiatic Society and the Royal Society of Asian Affairs, where Sophie is also a member of council. Both Sophie and Max return to central Asia several times a year, and Sophie continues to develop and promote investment and tourism opportunities there.

UPDATER

Ernest White II is a storyteller, explorer, and proponent of reasonable recklessness who has circumnavigated the globe five times. He is the producer and host of global reality-travel television series *Fly Brother*, host of the travel- and culture-focused *Fly Brother Radio Show*, and publisher of multicultural travel portal *FlyBrother.net*. Ernest's writing includes fiction, literary essay, and travel narrative, having been featured in *Time Out London*, *USA Today*, *Ebony*, *The Manifest-Station*, *Sinking City*,

Lakeview Journal, Matador Network, and at TravelChannel.com. He is also nonfiction editor at literary travel journal *Panorama*, former assistant editor at *Time Out São Paulo*, and founding editor of digital men's magazine *Abernathy*. A Florida native, Ernest's obsessions include Indian curry, the city of São Paulo and Rita Hayworth.

AUTHORS' STORY

In fairy tales a hero rides in on a white horse; in Tajikistan he's more likely to be driving a 4x4. We've always considered ourselves to be fairly accomplished overlanders, but Tajikistan's roads (and sometimes lack thereof) have tested us to our limits, and we'd never have completed a fraction of the journeys we've made if it weren't for the kindness of strangers. We've been dug out of the river mud by soldiers, had the dangling bits of our engine cable-tied back into place on the Pamir Highway, and been rescued by the British Embassy car (complete with spare wheel-nut key) at midnight in a car park in Khujand. All our saviours appeared from nowhere, with few of them did we share more than half a dozen words in common, and in every case we were left feeling our new friends were even more grateful than we were for the meeting. In Tajikistan a guest is king.

PUBLISHER'S FOREWORD   *Adrian Phillips, Publishing Director*

Bradt now has several 'Stans' on its list. And Tajikistan is a particularly fascinating 'Stan' – where a mono brow is a sign of beauty and where the national sport is a game of polo played with the body of a dead goat. Beyond such quirky claims to attention, however, the country has epic landscapes and a culture textured by its position at the heart of the Silk Road. I recently met a seasoned traveller who rated cycling the Pamir Highway as her favourite travel experience. Her only complaint was an absence of any decent information to help her along the way; we hope you'll find that Sophie and Max have put that right with this superb guidebook.

Second edition published January 2018
First published 2013

Bradt Travel Guides Ltd
IDC House, The Vale, Chalfont St Peter, Bucks SL9 9RZ, England
www.bradtguides.com
Print edition published in the USA by The Globe Pequot Press Inc,
PO Box 480, Guilford, Connecticut 06437-0480

Text copyright © 2018 Bradt Travel Guides
Updated by Sophie Ibbotson and Ernest White II
Maps copyright © 2018 Bradt Travel Guides Ltd; includes map data © OpenStreetMap contributors
Photographs copyright © 2018 Individual photographers (see below)
Project Managers: Claire Strange and Laura Pidgley
Cover research: Pepi Bluck, Perfect Picture

The authors and publisher have made every effort to ensure the accuracy of the information in this book at the time of going to press. However, they cannot accept any responsibility for any loss, injury or inconvenience resulting from the use of information contained in this guide. All rights reserved. No part of this publication may be reproduced, stored in a retrieval system, or transmitted in any form or by any means, electronic, mechanical, photocopying, recording or otherwise without the prior consent of the publisher. Requests for permission should be addressed to Bradt Travel Guides Ltd in the UK (print and digital editions), or to The Globe Pequot Press Inc in North and South America (print edition only).

ISBN: 978 1 78477 054 9 (print)
e-ISBN: 978 1 78477 508 7 (e-pub)
e-ISBN: 978 1 78477 409 7 (mobi)

British Library Cataloguing in Publication Data
A catalogue record for this book is available from the British Library

Photographs Alamy Stock Photos: Aurora Photos (AP/A), dbimages (DBI/A), ITAR0TASS Photo Agency (IT/A), Theodore Kaye (TK/A), Michael Runkel (MR/A); Shane Dallas (SD); Dreamstime. com: Jakub Cejpek (JC/DT), Nazar Nyazov (NN/DT); www.flpa.co.uk: Imagebroker (I/FLPA), Donald M Jones/Minden Pictures (DMJ/MP/FLPA), Mark Newman (MN/FLPA), Paul Sawer (PS/ FLPA), Jurgen and Christine Sohns (JCS/FLPA); Getty Images: Mattieu Paley (MP/GI); Kalpak Travel (KT); Maximum Exposure Productions (MEP); Shutterstock.com: Viktoria Gaman (VG/S), Michal Knitl (MK/S); mbrand (m/S), Milosz Maslanka (MM/S), Alisher Primkulov (AP/S), Truba 7113 (T7113/S), Nickolay Vinokuravo (NV/S), Abeselom Zerit (AZ/S); SuperStock (SS); Tourism Development Centre, Tajikistan (TDC), Raven Valentine (RV); Wikimedia Commons: www.foto.tj (FTJ/WC)
Front cover Horsemen riding at speed (MP/GI)
Back cover Musician (VG/S); Wakhan Corridor (MR/A)
Title page Hisor fort (SS); snow leopard (AZ/S); Tajik man (SS)

Maps David McCutcheon FBCart.S; relief base map by Nick Rowland FRGS

Typeset by Ian Spick and Dataworks, India
Production managed by Jellyfish Print Solutions; printed in the United Kingdom
Digital conversion by www.dataworks.co.in

Foreword

Robin Jeremy Ord-Smith

I was fortunate to be the British Ambassador to Tajikistan from 2012 to 2015, a position I coveted since 2008 when I first set foot in Dushanbe, glimpsed the magnificent mountains that surround the capital and experienced the warmth of the climate and the people. I have travelled widely through this extraordinary country, over the 'Roof of the World' in the Pamir Mountains to thousand-year-old fortresses in the Wakhan Corridor, across sun-baked southern plains to the border with Afghanistan, and along twisty dirt roads in the Fann Mountains to the verdant Fergana Valley in the north. Throughout, I have been stunned by the beauty of the countryside, the extraordinary wealth of history and the generous hospitality of the Tajik people.

Tajikistan is a young republic, gaining independence from the Soviet Union in 1991, but its historical roots are deep and rich. Standing at the crossroads between east and west, north and south, important arteries of the Silk Road crossed its territory. Modern Tajikistan was once part of the Achaemenid Empire, and was occupied briefly by Alexander the Great as the Graeco-Bactrian Kingdom in the 4th century BC. It also formed part of the Samanid Empire in the 10th century AD (from which the roots of the current Tajik republic originate), was attacked by Mongol hordes in the 14th century and subsequently came under Persian and later Bukharan rule before playing host to some of the most famous incidents of the Great Game. It was later absorbed into the expanding Russian Empire and, in 1929, became part of the USSR. Today, Tajikistan blends all of these historical elements into a unique and fascinating cultural identity that is readily accessible to the visitor in the bazaars of Dushanbe, the mosques of Istaravshan, the remote rural villages where some still speak Sogdian (the language of Alexander the Great) and in Tajik handicrafts, artwork, literature and poetry.

If the stunning mountain scenery and wealth of history have an immediate impact on the visitor, it is the warmth of the Tajik people that never fails to leave a lasting impression. It is difficult to walk through a village without being offered tea and a selection of dried fruits, nuts, biscuits or sweets by welcoming and gracious locals. In my time here, I have been overwhelmed by the generosity of the Tajiks – the old etiquette of the honoured guest is alive and well.

Should the combination of remarkable countryside, fascinating history and lavish hospitality not be enough to entice you, then perhaps the fact that Tajikistan enjoys more than 300 days of sunshine each year might. There has never been a better time than now to visit Tajikistan and I hope this important new travel guide helps you to plan your visit so that you too can experience everything this vibrant country has to offer to its visitors, guests and friends.

Acknowledgements

Travelling in central Asia is always a team effort, and from the Tajik consul in London who issued our first visas to the very last customs official to pass a covetous eye over the Land Rover, we have plenty of people to thank.

For the first edition, Jack Barkley-Smith and Ainura Temiralieva made invaluable contributions. Ben Tavener, Bryn Kewley, Helen Watson, Steve Dew-Jones, Jim O'Brien and Bijan Omrani all wrote great material on their various areas of expertise, and in doing so gave greater breadth and depth to this guide. We are forever indebted to Robin Ord-Smith for the well-timed pizzas and beer in Khujand, and also for his thought-provoking foreword to this guide. Thank you to the Royal Society for Asian Affairs (*www.rsaa.org.uk*) for hosting the *Tajikistan* book launch, and to all our friends for celebrating with us there.

Ernest White II did a sterling job travelling all over Tajikistan for the second edition, and it's to his credit that he jumped at the challenge with such little notice. Thank you for giving *Tajikistan* the TLC it needed to bring everything up to date, and making it ready for the next few years of visitors.

Alovaddin Kalonov of Paramount Journey (*www.paramountjourney.com*), Shagarf Mullo-Abdol of Pamir Silk Travel (*www.pamirsilk.travel*), and Zhandiya Zoolshoeva (*www.pecta.tj*) also gave us a great deal of their time and expertise, especially for the chapters relating to the Pamirs and Zarafshan Mountains, and Huw Thomas, Jan Bakker and Jonathan Hibbert-Hingston provided much-appreciated comments and suggestions. Thank you to you all.

FEEDBACK REQUEST AND UPDATES WEBSITE

At Bradt Travel Guides we're aware that guidebooks start to go out of date on the day they're published – and that you, our readers, are out there in the field doing research of your own. You'll find out before us when a fine new family-run hotel opens or a favourite restaurant changes hands and goes downhill. So why not write and tell us about your experiences? Contact us on ☏ 01753 893444 or e info@bradtguides.com. We will forward emails to the authors, who may post updates on the Bradt website at w bradtupdates.com/tajikistan. Alternatively you can add a review of the book to w bradtguides.com or Amazon.

Contents

Introduction

Tajikistan is the roof of the world. When you first start to read about the country, or talk to people about it, this same cliché pops up time and again. Initially it may seem that such repetition shows a lack of imagination among writers (at least a century of them, and counting), but when you finally come to stand atop a peak in the High Pamir, staring down as a concertina of meringue-like peaks unfolds beneath you, or even swoop down to land on a scheduled flight, holding your breath else the pilot brushes the snow off the mountaintops with the underside of the plane, you too will find the same phrase tripping off your tongue. Tajikistan *is* the roof of the world.

For those visitors with vertigo or for whom battling the elements on the mountainside holds limited appeal, the country does, fortunately, have somewhat more to offer. Its numerous attractions, often hidden away from the well-worn path, together build a picture of a country at a crossroads: one that lies where tectonic plates collide, where the world's fiercest armies fought and most successful merchants traded, and where the tumultuous past and an uncertain future are caught in an interminable, unpredictable embrace.

Nature has been kind to Tajikistan, bestowing the country not only with breathtaking beauty but with a moderate climate too. Mountains and glaciers, lush river valleys and dense forest support a bewildering array of flora and fauna, including the famed (but sadly camera-shy) Marco Polo sheep and the even rarer snow leopard. Hot springs – either the result of geological faults or miracles enacted by ancient holy men – are scattered through the valleys, their warm, mineral-rich waters both a pleasant diversion on a journey, and, for local Muslims, important pilgrimage sites. Alpine meadows bursting with the bright colours of spring flowers create a patchwork rainbow that streaks across the horizon, the pastures welcome picnic spots for road-weary tourists and grazing goats alike.

Tajikistan's rich past has left ample mark on its present. Though the Buddhist temples of Ajina Tepa and Takht-i Sangin are now broken shadows of their former, prestigious selves, walking along the ruined walls here, in ancient Panjakent or in Sarazm, is a poignant reminder that Tajikistan has not always been a remote and isolated place. For much of its past it has been at the centre of the Silk Road, at the meeting point of mighty empires, and as a consequence its people and cities have thrived financially and culturally, drawing strength and the ability to adapt and survive from the cosmopolitan societies that settled here.

The Soviet and post-independence periods are also not without their visual legacies. Though Lenins and Marxes have more often been ousted from their once prominent plinths, a few still stand as reminders of the enduring impact of communism on Tajikistan. Manmade dams and reservoirs, cotton fields, mines and industrial units, all legacies of Soviet planning, still dot the landscape, some contributing to the modern economy but others laid to waste.

In Dushanbe, more than any other city, the desire of President Rahmon to make a statement and to be remembered is clear: the wide, tree-lined streets may date from earlier years, but the architectural statements – the Palace of Nations with its gleaming, golden dome; the world's second-tallest flagpole; and the imposing statue of Ismoili Somoni, flanked by uniformed guards – are all his doing. A quarter-century after independence, the country's cultural identity is still being created, as Tajiks living abroad return to plant new ideas and dreams in timeless soil, and younger generations mature with hope and optimism. Tajikistan is a resilient place, where exceptional beauty is found through every tunnel and mountain pass.

FOLLOW BRADT

For the latest news, special offers and competitions, subscribe to the Bradt newsletter via the website w bradtguides.com and follow Bradt on:

f BradtTravelGuides
🐦 @BradtGuides
📷 @bradtguides
𝒫 bradtguides

HOW TO USE THIS GUIDE

PRICES Prices in this guidebook are given in either US dollars or Tajik somoni. The currency used in each instance is the one that the company or organisation advertises for itself.

WEBSITES
Although all third-party websites were working at the time of going to print, some may cease to function during this edition's lifetime. If a website doesn't work, you might want to check back at another time as they often function intermittently. Alternatively, you can let us know of any website issues by emailing e info@bradtguides.com.

MAPS
Keys and symbols Maps include alphabetical keys covering the locations of those places to stay, eat or drink that are featured in the book. Note that regional maps may not show all hotels and restaurants in the area: other establishments may be located in towns shown on the map.

Grids and grid references Several maps use grid lines to allow easy location of sites. Map grid references are listed in square brackets after the name of the place or site of interest in the text, with page number followed by grid number, eg: [76 C3].

Part One

GENERAL INFORMATION

Location Landlocked country in heart of central Asia
Neighbouring countries Afghanistan, China, Kyrgyzstan and Uzbekistan
Area 144,100km² (55,637 square miles)
Climate Continental, subtropical and semi-arid with some desert areas
Status Republic
Population 8.33 million (2016 est.)
Life expectancy 65 years for men, 71 years for women
Capital Dushanbe (population c822,000)
Other main towns Khorog, Khujand, Qurgonteppa and Kulob
Main exports Aluminium, cotton and foodstuffs
GDP (PPP) US$28.81 billion (2016 est.), GDP (PPP) US$3,000 (2016 est.)
Official languages Tajik and Russian
Religion 90% Muslim (85% Sunni, 5% Ismaili), 10% Russian Orthodox and other minorities
Currency Tajik somoni (TJS)
Exchange rate £1 = TJS11.7; US$1 = TJS8.8; €1 = TJS10.2 (November 2017)
National airline Tajik Air
International dialling code +992
Time GMT+5
Electric voltage 220V, round two-pin plugs
Weights and measures Metric
Flag Horizontal stripes of red, white and green with a golden crown and stars
National anthem *Surudi Milli*
National sports Wrestling, judo, football and *buz kashi*
Public holidays 1 January (New Year's Day), 8 March (International Women's Day), 21–23 March (Navruz), 1 May (International Labour Day), 9 May (Victory Day), 27 June (National Unity Day), 9 September (Independence Day), 6 November (Constitution Day)

SEND US YOUR SNAPS!

We'd love to follow your adventures using our *Tajikistan* guide – why not send us your photos and stories via Twitter (*@BradtGuides*) and Instagram (*@bradtguides*) using the hashtag #Tajikistan. Alternatively, you can upload your photos directly to the gallery on the Tajikistan destination page via our website (w *bradtguides.com/tajikistan*).

1

Background Information

GEOGRAPHY AND CLIMATE

Tajikistan's epic landscapes are the first thing to strike a casual visitor: mountains soar to the heavens, great torrents of foaming water move these same mountains and destroy everything in their path, and silent plateaus, seemingly empty of life, captivate the imagination with their scale and isolation.

GEOGRAPHY Tajikistan is the smallest of the central Asian republics, with a total land mass of just 144,100km² (55,637 square miles). The Pamir-Alay mountain range covers more than half of the country and includes two of the three highest peaks in the former Soviet Union: Ismoili Somoni Peak (7,495m/24,589ft) and Ibn Sina Peak, also called Lenin Peak (7,134m/23,537ft). The Fedchenko Glacier is the largest non-polar glacier in the world.

Tajikistan's glaciers and snow-melt feed numerous mountain lakes, the largest of which is Lake Karakul (see box, below). Major rivers include the Amu Darya (also known as the Oxus), the Syr Darya (or Jaxartes) and the Vakhsh. The Amu Darya and its tributary, the Panj, form much of the western and southern border between Tajikistan and Afghanistan, while the northern and eastern borders with Uzbekistan, Kyrgyzstan and China are much less clearly defined.

Although Tajikistan has a widespread river network but, due to poor soil quality and the steepness of its mountain slopes, only about a quarter of the land area is suitable for farming. The vast majority of this is pasture and meadow, ideal grazing lands rather than fields where food crops can be grown. Commercial farming

LAKE KARAKUL

When British explorers discovered Tajikistan's largest lake in the 19th century, they named it Lake Victoria in honour of the queen and marked it accordingly on their maps. This name fell into disuse during the Soviet period, and it was replaced with the current Kyrgyz name (which means 'black lake').

Karakul stretches 52km across the Pamirs and lies at an altitude of 3,900m (12,800ft). It is divided by a peninsula into two basins, the shallow eastern basin and the significantly deeper western basin.

It is thought that the basins were created by meteor impact some 25 million years ago. Russian scientists have established this by looking at images taken from space. It is believed that the water level was previously significantly higher, perhaps as much as 60m above its present level, and that it flowed into the Panj and then into the Amu Darya. The reduction in water height means that the lake no longer has an outflow and hence it has turned saline.

From the ancient times to the modern, Tajikistan has been a significant metal and mineral producer. By the 9th century AD mining operations in the Karamazar (now in Uzbekistan) and the Pamir Mountains were producing raw silver and worked goods for export along the Silk Road. This both generated revenue and projected Tajik culture beyond its nascent borders.

The products of Tajik mining efforts are mentioned throughout antiquity. The Book of Job speaks of sapphires that contain 'dust of gold', a reference to lapis lazuli from Badakhshan, and Marco Polo writes of the mining of balas ruby, which is still mined south of Andarob. Less valuable, but still present in Tajikistan in large quantities, is coal; Pliny the Elder refers to the mountains of it burning at night. These same coal deposits (still burning) can be seen even today near Rabat (page 104).

With the arrival of the Soviet Union and industrialisation, thousands of mining and smelting specialists were brought to Tajikistan to identify and exploit its mineral resources. They found deposits of everything from silver and gold to uranium, lead and zinc. They also established the country's major aluminium works at Tursunzoda (see box, page 93).

The disintegration of the Soviet Union caused an exodus of skilled workers from Tajikistan, including many of its geologists and mining specialists. The mining and metal extraction industries collapsed. Much of the infrastructure related to mining or processing was destroyed during the civil war, or simply fell into disrepair, and the environmental legacy is marked: in January 2017, the European Bank of Reconstruction and Development (EBRD) signed an agreement with the Tajik government to clean up sites contaminated with uranium tailings, but it will be a long time before the work is done and it is by no means the only contamination issue.

The last decade has seen a slight up-tick in the mining industry. China is investing heavily in the gold sector, and the Beijing-owned Zijin Mining Group has a 75% stake in the Zarafshan concession, which produces around two-thirds of Tajikistan's annual gold output. The core minerals of interest are the following.

GOLD Perennially alluring, gold continues to shine for investors both due to the current high spot price and the reasonably high grades to be found in Tajikistan. Production is increasing year on year, and in 2015 the country's total output was approximately three tonnes. This was the result of joint ventures between foreign companies and local partners (both governmental and private), the largest of which is SP Zarafshan, a Chinese–Tajik venture. Most of the gold is mined in the Sughd province in the north, and in the Pamirs. Most of the mineralogical surveying was done during the Soviet period, but significant newly identified deposits are still being proven.

The Tajik government is aware that it needs to increase its revenues and so has announced that it will look favourably on Western mining juniors (small companies looking to prove new reserves) seeking gold exploration licences. JV Darvaz and

efforts are therefore concentrated in the warmer, more fertile river valleys of Sughd and Khatlon provinces, where you'll see wheat and cotton fields as well as orchards of fruit and nuts.

For administrative purposes Tajikistan is divided into the Sughd, Khatlon and Gorno-Badakhshan Autonomous Oblasts (GBAO), *oblast* being the Russian for province and *viloyat* its Tajik equivalent, and the Region of Republican the Zeravshan Gold Company, both of which are registered in Tajikistan, dominate the gold-mining industry, albeit backed by foreign money and expertise.

SILVER One of the world's most significant proven reserves of silver is placed in the north of Tajikistan near to Kon-i Mansur: there is thought to be as much as 50,000 tonnes below ground, with 49 grams of silver per tonne of ore. It occurs with significant amounts of lead and zinc, though realisation of the full potential of this reserve has yet to occur. The Akdzhilga and Mirhantskiy deposits are the two most likely to be developed, and if they are then Tajikistan will become one of the world's largest producers and exporters of silver.

COAL Despite Tajikistan's own large coal reserves, it remains a net importer of coal and other fossil fuels. This is because although the domestic reserves are suitable for open-pit extraction, they are in logistically challenging locations and so cannot be economically extracted at the present time. Utilisation of these reserves would reduce dependence on neighbouring countries.

OTHER RESOURCES Antimony, arsenic, boron, fluorspar, mercury, molybdenum, natural gas, petroleum, strontium, tin, tungsten and uranium have been, or continue to be, produced in Tajikistan with varying degrees of success. The collapse of the Soviet Union simultaneously destroyed both their traditional marketplace and the skills for their extraction.

Rare earth elements are not as rare as the name suggests, but are widely dispersed throughout the earth's crust. Their extraction in most cases only becomes economic when extracted in parallel with other metals. The US Geological Survey (USGS) is actively promoting, and assisting in, the mining of rare earths in Tajikistan as the USA is aware of the strategic complications for many countries if China continues to enjoy a near monopoly on rare earth extraction and refining. Production of rare earths in Tajikistan is a viable option given its shared geological features with China, and from a political perspective having secured rare earth supplies from a country on China's doorstep might make the USA feel vindicated in its investment.

Looking to the future, although Tajikistan does have significant natural resources, their development is likely to remain slow on account of the logistical challenges of moving goods and equipment in-country, and the unpredictable bureaucracy. The seasonal nature of the hydro-power supplies needs to be resolved to add value to the primary product. Tajikistan's location next to China needs to be more fully exploited for the benefit of the mineral industry. Currently the political will is in place to get some successful mineral extraction projects started, but sovereign risk will continue to be the main deterrent to a long-term view being taken by the mining majors.

Subordination (formerly known as Karotegin), ruled directly from Dushanbe. The provincial capitals of the three oblasts are Khujand, Kulob and Khorog respectively.

CLIMATE Tajikistan's climate is continental, and varies dramatically according to elevation. It is the wettest of the central Asian republics, but again rain and snowfall depend on location, from the relatively dry valleys of Kafiristan and Vakhsh

(500mm a year), to the Fedchenko Glacier, which receives more than 2,200mm of annual snowfall.

Temperatures in Tajikistan's lowlands range on average from −1°C in January to as much as 30°C in July. The climate is arid, and artificial irrigation is required for agriculture. In the eastern Pamirs it is far colder: winter temperatures frequently fall to 20° below freezing, and the average temperature in July is just 5°C.

As the earth's climate changes due to global warming, Tajikistan is on the front line of the struggle. Approximately 30% of the country's glaciers have been lost in the past 70 years, and the rate at which they are melting is accelerating. The glaciers are Tajikistan's primary source of clean drinking water and water for crop irrigation, and they are also the most important resource for the country's hydro-electric power stations. Even a degree increase in average temperatures would have catastrophic consequences for the country.

NATURAL HISTORY AND CONSERVATION

With thanks to Helen Watson for her contributions on flora and fauna

GEOLOGY Tajikistan lies close to the meeting point of the Indian and Eurasian tectonic plates, its mountains the product of a collision between the two some 50 million years ago. The Indian plate is continually inching northward, further pushing up the earth's crust towards the sky, and hence the Pamirs and their sister range, the Himalayas, are still growing.

As a result of this movement Tajikistan is seismically active, and earthquakes are particularly common, particularly in the Pamirs and Tian Shan ranges. In 2016 scientists recorded nine earthquakes stronger than 4 on the Richter scale occurring in Tajikistan, the largest of which happened 130km from Kulob and measured 5.4.

Most of Tajikistan's earthquakes are relatively minor; you may not even feel them. However, there is some concern that the natural dam currently holding back Lake Sarez, a body of water half the size of Lake Geneva, could one day be dislodged by an earthquake in the area, and destroy villages in the valley below with a tidal wave, causing flooding as far downstream as Uzbekistan and Turkmenistan.

Though 19th-century explorers did comment on Tajikistan's geology, the country was only properly surveyed during the Soviet period. Today the Tajikistan Geological Survey (TGS) collaborates with other countries' geological surveys, the ministries of the economy, energy and mines, as well as private companies, to better understand Tajikistan's mineral wealth and to exploit it commercially.

PALAEONTOLOGY Central Asia has its fair share of fascinators from the ancient to the modern, but perhaps the oldest draws for tourists are those from prehistory: fossils and dinosaur footprints. Though not as impressive as Turkmenistan's 'dinosaur plateau' at Koyten Dag Nature Reserve, Tajikistan does have two sites in the Shirkent Valley that are of interest to dinosaur hunters.

Alongside the right tributary of the Shirkent River are the fossilised footprints of *Macrosaurus gravis* (literally the 'heavy kangaroo-anteater'), a dinosaur that may well be unique to this region. Each footprint is around 50cm in diameter, giving a good idea of the scale of the reptiles that created them. You will need a guide to locate the prints, but it's well worth the hike up into the hills.

The second site lies near to Pashmi Kuhna village. Here there are the footprints of a giant Tridactylus, each print being over 70cm in length. You can sit in the depressions formed by the prints. If you look closely at the surrounding rocks you can see giant wave ripples and mollusc shells, reminding us that this now elevated point was once a seashore. It's humbling.

FLORA At the upper limits of vegetation in the Pamirs (4,400m), plants must battle against the extremes of cold and drought. They grow in sparse clumps to conserve warmth, have fleshy leaves to prevent desiccation and large roots to store energy during the winter (eg: *Saxifraga*, *Rhodiola* and *Saussurea* species). In the high valleys, by rivers such as the Murghab, alpine sedge meadows provide grazing for yak and grow a variety of montane flowers such as buttercup, gentian and primrose. Where there is little access to water, plant life is sparse and restricted to clumped prickly species (eg: *Acantholimon*, *Artemisia* and needle grass), which ward off hungry grazers and halophytic species such as the *Saliconia* that can grow in the high levels of salt left by evaporation.

The first trees appear at around 3,500m along the river valleys. Here stands of willow, birch, poplar and tamarisk add a splash of emerald to the ochre landscape. It is very noticeable that the tree growth follows close to riverbanks and manmade irrigation channels. Juniper forest can also be found at this altitude, particularly in the Hisor, Turkestan, and Zarafshan mountains. By around 2,500m broadleaved species appear, such as walnut, maple, plane (chenar), apple and rose.

Evidence from DNA analysis has revealed that wild apple found in the mountains of central Asia is the progenitor of the c7,500 apple varieties that we eat today. It is thought that the plant was carried out of central Asia in the Bronze Age to Mesopotamia where it underwent domestication before eventually being brought to western Europe by the Romans. Apart from walnuts and apples, apricots and cherries grow in abundance. Pistachio, almonds (with stunning pink blossom) and pomegranate are also found in the lower forests (600–1,700m) in southern parts of the country. Mulberry trees often grow in villages and courtyards. The berries, which are white and very sweet, fall in enormous numbers and can often be seen laid out to dry on porches. The leaves of the tree are used in the farming of silkworms.

The tugai forests (300–600m), situated on the banks of the Amu Darya and its tributaries, are some of Tajikistan's most threatened habitats. Poplar, oleaster and tamarisk grow on these warm floodplains along with reed grass, bulrush and liana. The land is often used to grow cotton, because it is easy to irrigate and initially very fertile. Within a few years of conversion, however, it accumulates salt and becomes unusable. This results in more forest being cut down. A number of the tugai fragments have nature reserve status, for example the Tigrovaya Balka reserve on the Vakhsh River.

FAUNA When you think of Tajikistan, you think of the mountains. But among those rugged peaks, grazing in flower-filled meadows alongside the fertile river valleys, is a wealth of wildlife. Everyone hopes to spot the endangered rare mammals such as snow leopard, Marco Polo sheep, ibex and brown bear, but even if these shy creatures remain elusive (or your trip is based on Tajikistan's cities and towns) you can still expect to see birdlife, butterflies, hares, Bactrian camel and domesticated yak.

With its smoky-grey spotted coat, luminous eyes and wide paws for walking on snow, the snow leopard (*Panthera uncia*) is the poster child of Tajikistan's fauna. This is the creature we all hope to see. These magnificent cats roam the highest mountain passes, but are notoriously shy, so it is exceptionally difficult to spot them.

Around 200 snow leopard are thought to be resident in Tajikistan's high mountains, making up around 5% of the world population. Their survival, here as elsewhere, is threatened by habitat loss, depletion of prey and illegal hunting: sadly, although the snow leopard is included on the IUCN (International Union for Conservation of Nature) red list of threatened species, hunters continue to track and kill them for sport.

Snow leopard inhabit alpine and subalpine zones, usually at altitudes over 3,000m. Most individuals in Tajikistan have been recorded in the Murghab District in the Pamirs, so if you do hope to see one, this is the best place to go. META, the Murghab Eco-Tourism Association (page 175), will be your best source of trekking guides. You will need exceptional patience: even spending a week to ten days in the Pamirs, there is no guarantee you will see a snow leopard, though we wish you the best of luck!

Tajikistan is a hot spot for rare mountain ungulate species, namely the mighty Marco Polo sheep, the Central Asian ibex, the Tajik markhor, and the urial (a kind of wild sheep).

The Tajik markhor (*Capra falconeri heptneri*) is a near-threatened species of goat. A beardy creature, it has long corkscrew horns that look like snakes, giving it a rather demonic appearance. Like the ibex, it has an impressive ability to climb cliffs. There may be fewer than 700 markhor left in Tajikistan, and globally fewer than 5,500 spread across isolated regions of the central Asian massif. Markhor sightings in Tajikistan have declined significantly in recent years, and are now only recorded in the Darvaz and Shurabad ranges.

The urial (*Ovis orientalis vignei*) is a species of wild sheep, with long rather ragged fur, which is reddish in colour in summer but fades during the winter months. The male urial has a dark ruff around the neck. Found from Iran to India, urial live on the lower mountain slopes, preferring grassy meadows. Unfortunately so do humans, and the result is that the urial's habitat is being steadily encroached on. The urial subspecies you can see in Tajikistan is the Bukhara urial (*Ovis orientalis bochariensis*), and it tends to live in the mountains along the Amu Darya River.

The central Asian ibex (*Capra sibirica*), also known as the Siberian ibex, is widely distributed across Tajikistan, and hence is the mountain ungulate species you are most like to see. There is a significant population of ibex in the eastern Pamirs, and some also in the Zarafshan and western Pamir ranges. Typically tan in colour, both the male and female ibex have horns, though the horns on the males tend to be larger. The ibex lives above the vegetation line out of choice, but will descend to find food, especially if there has been snowfall.

To learn more about the Marco Polo sheep, see box, page 168.

Sentinel marmot are commonly heard whistling to warn their colonies of danger. These large golden rodents are eaten by land-dwelling carnivores and birds of prey alike (see box, opposite), as are Tolai hares, grey hamsters and Pamiri voles.

Herds of the shaggy domestic yak are a common sight grazing the alpine sedge meadows. If you are lucky you may also encounter Bactrian camels along the Wakhan or the Pamir Highway.

The lower forested environments are home to brown bear, wolf, fox, wild boar, urial sheep and porcupine. The tugai forests are a key habitat for endangered Bukhara red deer, a relative of the European red deer. The tugai was once roamed by the now extinct Caspian tiger and is still home to the golden jackal and striped hyena more commonly found in the neighbouring steppe of Turkmenistan, Afghanistan and Uzbekistan. Goitered gazelle used to live in the tugai and steppe, but in the last century numbers dwindled to virtual extinction through hunting and habitat loss. The steppe tortoise can be found in low-lying open habitats.

Tajikistan is a global hot spot for the Apollo (*Parnassius*) butterfly, with 15 of the world's 40 species represented. Unfortunately, a number of these beautiful white

Around 350 species of birds can be found in the variety of habitats on offer in Tajikistan, which are especially good for mountain and river specialists, as well as being fantastic places to look for many species of birds of prey.

Of the many eagle species found here, white-tailed, short-toed, imperial, golden, Bonelli's and booted eagles will perhaps be highest on birders' lists, as well as the vulnerable Pallas's fish-eagle, Himalayan and Eurasian griffons, Lammergeier and the rare cinereous vulture.

Tajikistan is also home to eight species of owl, including pallid and European scops owls and European eagle-owl.

Lake and river habitats should provide views of many species of goose, duck (including the vulnerable marbled teal and white-headed and ferruginous ducks), plover and sandpiper, as well as some herons, storks and bitterns. Dippers are a common sight.

From the galliformes family, keep your eyes peeled for species such as the chukar, see-see partridge, rock ptarmigan and the beautiful Tibetan and Himalayan snowcocks.

Many species of finch (including black-headed mountain-finch, red-fronted rosefinch and white-winged snowfinch) are possible here.

Areas of woodland offer the opportunity to see some of the country's passeriformes, including a good range of corvids, up to six species of shrike (including long-tailed), and many larks, flycatchers and warblers.

Recently, the large-billed reed warbler was rediscovered in the Pamir Mountains, much to the excitement of scientists and the birding community.

butterflies, with black and red markings, are threatened due to the collecting trade. A new species of Apollo butterfly was discovered in neighbouring Kyrgyzstan in 2006, so it seems likely that there are other species of insects yet to be discovered in this largely inaccessible part of the world.

A large number of the animals mentioned here are rare or elusive, and are unlikely to be spotted by the casual visitor (apart from marmots, ibex, yak and various birds (see box, above). Binoculars, a large dose of patience and preferably the knowledge of a local guide are ingredients to successful wildlife watching.

A good selection of references and links for the wildlife of the Pamirs can be found at w pamirs.org/wildlife.htm.

Wildlife Tajikistan (w *wildlife-tajikistan.org*) is running a long-term conservation project to develop sustainable wildlife management practices in Tajikistan. Its work includes rehabilitating ungulate populations, conserving their ecosystems, and educating local communities about why conservation is important. The following conservation charities have also carried out work in the area: Flora and Fauna International (w *www.fauna-flora.org/explore/tajikistan/*) and the Wildlife Conservation Society (w *wcs.org*).

HISTORY

Tajikistan's location at the crossroads of the Silk Road, its strategic importance as a buffer between mighty empires, and the omnipresent greed for its natural resources, have given it a past more turbulent than most. Time and again the population has bounced back from the brink of annihilation at the hands of history's most barbaric invaders to rebuild their homes, their cities and families, to thrive for a brief period and then to start over again.

ANCIENT HISTORY Man has lived in Tajikistan since the Stone Age. A Neanderthal skull thought to be at least 120,000 years old was discovered in the Afghan part of Badakhshan, and excavations around Murghab in the early 1960s confirm there were already permanent settlements in the Pamirs in the 8th millennium BC.

The Zarafshan Valley has been inhabited for an estimated 5,000 years. The site at Sarazm (pages 112–13) demonstrates the early rise of proto-urbanisation in central Asia. Archaeological surveys there show that it was a sophisticated settlement of infrastructure and homes. The inhabitants would have exploited local mineral resources – Sarazm became an important centre of metallurgy – practised agriculture and produced handicrafts. The people who lived, worked and traded here were connected not only with other communities in the central Asian steppe, but with those as far afield as Mesopotamia and the Indian subcontinent.

Sarazm was abandoned around 2,000 BC when Andronovo settlers arrived in the Zarafshan Valley from the north. Originally a culture from western Siberia, the Andronovo were largely mobile, but did build fortified settlements. The Andronovo kept livestock, including camel, goat, sheep and horse, and agriculture was a vital component of their economy. They had mastered metalwork (copper and bronze) and were fine stonemasons: they buried their dead in stone and wood chambers, accompanied by models of chariots, livestock, weapons and household goods they might need in the afterlife.

The earliest written accounts of life in Tajikistan come from the Greek historian Herodotus (5th century BC) and chroniclers of the Achaemenid Empire (559–330BC). They refer to the existence of **Scythians** (also known as Sakas or Sacae) who inhabited central Asia and southern Russia from the 2nd century BC. Early historians believed that the Scythians were the offspring of Hercules and a snake goddess, but subsequent studies by anthropologists and archaeologists have come to the far more banal conclusion that they were in fact Eurasians and speakers of a language from the Indo-European group. Later Chinese sources suggest these people were blue-eyed and fair. When combined with ethnographic data, it would appear therefore that, prior to the Mongol invasion, Tajikistan's population was more Caucasian in appearance than it is today.

By 500BC much of Tajikistan was under Persian influence: **Cyrus the Great** had sent his forces to Bactria (what is now western Tajikistan, northern Afghanistan and southern Uzbekistan) and lost his own life fighting the Massagtae (a Scythian tribe) on the banks of the Syr Darya in 530BC. Two hundred years later **Darius III**, the last Achaemenid king, would also lose his life in Tajikistan, this time fleeing from the seemingly undefeatable forces of **Alexander the Great**. Alexander subjugated **Sogdiana** (see box, opposite) and married Roxana, daughter of a Sogdian chief.

Alexander died in 323BC and his empire collapsed. The successor states that emerged were first Graeco-Bactrian, then Kushan, Sassanid and Turkic. Greek baths and theatres, Zoroastrian fire temples, Buddhist monasteries and coinage and artworks from as far afield as Egypt, Turkey and India all made their historical mark on Tajikistan for archaeologists to find centuries later.

THE ARRIVAL OF ISLAM Central Asia's cultural diversity and cosmopolitanism was to be brutally crushed, along with many of its inhabitants, with the arrival of Arab invaders in the early 8th century. The Ummayads and, later, the Abbasids, made swift progress through Bukhara (AD709) and Samarkand (AD712), clashing with the Chinese Tang army at the **Battle of Talas** in 751. Their defeat of the Chinese was a game-changer: it made the Arabs the dominant power in the region, and the invaders switched from being raiders to rulers. For the first time since the death of Alexander the Great there was political unity in the region, and with political and economic stability came the opportunity for physical and cultural development.

Arab power waned by the 9th century but Islam was here to stay: the Persian **Samanids** (879–999) ruled Transoxiana (literally 'the lands beyond the Oxus', which approximates to modern-day Tajikistan, Uzbekistan and parts of southern Kazakhstan

THE SOGDIANS

For nearly three centuries, from the start of the 2nd century BC, Silk Road trade was dominated by the Sogdians. An Indo-Iranian-speaking group, they had settled in Transoxiana and controlled both the fertile lands around Samarkand and the mountain passes in what is still called Sughd Province. In short, the area occupied by modern-day Tajikistan and Uzbekistan was the heartland of Sogdiana.

The Sogdian tribes had inhabited this part of central Asia from approximately the 6th century BC. Their early mastery of metalwork meant that even in the Bronze Age they already had substantial regional settlements, including Sarazm (pages 112–13). When the Achaemenid Cyrus the Great invaded Sogdia in 546 BC, he incorporated Sogdian soldiers into his army, as they were respected for their prowess on the battlefield. At the time, the Sogdian population was largely nomadic, and most likely ruled from neighbouring Bactria.

The Sogdians began rising to prominence during the Hellenistic period. Alexander the Great besieged their fortress, the Rock of Ariamazes, and it was here that he first set eyes on Roxana, who would become his wife. This political alliance enabled the Sogdians to rise above other regional powers, as Alexander and Roxana's son, Alexander IV of Macedon, would inherit his father's throne. Intermarriage between Alexander's troops and local women was actively encouraged.

Now politically stabilised, the Sogdians thrived culturally and financially thanks to their location on the Silk Road. Their capital, Maracanda (now Samarkand in Uzbekistan), was a melting pot of ideas: Zoroastrianism, Manichaeism, Nestorian Christianity, and Buddhism were all practised here, though it seems that Zoroastrianism was the dominant faith. The Sogdians were major translators of religious texts, ensuring that religious teachings could be spread wherever the itinerant merchants travelled, and they built many religious structures, not only temples but also shrines.

Chinese manuscripts discovered at Dunhuang suggest the Sogdians had a virtual monopoly on trade between India, China, and Sogdia. The Sogdians were major slave traders, dominating the slave market at Turpan, but they also dealt in silks, ceramics, precious metals and stones, and foodstuffs.

The Sogdians remained politically, culturally and economically influential in the region until the Arab conquests in the early 8th century. Many native Sogdians had already converted to Islam, and their military was unable to hold back the superior forces of the Abbasid Caliphate. Pockets of Sogdian culture did survive, and in spite of attempts to eradicate Sogdian speakers entirely in the 20th century, their descendants and traditions do continue in Tajikistan's Yagnob Valley (pages 97–103).

The 'Great Game' is the term applied to the long-term contest between the British and Russians for influence in central Asia, and particularly Afghanistan, during the 19th and into the early 20th century.

Throughout the 1800s, the British Empire in India pushed its frontiers northwest through Sindh and the Punjab, gradually taking the area of modern-day Pakistan under its control. Similarly, the Russian Empire annexed huge swathes of territory in central Asia. This land was made up of a number of emirates based around the old Silk Road cities such as Bukhara, Samarkand and Khiva. Most of the area that comprises modern-day Tajikistan was dependent on the Emirate of Bukhara, which was taken into Russian control at the end of the 1860s.

With this territorial expansion, it became obvious that a major problem was looming: it was not clear where the two empires would meet. Much of Afghanistan and central Asia was little known to Western cartographers, and the lack of certainty as to where they might establish their frontiers gave rise to deep suspicion. On top of this, each side coveted the other's possessions in Asia. The British were eager to gain new markets for their manufactures in the old emirates. The Russians equally wished to lay their hands on British India and access to the Indian Ocean. They regarded these objectives as the ultimate prize.

The Great Game is also commonly known as the 'Tournament of Shadows', a phrase that gives accurate flavour to this period in central Asian history. The conflict never came to outright war between Britain and Russia, but nevertheless their agents, explorers and spies fervently competed throughout the region, racing to explore and map out the terrain, win over native allies and find ways of preserving and extending their nations' influence. Bearing in mind that Britain and Russia were also frequently at loggerheads in Europe, each would attempt to frighten the other into thinking that an outright attack in Asia was being planned, thereby tying up their military resources and wealth from use in the European theatre.

This is not to say that actual war was not a part of the Great Game. Britain's primary strategic interest in the 19th century was the desire to find a frontier that could securely be defended against Russia: Britain invaded Afghanistan in the First Afghan War (1838–42) and again in the Second Afghan War (1878–80).

and Kyrgyzstan) from their capital in Bukhara. Persian replaced the Bactrian and Sogdian languages, Islam was the prevalent religion, and Persian culture flourished. Abu Ali ibn Sina (known to Europeans as Avicenna), the founder of modern medicine, the great astronomer al-Biruni, and the poets Rudaki and Firdausi were all sons of the Samanid Empire. The cities of Bukhara and Samarkand – both ethnically and culturally Tajik, though now within Uzbekistan – reached their cultural zenith.

This cultural golden age crashed unceremoniously with the arrival of the Turkic **Ghaznavids** in 999. They fought bitter turf wars with the Karakhanids and Seljuks, frequently burning everything in their wake. But the worst was yet to come.

Temujin (Genghis Khan) began to ride west from the Altai in 1219. All those who stood in his way were destroyed. In Khujand the unfortunate governor had molten silver poured into his eyes as punishment for his city's resistance; the men of Khujand were butchered without exception, and the women and children sold as slaves. Many regional urban centres were destroyed, never to recover.

Genghis Khan's supposed descendant, **Timur** (also known as Tamerlane), caused similar upheaval in the late 14th and early 15th centuries, slaughtering civilians and

After 1880, the British came to terms with Afghanistan. They allowed a strongman named Abdur Rahman to take control, but the British themselves controlled Afghanistan's foreign policy. While this made the chances of a Russian attack through Afghanistan unlikely, the British were still worried about the Pamir Mountains. Strategically they were of vital importance, standing at the meeting place of the British, Russian and Chinese empires. Yet even by the latter part of the 19th century, they were still imperfectly known. At first, the British feared it was possible for Russia to march an army over the Pamirs into British India. However, as it became clear with further exploration that the difficulty of its passes would not allow this, the threat from Russia still did not recede. At the end of the 1880s, Russian agents searched out ways they could get through the Pamirs to towns on the very edge of British India – Gilgit, Hunza and Chitral – and made attempts to win over their rulers against the British.

It was in this context that one of the more famous encounters of the Great Game took place. In 1891, the British explorer and spy Francis Younghusband encountered a Russian colonel named Yanov in the isolated wilderness of Boza-i Gumbad on the northern fringe of the Wakhan Corridor. Being officers and gentlemen they greeted each other cordially in the frozen wastes and shared an excellent dinner, supplied by Yanov, washed down with vodka, wines and brandy. Over their aperitifs, however, Yanov made it clear that he was present with a Cossack detachment to annex large sections of the Pamirs that the British regarded as belonging to Afghanistan and China. Such an action would bring British territory face to face with Russia.

Three days after having shared dinner, Yanov was given the task of expelling Younghusband from what the Russians now regarded as their dominion, something he did with regret. However, the news of Younghusband's expulsion caused an outcry in London, and Russia withdrew from large parts of the territory they had just claimed. After the British had secured Gilgit, Hunza and Chitral against Russian intrigue, they came to a final border agreement with Russia in 1895. This finally fixed the frontier between them above the Wakhan Corridor, which itself became an Afghan buffer zone to prevent British and Russian lands from touching. This border, forged in the heat of the Great Game, was later inherited by Tajikistan and is still in operation today.

soldiers alike as he built up an empire stretching from Mesopotamia to the Indus Valley. Central Asia was Timur's birthplace and the empire's political, ideological and cultural heartland, and he revived the fortunes of Samarkand by designating it as his capital and developing it as a centre for the arts.

The **Timurid** Empire collapsed not long after Timur's death, though the Mughal Empire in India was one of its genetic and ideological descendants. Tajikistan endured a succession of Turkic rulers, including those of the **Shaybanid** and **Astrakhanid** dynasties. It is of note that, unlike the neighbouring peoples in central Asia, the Tajiks are ethically, culturally and linguistically Persians, not Turkic tribes, so this was another era characterised by foreign dominance.

THE KHANATES AND IMPERIAL RUSSIA   By the 18th century three khanates (Turco-Mongol kingdoms ruled over by a khan) controlled the bulk of central Asia: the **Kungrats of Khiva,** the **Mangits** of Bukhara, and the **Mins** of Kokand in the Fergana Valley. The Khan of Kokand's territory stretched deep into the Tian Shan Mountains and northern Tajikistan.

Kokand was famed for its slave markets and the despotism of its rulers. Merchant caravans were frequently raided, their goods stolen and their owners sold. Kokand's territory was expanded with the aid of a mercenary army, and both British and Russian travellers recorded with shock the viciousness of the regime they encountered. This brutality was to be the khans' undoing, however: the people rebelled and civil war seriously weakened the state. Tsarist Russia advanced into the breach.

Russia began moving into central Asia from the mid-1860s. Tashkent fell in 1865, swiftly followed by Bukhara in 1867 and Samarkand in 1868. Kokand became a Russian vassal state the same year thanks to a commercial treaty, its khan merely the titular head of his territory. He was forced into exile in 1875 and Tsar Alexander II brought Kokand and its people under his direct control. Russian and European migrants flooded south, and the arrival of the railways tied central Asia to Moscow.

Imperial Russia began the slow modernisation of Tajikistan, and the direction of development was largely linked to Russia's own economic needs. The American Civil War had cut off cotton imports from the Americas, so Russia needed new suppliers. From the 1870s onwards, they began to introduce industrialised agricultural methods, and to convert grain production to cotton.

The Russians had a dramatic military superiority to the predominantly poor, tribal groups they encountered in Tajikistan, so maintaining control was of little difficulty. There were relatively few occasions when the Tajiks resisted and rebelled (notably in Jadidist uprisings in Kokand and Khujand in 1910, 1913 and 1916). Treaties and opening areas to trade was more effective than open warfare.

THE SOVIET UNION Tajikistan was not an immediate convert to communism. After the 1917 Bolshevik revolution, White Russians had fled south, the indigenous *basmachi* movement (see box, opposite) fought a determined war of resistance, and a short-lived independent state was formed by young, Jadid-influenced nationalists in Kokand.

In the early years of Soviet control, it was uncertain where Tajikistan would lie. It was first of all part of the **Turkestan Soviet Socialist Republic** (1918–24), then an autonomous satellite to the Uzbek SSR (1924–29), and only in 1929 was the Tajik state upgraded to an SSR in its own right. Although Stalin theoretically divided central Asia on ethnic-linguistic lines, the **Tajik SSR** was a grotesquely deformed beast, with the Tajik-majority cities of Bukhara and Samarkand given to Uzbekistan, the Uzbek city of Khujand appended to Tajikistan, and the Tajik exclave of Vorukh entirely surrounded by Kyrgyzstan's sovereign territory.

Soviet rule was a mixed bag for Tajikistan. Around 10,000 people were expelled from the Communist Party of Tajikistan during Stalin's purges of the 1930s, and ethnic Russians typically replaced Tajiks in positions of power. One-sixth of the population was conscripted into the Soviet army during World War II, and between 60,000 and 120,000 soldiers – out of a national population of 1.5 million – are thought to have died during the conflict.

But on the other hand, the country developed rapidly. Agriculture was dragged more or less into the 20th century, and living standards improved, though Tajikistan did lag behind the other SSRs by almost every development index. Tajikistan did industrialise, in particular in the mining sector. The majority of the population became literate and, for the first time, Tajik women entered the workplace. The country became economically, culturally and linguistically linked to a global superpower. The downsides were political repression and purges, forced collectivisation leading to famine, and environmental damage, the consequences of which are still being felt.

THE BASMACHI

The roots of the Basmachi lay in the forced conscription of central Asian Muslims by the Russian army towards the end of World War I. Treated like animals, the potential conscripts resisted, attacking Russian civilians as well as militias. The Russian response was brutal: whole villages were massacred and their property burned to prevent any survivors' return. Many more families died fleeing across the mountains to China.

The Basmachi developed largely as a Muslim resistance force against the 'godless' Bolsheviks. In Tajikistan, they were led by Ibrahim Bek, a peasant who bore the mighty moniker Commander in Chief of the Armies of Islam. They were supported by White Russians and even British agents keen to stem the rise of Russian influence in central Asia.

Bek's Basmachi ambushed Red Army troops with a large but unsophisticated guerrilla force. Every violent reprisal served only to swell his ranks with yet more disgruntled Tajiks, ordinary people who realised their lifestyle and livelihoods were under threat. Their apparent strength attracted the services of the Turkish general Enver Pasha (see box, page 143), they overpowered the Russian garrison at Dushanbe and seemed a genuine force to be reckoned with.

It was not to be. Infighting and poor communication broke the Basmachi. The Red Army retook their garrison and began an effective propaganda campaign that suggested the Basmachi were Islamic extremists and backward. Running out of money and swiftly losing support, Bek fled with 50 followers across the river to Afghanistan in June 1926. When he returned to Tajikistan five years later, Bek lasted just two months: he was captured by local police, found guilty of armed rebellion and summarily executed. The Basmachi movement in Tajikistan died with him.

INDEPENDENCE AND THE CIVIL WAR Independence came to Tajikistan suddenly and unexpectedly in 1991. The failed coup in Moscow triggered declarations of independence in other central Asian states and Tajikistan followed suit. **Rahmon Nabiev**, First Secretary of the Communist Party of Tajikistan, was elected as the country's first president but he lacked widespread support away from his power base in Khujand, and anti-government protests in 1992 escalated into full-scale civil war.

Tajikistan was deeply divided along clan lines, and each clan had its own geographical stronghold. The Khujandis (Leninabadis), Kulobis, Garmis, Pamiris and the clans centred around Qurgonteppa all struggled for eminence, and their methods were brutal: scorched earth policies, ethnic cleansing and deliberately causing famine. More than 60,000 people died, and half a million fled their homes.

When the **peace agreement** was finally signed in 1997, Tajikistan was on its knees. The country's GDP had shrunk by 70% and infrastructure was in tatters. **Emomali Rahmon** (see box, page 18), a native of Danghara sworn in as president after unopposed elections in 1992 and again in 1994, was forced to co-operate with the opposition leader Sayid Abdullo Nuri in a new power-sharing organisation, the National Reconciliation Commission. Rahmon again won controversial elections in 2006 and 2013, with 79% and 84% of the vote, respectively. Though the country recently celebrated 25 years of freedom from direct Russian control, over 10% of the population is dependent on Russia for employment and an even larger number are dependent on remittances sent home. The people of Tajikistan soldier on.

GOVERNMENT AND POLITICS

Tajikistan is a presidential republic: the president is both head of state and head of government. He appoints the prime minister (a largely ceremonial post) and members of government. Legislative power is divided between the executive and a bicameral parliament.

Tajikistan's 2003 constitution states that the president and parliament are to be democratically elected and that the president may serve a maximum of two seven-year terms. The reality is that though concessions were made to the opposition following the end of the civil war (most importantly a guarantee that the **United Tajik Opposition** would occupy 30% of government positions), Tajikistan is now in effect a one-party state in which the president's party, the **People's Democratic Party of Tajikistan (PDP)**, has almost total control. OSCE (Organization for Security and Co-operation in Europe) and other international election monitoring bodies do not consider Tajikistan's elections to be free and fair, and restrictions on the press (including foreign news websites) make it difficult for opposition parties and candidates to have their voices heard. The president controls the Central Election Commission and, therefore, has substantial influence over both the registration of parties and candidates and election procedures.

The judiciary has nominal independence but no actual power to enforce rule of law. As a court decreed in 2006 that President Rahmon's first two presidential terms did not in fact count, and his reign is continually extended through referendums and decree, he is likely to remain in power until he either dies or decides to step down (see box, page 18).

Tajikistan is a member of several international organisations, including the UN, NATO, OSCE, IMF and the World Bank. More locally, Tajikistan belongs to the CIS Customs Union, CSTO and the Shanghai Cooperation Organisation. The country still has a strong reliance, both military and economic, on Russia, and increasingly with China, too. Tajikistan has an uneasy relationship with its neighbours due to various border disputes and ongoing concern about cross-border security and the narcotics trade.

ECONOMY

The combination of the fall of the Soviet Union and the ensuing civil war spelled economic disaster for Tajikistan. In less than a decade it went from being part of a global superpower to one of the poorest 30 countries on earth. Some 70% of the population still lives on less than US$2 a day, infrastructure is crumbling, and foreign investors are put off by red tape, an unpredictable tax regime and rampant corruption. Public debt in 2016 equalled 35% of the country's GDP and some one million Tajiks work abroad, mostly in Russia, due to lack of employment opportunities at home.

Prior to the global economic downturn, the Tajik economy was growing at around 8% a year, and the country's substantial mineral reserves (see box, pages 4–5) are ripe for exploitation. But with the Russian and Chinese economies in the doldrums, the dollar value of remittances sent by Tajiks in Russia dropped by over 65% in 2015 and commodities continue to drop in price.

Tajikistan's largest export is aluminium, and a single aluminium works at Tursunzoda (the third-largest aluminium producer in the world) reputedly consumes 40% of the country's electricity. Production methods are outdated (technology from the 1970s is still the industry's staple) but this single factory still accounts for more than 50% of Tajikistan's export revenues. For greater detail, see box, page 93.

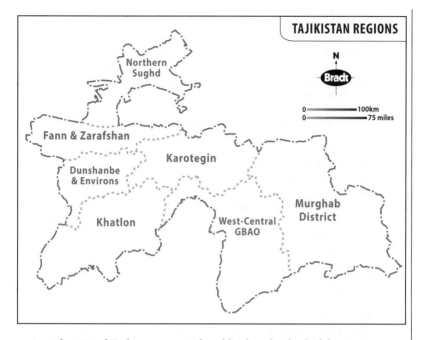

N

Bradt

0 ▬▬▬▬▬▬▬ 100km
0 ▬▬▬▬▬▬▬ 75 miles

Northern Sughd

Fann & Zarafshan

Karotegin

Dunshanbe & Environs

Khatlon

West-Central GBAO

Murghab District

A modest 7% of Tajikistan is agricultural land, and a third of this is given over to cotton production. Cotton is a water-intensive crop and, as in neighbouring Uzbekistan, the government has been criticised for using forced labour to harvest the crop. Other agricultural produce includes fruits (in particular melons, grapes, apricots and apples), nuts, vegetables and small quantities of wheat, barley and tobacco.

For information on Tajikistan's hydro-power production, see box, page 148.

PEOPLE

Inhabited at least since the Neolithic period and situated at the meeting point of numerous Silk Roads, it should come as little surprise that Tajikistan is a melting pot of ethnicities and that even those who claim to belong to a single ethnic group may in fact have a diverse genetic heritage.

TAJIKS Around 84.3% of Tajikistan's population are ethnically Tajik and give the country its name. They are by no means the only Tajiks, however: considerably more Tajiks actually live in Afghanistan than in Tajikistan (an estimated 8 million) due to the annexation of Badakhshan in the 18th century and the mass exodus to escape Soviet persecutions in the 1920s and 1930s, and the cities of Bukhara and Samarkand (both now in Uzbekistan) also have Tajik-majority populations.

Tajiks are essentially Persians, the division between the two groups being the result of a 20th-century political decision (page 14). They consider themselves to be the oldest ethnic group in central Asia and trace their ancestry right back to the Bactrians and Sogdians (see box, page 11). The Tajiks are not a homogeneous group, however, and are deeply divided on clan-based lines with strong regional affiliations and blood ties.

At independence in 1991 few people had heard of Emomali Rahmon (or Rahmonov in Russian), and even fewer could have anticipated his meteoric rise to power. Born to a peasant family in Danghara, Khatlon Province in 1952, he served for three years in the Pacific Navy Military Force in the early 1970s, then worked on a collective farm. He took a degree in economics from the Tajik State National University in 1982, then held a series of bureaucratic roles, working in party bodies and building up significant support in the Kulob region.

Shortly before independence, Rahmon was elected as People's Deputy to the Supreme Council of the Tajik SSR. Qahhor Mahkamov became Tajikistan's first president in November 1990, followed in quick succession by Rahmon Nabiev and acting president Akbarsho Iskandarov. It was only when Iskandarov resigned in a bid to quell growing civil unrest that Rahmon, by then Chairman of the Executive Committee of the Council of the People's Deputies of Kulob Province, was unceremoniously dumped in the driving seat. He was elected to the presidency in November 1992, and holds the role to the present day.

Rahmon inherited a poisoned chalice: Tajikistan's civil war was just beginning. In the five years of war he masterfully survived an assassination attempt and two attempted coups. When elections finally took place in 1999, seven years after he began running the country, he polled 97% of the vote. Given the absence of opposition, however, this outcome was little surprise.

Today, President Rahmon divides opinion. While the international community periodically levels accusations of corruption and human rights abuses against him, it nonetheless recognises his role in maintaining a relatively stable buffer state against Islamic extremists pushed north from Afghanistan. In Tajikistan itself, he remains reasonably popular, probably in equal parts due to government policies, state propaganda, the absence of a viable alternative, and a fervent desire not to return to the bloodshed of the civil war years.

In a series of decrees and referendums in 2015 and 2016, Rahmon secured lifelong immunity from prosecution, ironclad veto power over state decisions, the abolition of presidential term limits, and the title 'Founder of Peace and Unity, Leader of the Nation'. Two of Rahmon's children are senior officials in his government, and it is assumed that his son, Rustam Emomali (who his father has appointed as Mayor of Dushanbe) will ultimately succeed him.

UZBEKS The Uzbeks are a Turkic people who today comprise around 13.8% of Tajikistan's population. They are mostly found in the west of Tajikistan around Hisor and Vakhsh, and also in the northern patchwork of territories that is the Fergana Valley (pages 115–30). It is likely they originated in southern Siberia and the Altai Mountains and came south in the wake of the Mongols in the early Medieval period. The Uzbek community tends to be more urbanised than other ethnic groups, probably due to their history of conquest and trade in place of nomadism.

KYRGYZ An estimated 0.8% of Tajikistan's population are Kyrgyz, and most of them live in the eastern Pamir around Murghab, with another smaller group in the Wakhan Corridor. The origins of the Kyrgyz are distinctly hazy (indeed sources as late as the 19th century tended not to differentiate between Kyrgyz and Kazakh clans) but it is likely that, as with the Uzbeks, they migrated to central Asia from Siberia between the 10th and 15th centuries. The Kyrgyz language is Turkic and, though a few nomads do retain their traditional lifestyle, the majority of the population was forced to become sedentary (with great loss of life) by the Soviets.

RUSSIANS In the late 1980s Russians and other Slavic groups comprised around 10% of Tajikistan's population. Today they are little over 0.5% of the population as many people returned 'home', even if they were born in Tajikistan, upon the break-up of the Soviet Union or fled to escape the violence of the civil war. The remaining Russian population is mainly based in Dushanbe (formerly Stalinabad) and Khujand (formerly Leninabad).

OTHER ETHNIC GROUPS The Soviet policy of deporting subversive and other undesirable elements to central Asia (the alternative place of exile to Siberia), mixed with a few self-orchestrated migrations, has left Tajikistan with notable populations of Koreans (more than half a million were deported to the region during World War II), Volga Germans, Poles, Ukrainians, Dungans, Uighurs and even Kurds. Afghans have also fled across the border to escape the violence and to seek work. Though these groups have frequently intermarried, and many have now emigrated, it is still possible to hear snatches of their languages and, more importantly for those fed up with the ubiquitous *shashlik*, to feast on their various cuisines.

LANGUAGE

Tajikistan's constitution states that 'The state language of Tajikistan is Tajik. Russian is the language of inter-ethnic communication.' A number of other languages are also spoken by minority groups, among them various Pamiri dialects, Kyrgyz, German and Yagnobi, the closest living language to ancient Sogdian.

TAJIK Tajik is an Indo-European language closely linked to Persian and Dari, and hence these three languages have a shared literary heritage. Unlike most central Asian languages, it is not related to Turkish. From the 9th century Tajik was written in a modified version of the Perso-Arabic script (it had previously been written in Sogdian), and the Arab invasions of this time account for its Arabic loan words. It was only with Stalin's division of central Asia in the 1920s that Tajik began to be seen as a linguistic entity distinct from Persian.

Tajik was designated as the state language of the Tajik SSR in 1929. For the first decade, it was written in a modified Latin script, but in 1939 it was again replaced, this time by Cyrillic. Over the course of the 20th century Tajik has acquired a significant amount of Russian vocabulary, in particular technical terms for which there is no immediately obvious Persian root.

Today an estimated two-thirds of Tajikistan's population speak Tajik as their mother tongue and it is the main language of education.

RUSSIAN Even 25 years after independence, Russian remains the lingua franca of central Asia, and it has been reintroduced as a compulsory part of the school curriculum in Tajikistan. It remains the language of government, of academia and of any technical conversation, and a knowledge of Russian still provides a cultural connection with (and, more importantly, the ability to work in) other parts of the former Soviet Union.

ZABON DONI JAHON DONI **(KNOW LANGUAGE, KNOW THE WORLD)** Proverbs give you an important insight into a country and how its people think. What is more, learning just a few and being able to use them in conversation shows your host that you are taking an active interest in their culture, their country and their language. Here are a few of our favourites:

- One who is always laughing is a fool, but the one who does not laugh is unhappy.
- Anyone who has sown the seed of evil opens the gates of his death.
- He who stole the eggs will steal the donkey.
- The walls have mice, and the mice have ears.
- A sick horse can no longer gallop.
- A person's navel is on his belly, while the world's navel is on the Pamirs.
- If you sit with the moon you become the moon. If you sit in a *deg* (cooking pot) you become black.
- The sun cannot be covered with a skirt.

PAMIRI LANGUAGES In the Pamirs it can seem that every valley has its own language, and this is not far from the truth. The linguistic diversity of the region has attracted academics since the late 19th century when it caught the attention of Russian and British explorers. It was investigated more seriously by Soviet scholars and a Department of Pamir Languages was established in the Dushanbe Institute for Language and Literature in 1967. It continues to undertake research in and around Khorog, to where it moved in the early 1990s.

Many of the Pamiri languages derive from ancient Iranian, though this does not mean that they are mutually intelligible. They are predominantly oral; the only alphabet developed for Shughni, for example, was banned in 1939, and, in any case, was never widely used.

In the eastern Pamirs, particularly around Murghab, Kyrgyz is widely spoken, though typically in addition to Tajik or Russian, and it is also taught in schools. Kyrgyz is a Turkic language also written in the Cyrillic script.

See also *Appendix 1, Language*, pages 184–6.

RELIGION

The Tajik constitution allows for freedom of religion, but since 2009 **Sunni Islam** has been recognised as the country's official religion. Tajikistan is, in fact, the only former Soviet state to have an official religion due to widespread suppression of all religions during the communist period.

Around 85% of Tajikistan's population is Sunni (at least on paper), and it has been the dominant religion since the time of the Arab invasions in the 8th century. Most of these Muslims follow the Hanafi school, and in 2009 the country hosted an international symposium to commemorate Abu Hanifala's teachings.

Tajikistan also has a small number of **Shia Muslims** (about 5% of the total population) who belong to the Ismaili sect. There have been Ismailis in Tajikistan (predominantly in the Pamirs where they fled to escape persecution) since the early 10th century, and they follow the religious leadership of the Aga Khan (see box, page 21).

After Muslims, the next largest religious group in Tajikistan are **Christians**, most of whom are **Russian Orthodox**. The Christian community decreased significantly in the 1990s with the exodus of Russians and Ukrainians, but the St Nicholas Cathedral in Dushanbe continues to serve the city's adherents. Tajikistan also has a very small number of **Catholics** (mostly of German origin), **Baptists, Gregorians, Zoroastrians** and **Jews**, many of whose ancestors were deported to central Asia by Stalin.

Communism was supposed to supplant religion during the Soviet period, but attempts to secularise Tajik society were less successful than elsewhere in the USSR and many people retained their faith in private even if they publicly claimed to be atheist. The post-independence years have seen a marked rise in religious practice, including mosque building and the reopening of *madrasas*, which has caused concern among the political elite and the international community. Fear of Islamic extremists was a key component of Tajikistan's civil war (page 15), and the government remains extremely concerned about any religious group that might become an alternative centre of power.

EDUCATION

The official **literacy rate** in Tajikistan is 99.8%, a legacy of the effective, if somewhat narrow, curriculum implemented across the Soviet Union. Since independence, however, it is likely that literacy levels have dropped significantly for the reasons outlined below, though this has not been recognised in government figures.

State education in Tajikistan comprises four years of primary school (from the age of seven) and five years of secondary school, with an optional two final years for those aged 17–19. Classes are taught in Tajik, but since 2003 there has once again been mandatory teaching in Russian too.

Educational standards have been falling for several reasons, many of them intrinsically linked to Tajikistan's economic and security problems. Teachers earn, on average, just US$56 a month and many supplement their income with other forms of employment or by taking bribes from students. There is an extreme shortage of qualified teachers, because those who have graduated from university tend to leave the country to find better-paid work elsewhere. One-fifth of all school buildings were destroyed during the civil war and those that remain are in a poor state of repair and underequipped. Those resources they do have are decades out of date.

THE AGA KHAN

If you were asked to pick out from a crowd in South Kensington the spiritual leader of the Ismailis, an obscure Shia sect with a significant population in the Pamirs, a Swiss-born businessman and horse breeder would probably not be your immediate choice. His Highness Karim al-Hussain Aga Khan (b1936) is full of surprises.

'Aga Khan' is the hereditary title of the imam of the Ismaili community, a Shia denomination with around ten million adherents, the majority of whom live in the Pamirs, Afghanistan and northern Pakistan. The current Aga Khan is the 49th imam and claims descent from the Prophet's son-in-law, Ali.

In his 60 years as Aga Khan (he succeeded his grandfather at the age of 20), Karim has founded both the Aga Khan Development Network (AKDN) and the Aga Khan Trust for Culture (AKTC). The AKDN is one of the largest private development organisations in the world. Its annual budget exceeds US$925m (2017) and it works in more than 30 countries in the fields of education, health, culture and economic development.

The **gender disparity** in schools is also increasing, and it becomes more acute among older children. While the boy:girl ratio is 52:48 in the first grade, it changes significantly to 62:38 by 11th grade, and in universities and colleges just 26% of students are female. Girls often stay home to help care for younger children or to work and, as uniforms and school books are expensive, preference is given to the education of male siblings when money is tight.

There are also significant problems in **higher education**. Although there are more than 20 universities in Tajikistan, even the Tajik State National University (the best in the country) does not make it into the top 10,000 list of universities worldwide. Corruption is endemic, with bribes for admission ranging from US$200 for a course at one of the regional institutions, to an eye-watering US$4,000 for medical degrees in Dushanbe. Students frequently have to pay to pass a class, and this is on top of the official tuition fees.

Hope for higher education comes in the form of the Aga Khan (see box, page 21) and the Khorog campus of the University of Central Asia (w *ucentralasia. org*). Built across three sites (the other two being Naryn in the Kyrgyz Republic and Tekeli, Kazakhstan), the university ultimately plans to serve the 40 million-strong population of central Asia's mountain communities, providing courses such as teacher training, languages and development. Though the university has been beset by bureaucratic and infrastructure problems (in both cases inevitable given the locations involved), the Aga Khan Development Network (AKDN) has a strong track record in the region and a desire to engage groups beyond the traditional reach of state-run institutions.

CULTURE

MUSIC Tajikistan has a rich musical heritage and, for those who are so inclined, there are ample opportunities to experience traditional forms of music and dance.

Classical music can loosely be divided into *shashmaqam*, the traditional Islamic style, and the Russian-influenced operas and symphonies produced during the Soviet period. **Ziyadullo Shahidi** (d1985) is probably the most significant Tajik composer in the latter style, and a visit to his house-museum in Dushanbe (page 88) is the best way to appreciate his music and the cultural context in which he worked.

The **Gurminj Museum** (page 88) is Tajikistan's de facto centre for ethnomusicology and houses an excellent collection of traditional instruments, including those used in Pamiri folk styles (see box, page 179).

Tajikistan's pop stars tend to be on loan from Iran, Afghanistan and Russia. There are a few home-grown talents, however, including songstresses **Manija Davlatova** and **Shabnam Soraya**, suave crooner **Sadriddin**, and Tajik migrant worker **Tolibzhon Kurbankhanov**, whose veritable love song to Putin became a controversial YouTube hit in the run-up to Russia's 2012 elections. Meanwhile, popular singer **Nigina Amonqulova** has captured a new audience for Tajikistan's folk music with her youthful interpretations of the classics, while **Ozoda Ashurova's** repertoire spans the centuries, from *shashmaqam* to folk to pop.

LITERATURE Given the close relationship between Tajik and Persian (page 19), it is perhaps unsurprising that their literatures have become entwined, with Tajiks absorbing many works from the Persian literary canon into their own. Tajiks have retained this sense of a united literary identity in spite of their community being split by the geographical borders of numerous nation states, and hence Bukhara and Samarkand (both now in Uzbekistan) are still seen as centres of Tajik literary culture.

The writer and philosopher **Abu Abdullah Rudaki** (see box, below) is considered to be the father of Tajik literature. Along with **Firdausi** (934–1020), author of the epic poem *Shahnama* (The Book of Kings), and the scientist **Hussayn ibn Abu Ali Ibn Sina** (980–1037), known in the west as Avicenna, he is a pillar of classical Tajik literature, and rightly commemorated with street names and monuments across the country. The most visually appealing memorials to Rudaki are the mosaic arch and statue in Central Park, and the Writers' Union Building (both in Dushanbe, pages 65–91), which also commemorates Tajikistan's other literary heavyweights.

Moving forward to the immediate pre-Soviet and Soviet periods, three writers dominate. **Sadriddin Ayni** (1878–1954) was a Jadidist writer, educator and poet. He became a communist and began writing prose in the Soviet era. His works include several novels (including his most famous works *Slaves* and *Dokhunala*), and also memoirs depicting life in the Bukharan Khanate. Several of his works have been adapted for the screen. Ayni was the first president of Tajikistan's Academy of Sciences.

Abu'l-Qasem Lahuti (1887–1957) was born in Iran but was politically drawn to the Soviet Union and settled in Tajikistan in the 1920s, encouraged no doubt by the fact he had been sentenced to death by a court in Qom for his part in a failed coup against the Iranian government. He wrote both lyric poetry and 'socialist realist' verse, and was also the author of the official anthem of the Tajik SSR. His poetry was published in six volumes in 1960–63.

Another poet, **Mirzo Tursunzoda** (1911–77), collected Tajik oral literature and wrote his own poems inspired by political and social change. For more about his life and work, see box on page 94.

It is possible to visit the house-museums of both Ayni and Tursunzoda in Dushanbe (pages 87–8 and 91).

ARTS AND CRAFTS A visit to any of Tajikistan's museums will demonstrate the skilled craftsmanship of ancient metalworkers, woodcarvers, potters, painters and weavers. While many of these skills have been lost, in large part due to the industrialisation of the 20th century and ongoing reliance on the import of cheap consumer goods first from Russia and now from China, a few workshops do

RUDAKI

It is sometimes said that Rudaki is to the Tajik as Shakespeare is to the English: despite the passing of centuries, everyone knows a few lines and allusions to his work still permeate modern poetry and prose.

Abu Abdullah was born in the village of Rudak (hence his moniker) in what is now Tajikistan in 857. Many of his biographers believe him to have been blind, but doubt is cast over this assertion by the vivid descriptions of colour in his poems, around 2,000 lines of which survive.

At the height of his career, Rudaki was appointed court poet to Nasr II, the Samanid ruler of Bukhara, and it was here that Rudaki produced his greatest works. His lyrical poems were philosophical in nature and included messages of patriotism (popular with the ruler) and messages of freedom (popular with the ordinary people but somewhat less popular with the ruler).

A refusal to stop preaching liberty to the masses ultimately ended Rudaki's life at court; he fell from favour and, without the support of a wealthy patron, he died in poverty at the remarkable age of 84.

THE PAMIRI HOUSE

The design of the *chid*, or traditional Pamiri house, is deeply symbolic and dates back more than 2,500 years. Though the symbolism of each architectural feature would originally have resonated with Zoroastrian philosophy, they are now typically associated with aspects of Ismaili Islam.

You enter the flat-roofed building through a small lobby area where you are expected to leave your shoes. This opens on to a large, square room lit by a skylight comprised of four concentric wooden squares: each square represents an element with the highest square (the one first touched by the rays of the morning sun) being associated with fire.

Wooden beams support the ceiling. The number of beams is dictated by the size of the room and local tradition: six beams are for the Prophets recognised by Islam; seven beams are for the first seven Imams or, for Zoroastrians, the seven Holy Immortals; 18 beams correspond to elements of Ismaili cosmogony; 49 beams are for the 49 Ismaili Imams; and if your roof is large enough to require 72 beams, each one is for a soldier in the army of Ali.

The beams are set upon five carved pillars. These are the principles of Islam or, alternatively, the Prophet Muhammad, his son-in-law Ali and daughter Fatima, and their two sons Hassan and Hussein. The pillar linked with Muhammad (the one to the left of the entrance) was traditionally made with sacred juniper wood. A child's cradle may be placed by this pillar to give the child protection. At a wedding the bride and groom will be seated next to the pillar of Ali so that they are blessed with good fortune and children. The stove is situated closest to the pillar of Fatima, and this is also where the bride sits at her engagement party. The fourth and fifth pillars, those of Hassan and Hussein, are joined together, symbolising their closeness. Important guests sit by the Hassan pillar, which is also a place for private prayer, and a lamp is lit for the dead by the Hussein pillar during the three-day period of mourning.

You will frequently see the inside of a Pamiri House painted in bright colours. Of these, the two most important colours are red and white. Red is for the sun (the source of life), for fire and for blood. White represents a mother's milk (which enables us all to grow) and also light.

continue to produce beautiful handicrafts in traditional ways, and their methods are being recorded and their goods promoted with the assistance of various NGOs.

Woodwork is probably the best preserved of Tajikistan's ancient crafts, largely because it has a practical, domestic application. The roofs and interiors of Pamiri houses are often richly carved, as are the doors of mosques and many of Tajikistan's other ancient buildings. There is a constant need for repairs and replacement timbers, and this has kept skilled carpenters in work. The best workshops are in Istaravshan and Isfara, though there are often individual craftsmen in smaller villages who are delighted to show off their skills.

Tajik women are traditionally the creators of **textiles**, and their work includes everything from hand-rolled felt and woven yak-hair carpets, to colourful knitwear and fine embroidery. The Murghab Eco-Tourism Association (META)-sponsored Yak House and De Pamiri Handicrafts both support women in remote communities and encourage them to produce well-made pieces for the tourist market. The garishly striped Pamiri socks are a particular favourite among our friends.

Tajikistan is rich in minerals, including precious stones (see box, pages 4–5), and historically a huge amount of **jewellery** was produced. Though gold is still popular (you only have to look at the shiny gold teeth), it is prohibitively expensive for most people, and so the jewellery produced for sale locally now tends to be made from silver and/or brightly coloured beads. Big earrings and necklaces make popular souvenirs; rings are a little less common.

SPORT Tajikistan's national sport is *gushtigiri*, a local form of wrestling, though it is the more exciting and impressive *buz kashi* (see box, page 178) that typically captures the eye of visitors and photographers. Traditionally each community had its own *alufta* or strongman, on whose shoulders the reputation of the village rested: those who challenged his authority would wrestle in a bid to improve their social rank. As in the rest of central Asia, **horse racing** and **horseback games** remain a popular source of entertainment, particularly in rural areas.

Football is, unsurprisingly, the sport of choice among young Tajiks. The Tajik National Football Federation was admitted into FIFA in 1994, and they also play in the AFC league. As of January 2017, the Tajik team was officially ranked 132 out of 211 in the world, and plays its home matches at the Pamir Stadium in Dushanbe. Tajikistan's top goal scorer is Manuchekhr Dzhalilov (b1990) who also plays for Tajikistan's national champions, Istiklol Dushanbe.

In other sports, Tajikistan has competed in the **Olympics** since 1996, and the Winter Olympics since 2002. Rasul Boqiev won the country's first-ever Olympic medal when he took bronze in men's judo (73kg) in Beijing in 2008. Yusup Abdusalomov claimed silver in the men's freestyle wrestling (84kg) at the same games, and then in 2012 Mavzuna Chorieva beat the odds to win bronze in the women's boxing. Dilshod Nazarov brought home Tajikistan's first gold medal, placing first in the hammer throw at the 2016 Summer Olympics in Rio de Janeiro.

TAJIKISTAN ONLINE

For additional online content, articles, photos and more on Tajikistan, why not visit **w** bradtguides.com/tajikistan.

Travel the world
from your armchair

Bradt's travel literature features true-life tales of adventure, discovery and danger, from the plains of Africa and beyond.

For a **25% discount** on all our travel literature titles visit our website and use the code **TRAVEL** at checkout.

www.bradtguides.com

2

Practical Information

WHEN TO VISIT

The core tourist season in Tajikistan is from April to October, though the season shortens substantially if you want to visit the Pamir or trek: to do that you should plan to visit between June and mid-September. That said, Tajikistan has its charms at every time of the year, you just need to plan your route (and clothing) with consideration for the sub-zero temperatures and snow.

Tajikistan explodes into life in the **spring**. As the snows subside and the higher parts of the country once again become accessible, the lower mountain slopes and pastures are a riot of colour. Tajiks celebrate Navruz, the Persian New Year, on the spring equinox, 21 March, with feasting, dancing and adrenalin-charged games of *buz kashi*, Tajikistan's answer to polo. When spring comes will depend entirely on your location, but expect the thaw and spring bulbs in Dushanbe from late February onwards, and for the snow to melt up on the Murghab Plateau from May.

In the **summer** months, when temperatures in Dushanbe and the lowlands soar to uncomfortable levels, the Pamirs come into their own: you can drive the Pamir Highway without the risk of snow from June to September, and at the same time climb the higher peaks. Glacial meltwaters have slowed, the rivers are no longer in spate and, though an occasional blizzard may still catch you unawares, you can join the shepherds as they drive their flocks up into the mountains to grow fat on the grasses of high pastures.

Tajikistan marks its Independence Day on 9 September, and the crops in the Fergana Valley and other agricultural areas are harvested. The fresh fruits at this time of year are divine. Nights in late September will already be cold in the Pamirs, and from October roads in the higher mountains will be impassable due to snowfall and ice. As the **autumn** progresses the emerald-green trees that form ribbons through the bottom of each river valley turn almost overnight to a fiery red and orange. In Tajikistan's lower regions, which include most of the north and southwest, there's a bite to the air come nightfall, but bright sunshine still warms up the day.

The **winter** is hard in Tajikistan, with many communities cut off and, if the harvest has been poor, dangerously short of food. For those with money, however, the snowfall marks the start of the ski season, and the Takob ski resort becomes busy with day trippers from Dushanbe.

HIGHLIGHTS

Tajikistan's attractions are deeply varied, from dinosaur footprints to Soviet hydro-electric dams, and your itinerary is likely to be influenced by your personal interests, mode of transport and the areas in which you travel. To provide food for thought, however, here is an eclectic selection of what we feel are the country's highlights.

ANCIENT PANJAKENT AND SARAZM Five thousand years of archaeological history at Tajikistan's first UNESCO World Heritage Site and the so-called Pompeii of central Asia are scarcely a stone's throw from one another, close to the Tajik–Uzbek border. Though the most important archaeological finds have been removed to museums in Dushanbe and Russia, the well-preserved ruins and their small museums give a fascinating insight into Tajikistan's early history. Few foreign tourists venture this far along the road, so you might well have the place to yourself.

BUZ KASHI The traditional sport of *buz kashi*, aka dead goat polo, is an adrenalin-fuelled rugby scrum on horseback played in mountain villages across Tajikistan and Afghanistan. Derived from goat raiding, teams of men (often from rival villages) race and wrestle the decapitated carcass of a goat with the aim of throwing it into a goal at the end of the pitch. Your best chance of seeing a match is at Navruz (which coincides with the vernal equinox in late March) and, following that, on other public holidays in spring and summer.

GARM CHASHMA The hot springs of Garm Chashma, just south of Khorog, are naturally occurring and have purportedly curative properties. Over thousands of years the mineral deposits have created a giant rock meringue, and you can sit and soak at the heart of it while staring up at the hillside in nothing more than your birthday suit. Men and women bathe separately, and it is a great way to relax and soothe tired muscles after a bumpy, dusty drive along the Pamir Highway.

ISKANDERKUL This turquoise-blue lake surrounded by the snow-capped peaks of the Fann Mountains is an understandable favourite with Tajik day trippers and foreign trekkers alike. Easily accessible from Dushanbe it can be combined with the Seven Lakes for a five-day trek or, for those seeking something a little less strenuous, it's an idyllic spot to camp, have a barbecue and rent a boat on the lake. If you are camping here during a full moon, do keep your eyes fixed on the surface of the water: it is said that the ghost of Alexander the Great's favourite horse, Bucephalus, rises from the lake and comes ashore to graze!

PAMIR HIGHWAY The prize for the world's best drive is hotly contested, but the Pamir Highway certainly comes close to perfection (at least in terms of thrills and views). Magnificent mountains, gushing rivers and waterfalls, summer settlements with nomads and sheep, and scarcely another vehicle in sight are all points in its favour. While it's not a route for the faint-hearted, if you have the physical and mental stamina it's a once in a lifetime experience whether you're travelling by two wheels or four. Be sure to visit in the summer months as the road is impassable during the rest of the year.

TAKING TEA Tajikistan runs on tea, and it's as significant for the social interaction that occurs while you drink as for the beverage itself. Whether you go to a *chaykhona* (literally a 'tea house') or are invited to join someone for a cup at their home, make sure you take the time to stop, drink and chat as the Tajiks do: hospitality and tea are virtually interchangeable and certainly not to be missed.

YAGNOB VALLEY Isolation saved the Sogdians. Fleeing from Panjakent when the Arabs invaded Tajikistan, almost all of the local population was slaughtered. Only those hidden in the mountains, cut off from the outside world, survived. Some 1,300 years on, their few descendants still live in the Yagnob Valley, among them the last speakers of Sogdian, the tongue Alexander the Great would have heard on the battlefield when he rode into Bactria in the 4th century BC. The lower parts of the valley can be explored by 4x4, but the remotest reaches are only accessible on foot.

SUGGESTED ITINERARIES

The challenge with Tajikistan is not selecting what to include in an itinerary but rather what to leave out: time is always a limiting factor, particularly when the hours spent travelling from A to B can be a significant part of your trip. If your time is short, select a city and make it the hub of your journeys. If you have longer to play with, think of getting to your destination as part of the adventure, sit back and enjoy the views.

TWO DAYS Just a couple of days is sufficient time to explore the main sights of Dushanbe. Start with a stroll along Rudaki to orientate yourself, and head for the National Museum for an overview of Tajikistan's history and to see the remarkable sleeping Buddha from Ajina Tepa. The neighbouring Ethnographic Museum is also worth an hour of your time. Take lunch in the square outside the Ayni Opera and Ballet Theatre, and while you're there buy a ticket for the evening's performance. Spend the afternoon in Central Park looking at the monuments to Rudaki and Ismoili Somoni, and also the dazzling Palace of Nations, or take a tour of the ornate Navruz Palace. Return to the theatre to soak up the atmosphere and enjoy the live orchestra, all washed down with Georgian champagne.

On the second morning, head to the north of the city for the botanical gardens. As the day progresses work your way back down Rudaki to the mosque, with an optional diversion to the house-museum of Mirzo Tursunzoda. Take lunch at the attractively painted Chaykhona Rokhat and then give your ears a treat with the sounds of traditional instruments at the Gurminj Museum. Finish up with souvenir shopping in Green Bazaar and the creaking old TsUM department store.

ONE WEEK One full week should give you ample time to get out of the city and to start exploring. Spend a day in Dushanbe, then head north to ancient Panjakent and Sarazm, taking an ethnographic tour of the valley with local company Pamir Travel (page 72) while you're there. From Panjakent head to Khujand with its attractive mosque, fort and lively bazaar, then return via the tiled mosques and *madrasas* of Istaravshan. Be sure to spend a night camping on the shores of Iskanderkul before you get back to the capital.

TWO WEEKS A fortnight will allow you to go trekking. Visit Dushanbe, ancient Panjakent and Sarazm as above, but then head for the Seven Lakes. Paramount Journey (page 31) will provide you with a knowledgeable, English-speaking local guide and all the equipment you need, and you can then trek the five-day route through the Fann Mountains to Iskanderkul. The physical landscape of Tajikistan is defined by its mountains and lakes, and there's no better way to appreciate their beauty and scale than on foot. Finish with Khujand and Istaravshan. You may also have time for a short diversion into the Yagnob Valley to meet the modern descendants of the Sogdians (pages 97–103).

ONE MONTH With a month at your disposal, the Pamirs open up to you. As two borders into southern Kyrgyzstan are now open, you can loop around most of Tajikistan. From Dushanbe, head east along the Rasht Valley into the wilderness

2

with its wildlife and occasional forts and shrines. Leave Tajikistan at Jirgatal and re-enter south of Sary Tash, from where the entirety of the dramatic, remote Pamir Highway awaits you. Cross the Pamirs at a leisurely speed, being sure to stop in the town of Murghab on the Murghab Plateau, and on arrival in the university town of Khorog, soak up the cosmopolitan air, the museum and botanical gardens. A loop further south will take you to Garm Chashma (naturally occurring hot springs), the ruby mine, and the northern edge of the Wakhan Corridor. Follow the Amu Darya River along the Tajik–Afghan border to Khatlon, with its ancient sites of Ajina Tepa and Takht-i Sangin, and the reconstructed Khulbuk fort, before meandering back to Dushanbe via the resorts on the Nurek Reservoir.

TOUR OPERATORS

Although it is possible, and indeed relatively straightforward, to travel independently within Tajikistan, many first-time visitors choose to go with a recognised tour operator as it generally reduces the hassles of bureaucracy, arranging internal transport and the language barrier. The companies listed below, all of which offer specialist, small group tours, also provide knowledgeable guides, helping you to get the most out of the country.

All of the companies listed are based in the UK, USA and Canada, or Switzerland, and their group itineraries include Tajikistan, often combined with at least one other central Asian republic. If you wish to travel only to Tajikistan, Kalpak Travel has single-country cultural tours and treks, including to the Fann Mountains; Paramount Journey operates both small group and bespoke tours; and Indy Guide will connect you with local guides and drivers. Tajikistan-based tour operators, of which there are a number of experienced, professional outfits, are listed under the *Tourist information* and *Local tour operators* sections of the city in which their offices are located.

UK

Intrepid Travel 4th Fl, Piano Hse, 9 Brighton Tce, Brixton, London SW9 8DJ; ☎ 020 3308 9753; e ask@intrepidtravel.com; w intrepidtravel.com. Arranges 13-day tour through Pamirs into Kyrgyzstan.

Regent Holidays 6th Fl, Colston Tower, Colston St, Bristol BS1 4XE; ☎ 020 3811 3588; e regent@regentholidays.co.uk; w regentholidays.co.uk. Offers a 13-day tour featuring the Pamir Highway & 2 multi-country central Asian tours.

Responsible Travel Edge Hse, 42 Bond St, Brighton, East Sussex, BN1 1RD; ☎ 01273 823700; w responsibletravel.com. With a focus on sustainable tourism, offers several tailor-made & multi-country group tours in central Asia.

Steppes Travel Travel Hse, 51 Castle St, Cirencester, Glos GL7 1QD; ☎ 01258 787426; e enquiry@steppestravel.co.uk; w steppestravel.co.uk. Offers several tailor-made holidays to Tajikistan, as well as an overland trip going through all 5 of the central Asian republics.

Sundowners Overland ☎ 020 8877 7657; w sundownersoverland.com. Tailor-made & group tours on the Silk Road & Trans-Siberian railway.

Undiscovered Destinations PO Box 746, North Tyneside NE29 1EG; ☎ 0191 296 2674; e travel@undiscovered-destinations.com; w undiscovered-destinations.com. Offers a 16-day group trip along the Pamir Highway & into Kyrgyzstan.

Wild Frontiers 78 Glentham Rd, London SW13 9JJ; ☎ 020 8741 7390; e info@wildfrontiers.co.uk; w wildfrontiers.co.uk. Group & tailor-made tours to Tajikistan with either Afghanistan (Wakhan Corridor) or Kyrgyzstan.

World Expeditions 1B Osiers Rd, Wandsworth, London SW18 1NL; ☎ 020 8875 5060; e enquiries@worldexpeditions.co.uk; w worldexpeditions.co.uk. Specialists in adventure travel & trekking since 1975. Arranges 3 trekking itineraries lasting 14, 15 or 33 days.

USA AND CANADA

East Site Inc 3 Hadley Dr, Medford, NJ 08055; ☎ +1 877 800 6287; e travel@east-site.com; w east-site.com. Numerous Silk Road tours including a package to all 5 central Asian republics, with monthly departures during the tourist season.

MIR Corporation 85 South Washington St, Suite 210, Seattle, WA 98104; ✆ +1 206 624 7289; e info@mircorp.com; w mircorp.com. Award-winning tours to the Silk Road, Russia & the CIS since 1986. Option to visit just Tajikistan or to combine it with neighbouring countries.

Paramount Journey 1200 Bay St, Suite 202, Toronto, ON M5R 2A5; ✆ +1 647 483 4101; e info@paramountjourney.com; w paramountjourney.com. Tajikistan specialists with offices in Toronto & Dushanbe. Offers tours only to Tajikistan, with a focus on trekking, mountain biking, jeep tours & kayaking. Itineraries can be tailored to individual tastes & abilities. See ad in 2nd colour section.

Silk Road Treasure Tours 39 East Fox Chase Rd, Chester, NJ 07930; ✆ +1 908 719 7676; w silkroadtreasuretours.com. Scheduled programme of both cultural tours & mountain

treks to Tajikistan only or combined with the other central Asian republics as well.

Indy Guide Humbelrain 9, 8824 Schönenberg; ✆ +41 79 100 5500; e info@indy-guide.com; w indy-guide.com. Social enterprise set up to link independent travellers with approved local drivers & guides. Also provides visa support & can put you in touch with other travellers wanting similar itineraries.

Kalpak Travel Ringstrasse 13, 5415 Nussbaumem; ✆ +41 78 657 2701; e info@kalpak-travel.com; w kalpak-travel.com. Full-service tour operator specialising in central Asia. Offers small group tours, some of which are scheduled to coincide with special events such as Navruz & Independence Day. Options include a 23-day active tour of the Pamirs & Wakhan Corridor, & a 13-day trek in the Fann Mountains. Tour leaders & guides are English speaking. Highly recommended. See ad in 2nd colour section.

RED TAPE

All visitors to Tajikistan will encounter a certain amount of bureaucracy, though it's easier than it was in the past. Almost all visitors will require a visa, usually obtained from a Tajik consulate in advance of arrival, and those travelling to the Pamirs will also require an additional Gorno-Badakhshan Autonomous Oblast (GBAO) permit.

VISAS Unless you are a CIS national, you will almost certainly need a visa to enter Tajikistan. The Ministry of Foreign Affairs now offers an electronic visa for tourists that can be processed online through a special website (w *evisa.tj*). The process usually takes two business days, requires a scanned copy of your passport (with at least 6 months' validity remaining) and planned itinerary, and costs US$50, plus an additional US$20 if you wish to visit the GBAO. Otherwise, you should apply in good time (at least two weeks ahead of your intended arrival), and ideally in your country of residence (if it has a Tajik consulate). There is a list of Tajikistan's diplomatic missions overseas on pages 33–4. If your country does not have a Tajik consulate you can send your passport to a consulate in another country, apply in person in another country or, occasionally, arrange with a travel agent (pages 30–1) to collect your visa on arrival at Dushanbe airport. Visas will not be issued on arrival to the nationals of countries where there is a consulate, and will not be issued to anyone at the land borders.

The visa application process is relatively straightforward. A letter of invitation (LOI) is not required for the standard 45-day tourist visa, so if you do not wish to apply online, you can simply download the visa application form from the Ministry of Foreign Affairs website (w *mfa.tj*) and fill it in. If you require a double- or multiple-entry visa, be sure to tick the correct box. You will need to submit it with a photocopy of your passport, a passport photo and a printout of your airline ticket or other proof of onward journey. The last is a recent requirement. A copy of your planned itinerary is also advisable. Submit all the paperwork along with your passport and the appropriate fee. Processing usually takes one week, though some consulates can fast-track the processing for an increased fee.

The cost of visas is constantly in flux and depends both on your nationality and the location at which you are applying. At the time of going to print, the cost for a British national applying in London was £70, with GBAO permit included.

It is important to note that while the standard tourist visa grants up to 45 days in Tajikistan, the GBAO permit is only good for a maximum of 30 days. If you want to stay longer in Tajikistan but are coming to the end of your visa, it is possible to get an extension in Dushanbe at the Ministry of Foreign Affairs (*33 Sheroz;* e *info@mfa.tj;* ⏰ *08.00–noon & 13.00–17.00 Mon–Fri, 08.00–noon Sat*). You will need a photocopy of your passport and two passport photos and, having paid the requisite fee at the designated bank, your passport should be ready for collection two working days later. It may also be possible to get an extension at an Office of Visas and Registration (OVIR) but you should allow longer for this: in Khujand we were quoted ten days.

REGISTRATION If you are visiting Tajikistan on a tourist visa for 30 days or less, you do not need to register in Tajikistan. If you are on a non-tourist visa (such as a business or study visa), are staying longer than 30 days, or have entered without a visa (for example because you are a CIS national), you will need to register at an OVIR. Non-tourists and those without visas should register within three days of arrival; tourists should register within the first 30 days.

The registration process involves taking a passport photo and copy of your passport to the OVIR and filling in the forms they give you. You will need to pay the registration fee (usually around US$20 but dependent on your situation) at a designated bank nearby, then return to the OVIR with the receipt. Registration can theoretically be done the same day, but you may be asked to return as much as a week later to collect your passport and the accompanying registration slip. You will need to keep the registration slip and show it on departure.

There are OVIRs in most cities, though some are more efficient than others. We have found the staff at the Khujand OVIR to be particularly helpful, and the staff in Dushanbe rather less so. If you cannot face the hassle of submitting the registration yourself, a local travel agent will do it.

GBAO PERMITS If you wish to travel to Gorno-Badakhshan, which includes the Pamir Highway, Khorog and the Wakhan Corridor, or even to pass through these areas, you will need a GBAO permit. You can apply for this at the same time as your visa; online, they cost US$20, but at the Tajik embassy in London, they cost £50.

It is also possible to get a GBAO permit once you are in Tajikistan. Travel agencies in Dushanbe, Khorog and Murghab can all get you a permit for around US$50 and will email you a scan (to be exchanged for the real permit in Khorog) if you are entering GBAO from Afghanistan or Kyrgyzstan.

Your passport will be checked on entering GBAO and frequently at checkpoints within the province as well. If you do not have the requisite permit you will not be able to continue your journey.

It should be noted that the issuing of GBAO permits was suspended for several months in the late summer and autumn of 2012 due to security problems in the region (see box, page 159). Though the Pamirs have now reopened to foreigners and permits are once again being issued, the situation is always subject to change.

POLICE AND MILITARY Tajikistan has a large number of highly visible police and military personnel and you will encounter them on a regular basis, particularly when travelling long distances by road, in border areas and when entering Gorno-Badakhshan and other sensitive places. The majority of personnel you encounter, be they traffic police, checkpoint attendants or border patrols, will be polite and may even want to chat; it's not uncommon to be asked into a control post for tea. Even if you only share a few words in common, this can be a surprisingly entertaining and memorable experience.

However, there are also officials who will make life difficult. Even if your paperwork is in order and you have not done anything wrong you may be hassled and even asked for a bribe. Feigning ignorance of what is being asked for, and claiming a complete non-comprehension of Russian even if you do speak a few words, is often a helpful strategy as the official in question will usually get bored and move on to easier, local prey. If you are required to pay a fine or bribe, demand to pay it at the local police station rather than by the road, note down the name and badge number of the official making the request and ask for a receipt. If the fine is legitimate, the official will have no problem complying with your requests, and if it is not legitimate, your requests will often dissuade him from pursuing the matter. A smile and a wave go down well when you part company, regardless of how the situation has played out.

EMBASSIES

Tajikistan's overseas missions are typically small, and their consular departments have very limited opening hours: in the case of London, for example, they are open to receive visa applications and return passports only 10.00–noon Monday and Thursday. In all cases, you are advised to call or check the website of the relevant embassy before visiting in person. All embassies are closed for Tajikistan's national holidays, and often for public holidays in their host country too.

If there is not a Tajik embassy in your country, you may be permitted to collect your visa on arrival at the airport in Dushanbe (pages 67–8). A full list of Tajikistan's current diplomatic representations can be found online at w mfa.tj.

All the embassies listed under *Foreign embassies in Tajikistan* are in Dushanbe unless otherwise stated.

TAJIKISTAN EMBASSIES ABROAD

⊕ Afghanistan 15 Wazir Akbar Khan, Kabul; \+93 784 098 355; e tajembkabul@mfa.tj

⊕ Austria 8/1A Universitäts Str, Vienna 1090; \+43 140 9 8266; e tajembvienna@mfa.tj; w tajikembassy.at. Also covers Hungary & Slovakia.

⊕ Azerbaijan 20 Baghlar, Baku; \+994 12 502 1432; e tajembbaku@mfa.tj; w tajembaz.tj

⊕ Belgium 16 Bd General Jacques, Brussels 1050; \+32 2 640 6933; e tajembbrussels@mfa.tj; w tajikembassy.be. Also covers the Netherlands & Luxembourg.

⊕ China LA 01-04, Liangmaqiao Diplomatic Compound, Beijing 100 60; \+86 10 6532 2598; e tajembbeijing@mfa.tj; w tajikembassychina.com

⊕ Egypt 251 St, Villa 15, Digla Al-Maadi, Cairo; \+2 02 9519 9665; e tajembcairo@mfa.tj; w tajemb-eg.org

⊕ France 14 Av d'Eylau, Paris 75016; \+33 170 929 342; e tajembparis@mfa.tj; w tajembfrance.fr

⊕ Germany 43 Perleberger Str, Berlin 10559; \+49 30 347 9300; e tajembberlin@mfa.tj; w botschaft-tadschikistan.de. Also serves Poland.

⊕ India A-2/6, Vasant Vihar, New Delhi 110057; \+91 2615 4282; e tajembnewdelhi@mfa.tj; w tajikembassy.in

⊕ Iran No 10, 3rd Alley, Shahid Zain'ali St, Niyavaran, Tehran; \+98 21 2229 9584; e tajemb.iran@gmail.com; w tajembiran.tj

Japan 1-5-42 Kamioosaki, Shinagawa-ku, Tokyo 141-0021; ☎ +81 36721 7455; e tajembtokyo@mfa.tj; w tajikistan.jp

Kazakhstan 15 Karasakal Erimbet, Chubari Microdistrict, Astana; ☎ +7 7172 240 929; e tajembastana@mfa.tj; w tajembkaz. tj. Consulate also in Almaty (*16 Sanatornaya, Baganshyl Microdistrict;* ☎ *+7 7272 697 059;* e *tajconsalmaty@mfa.tj*).

Kuwait 27 Hamad Al-Humaidhi St, Block 1, Shamiya, Kuwait City; ☎ +965 2484 7773; e tajembkuwait@mfa.tj; w tajemb-kwt.org

Kyrgyzstan 36 Karadarinskaya, Bishkek; ☎ +996 312 511 637; e tjemb.kg@mfa.tj; w tajemb.kg

Malaysia 524 Jalan 6, Ampang Utama 68000, Ampang Selangor DE; ☎ +603 4265 4969; e tajembmy@mfa.tj

Pakistan 295 St 35, F 11/3, Islamabad 44000; ☎ +92 51 229 3462; e tajemb_islamabad@inbox.ru; w tajikembassy.pk

Qatar Cnr Ibn Zaidoun & Al Rabiya sts, Doha; ☎ +974 4412 3906; e tajembqatar@mfa.tj

Russia 13 Granatniy Pereulok, Moscow 103001; ☎ +7 495 690 4186; e tajembmoscow@ mfa.tj; w tajembassy.ru. Consulates also in Yekaterinburg (*2A Grajdanskaya;* ☎ *+7 343 370 2360;* e *tajconsek@mfa.tj;* w *tajgenconsul-eka. ru*) & Ufa (*149 Cyurupa;* ☎ *+7 347 276 5296;* e *tajconsufa@mfa.tj;* w *tajgenconsul-ufa.ru*).

Saudi Arabia Al Worood Qtr, Al-Mar'a Yusuf bin Al-Hanbali St, Aloroba Rd, 365945 Riyadh 11393; ☎ +966 1205 4708; e tajembsaudi@mfa. tj; w tajemb-ksa.org

South Korea 19-9 Daesagwanro, 31-gil, Hannam-dong, Yongsan-gu, Seoul; ☎ +82 10 6884 5625; e tajkoreaemb@mfa.tj

Switzerland 93 Rue de la Servette, Geneva 1202; ☎ +41 22 734 1140; e tajembgeneva@mfa. tj; w tajikistanmission.ch

Turkey 20 Ertugrul Caddesi, Diplomatik Site, ORAN, Ankara; ☎ +90 312 491 1607; e tajembankara@mfa.tj; w tajikembassytr.org. Consulate also in Istanbul (*14 Halkali Caddesi, Yeşilköy Mh, Bakirköy-Istanbul;* ☎ *+90 212 426 5052;* e *tajconsistanbul@mfa.tj;* w *tajconsist.org*).

Turkmenistan 19 Kurungan, Ashgabat; ☎ +810 99312 355 696; e tajembashgabat@mfa. tj; w tajembassytm.com

UAE Villa 2, Al Mushrif St, PO Box 75213, Abu Dhabi; ☎ +97 12 441 7950; e tajembabudhabi@

mfa.tj. Consulate also in Dubai (*Villa 7, 4C Al Safa St 2;* ☎ *+97 14 394 5814;* e *tajconsdubai@mfa.tj;* w *dubaitajcons.org*).

UK 3 Shortlands, Hammersmith Grove, London W6 7BA; ☎ +44 203 609 8788; e tajemblondon@ mfa.tj; w tajembassy.org.uk

USA 1005 New Hampshire Av NW, Washington, DC 20037; ☎ +1 202 223 60 90; e tajikistan@verizon.net; w tajemb.us

Uzbekistan 61 Abdulla Kakhor, Tashkent; ☎ +998 71 254 9966; e tajembuz@mfa.tj

FOREIGN EMBASSIES IN TAJIKISTAN

Afghanistan 59/1 Ismoili Somoni; ☎ 369 902; e info@afghanembassy.tj. The Afghan embassy has moved twice in recent years, so if anyone tells you to go to M Tursunzoda or Pushkin, ignore them. The new embassy is off Ismoili Somoni. Drive west past the Hyatt, go straight across the roundabout & take the first road on the left. The embassy is the large yellow building. There is an additional Afghan consulate in Khorog (*17 K Kermshayev;* ☎ *(03522) 02 492*), which may be of use if you decide to cross the border at Ishkashim.

China 143 Rudaki Av; ☎ (0372) 242 188; e chinaemb_tj@mfa.gov.cn; w tj.china-embassy. org. Tucked back from the main road.

France 2nd Floor, 17 Rakhimi; ☎ (0372) 215 037; e cad.douchanbe@diplomatie.gouv.fr; w french-embassy.com/tajikistan-dushanbe.html

Germany 59/1 Ismoili Somoni; ☎ (0372) 352 230; e info@duschanbe.diplo.de; w duschanbe.diplo. de. Next door to the new Afghan embassy (see above).

India 45 Bukhoro; ☎ (0372) 217 172; e info. dushanbe@mea.gov.in; w indianembassytj.com

Iran 18 Bokhtar; ☎ (0372) 210 072; e iran-embassy.tj@tagnetgmail.com

Kazakhstan 31/1 Husseinzoda; ☎ (0372) 218 940; e dipmiskz7@tajnet.com

Kyrgyzstan 50 Said Nosir; ☎ (0372) 242 611; e kg@kgembassy.tj; w kgembassy.tj

Pakistan 20A Azizbekov St; ☎ (0372) 230 177; e parepdushanbe_taj@yahoo.com; w mofa. gov.pk. Behind Grand Asia Hotel.

Russia 29/31 Abuali Ibn Sino; ☎ (0372) 359 827; e rambtadjik@rambler.ru; w russianembassy. biz. The Russian embassy also has a consulate in Khujand (*21 Syr Darya;* ☎ *(03422) 64 673*).

Turkey 17/2 Rudaki; ☎ 0922 929; e embassy. dushanbe@mfa.gov.tr; w dushanbe.emb.mfa. gov.tr

ⓔ Turkmenistan 10 Ahu-Babaev; ☎ (0372) 241 162; e turkmenembtj@gmail.com; w tajikistan. tmembassy.gov.tm

ⓔ UK 65 Mirzo Tursunzoda; ☎ (0372) 242 221; e dushanbe.reception@fco.gov.uk; w ukintajikistan.fco.gov.uk

ⓔ USA 109A, Ismoili Somoni; ☎ (0372) 292 000; e usembassydushanbe@state.gov; w tj. usembassy.gov

ⓔ Uzbekistan 30 Sanoi St; ☎ (0372) 247 539; e ruzintaj@rambler.ru

GETTING THERE AND AWAY

However you choose to travel, Tajikistan is not a particularly easy country to reach. Land borders open and close somewhat erratically, flights are irregular at the best of times and cancelled at the first sign of bad weather, and wherever you arrive from by train you'll require a passport full of visas and the patience of a saint.

BY AIR The vast majority of visitors arrive in Tajikistan on a flight to Dushanbe and this is, on balance, the easiest way to travel. Unless there are extenuating circumstances, you will need to have a visa before boarding the plane (pages 31–2) and may be prevented from flying if you do not.

The safety record of many of central Asia's airlines, including Tajik Air, is such that they are prevented from flying in European airspace. Tajik and Somon Air do, however, serve a number of more localised routes, including to Moscow and Istanbul.

Aircraft are typically far older than those in service elsewhere, and they have not always been maintained to international standards. It is likely, therefore, that if you take a flight originating in Europe or the USA you will need to get a connection in one of the regional hubs (Almaty, Istanbul or Moscow). Direct flights to Tajikistan tend to come only from the Middle East, Russia and the other CIS countries.

The arrivals procedure is relatively straightforward. When you enter the terminal building collect an immigration form (a long, thin slip usually covered in advertising for the Beeline mobile phone network), fill it in and then wait in the immigration queue. Everything will get stamped, and part of the slip will be returned to you. Don't lose it as you'll be expected to hand it over when you leave. The baggage hall is the usual scrum, and there is a bottleneck near the exit as you have to have your baggage sticker checked and then pass everything through the X-ray machine.

For details on commercial airlines flying into Dushanbe and also Khujand (which has a small number of international flights to Russia and the CIS), see *Getting there and away* in *Chapters 3* and *5* respectively.

BY RAIL There is a certain romance attached to train travel, and if you have the time to sit and watch the world pass by at a leisurely pace (very leisurely in the case of the old Soviet rail network), it is still a viable way to reach Tajikistan. Regardless of where the train originates, you will need to ensure you have a valid transit visa for every country *en route*, as well as a visa for Tajikistan.

Ticket classes are categorised in the Russian style. First-class or deluxe accommodation (*spets vagon*) buys you an upholstered seat in a two-berth cabin. The seat turns into a bed at night. Second class (*kupe*) is slightly less plush, and there are four passengers to a compartment. Third class (*platzkartny*) has open bunks (ie: not in a compartment) and, if you are really on a very tight budget indeed, a fourth-class ticket (*obshchiy*) gets you an unreserved and very hard seat. Bring plenty of food for the journey, and keep an eye on your luggage, particularly at night, as theft is sadly commonplace.

Practical Information GETTING THERE AND AWAY

2

There are three main train routes to Tajikistan. There are two trains a week in each direction between Moscow and Dushanbe, a weekly service between Moscow and Khujand, and a thrice-weekly service between Samara (Saratov) and Khujand. All these services pass through Tashkent; the Dushanbe train also passes through Samarkand. Tickets to Moscow (second class) start from just over US$145 and the trip takes four days.

The train timetable for the whole Russian rail network (including central Asia) is online at w poezda.net. The Man in Seat 61 (w *seat61.com/silkroute.htm*) also has detailed information, including personal observations, about train travel in the former USSR.

If you are coming to Tajikistan from China, it would theoretically be possible to take the twice-weekly train from Ürümqi to Almaty, change for Tashkent and then continue on to Dushanbe or Khujand. We have not, however, taken this route or met anyone who has, so if you do manage to ride it successfully we'd love to hear from you.

BY ROAD Our preferred way to enter Tajikistan is through a land border, not because customs and immigration make it a particularly easy or pleasant experience, but because of the freedom having your own transport gives you once you finally make it inside.

The information given below was correct at the time of going to press. However, border crossings open and close regularly, often with little warning, and some crossings are open only to locals and not to foreigners. Keep your ear to the ground and, if in doubt, contact a tour operator or Tajik consulate before confirming your travel plans. We have previously ignored our own advice, with the result that we had to drive overnight from Panjakent to the Oybek crossing north of Khujand to leave Tajikistan before our visas expired. We would not recommend you follow suit.

Reaching Tajikistan **from Afghanistan** tends to be fairly straightforward, as diplomatic relations between the two countries are generally good. The two main border crossings are between Kunduz and Dusti at Panj-i Poen (Khatlon province), and at Ishkashim on the northern side of the Wakhan Corridor. To enter Tajikistan at Ishkashim you will require a GBAO permit (pages 32–3) in addition to your Tajik visa. Pedestrians can also cross the suspension bridge over the Panj at Khorog and, if you have a transit visa for Uzbekistan, it would also be convenient (and a relatively quick drive) to cross from Afghanistan into Uzbekistan at Termez, then cross into Tajikistan at Denau.

These borders loosely operate 09.00–16.00 and are officially closed on Sundays and public holidays, though certainly at Ishkashim we've managed to look so downtrodden and miserable that the guards got the relevant officials out of bed and opened the border specially (there's not much to do in Ishkashim, perhaps). If your arrival happens to coincide with lunch you'll have to wait, but any food, drink (non-alcoholic if you're on the Afghan side) or cigarettes you have to share will certainly liven the experience. If you are entering Tajikistan, expect your baggage and vehicle to be thoroughly searched by customs. They are looking for narcotics.

Relations with **Uzbekistan** are a little more unpredictable, and hence at the time of going to press the most useful border between the two countries, the crossing between Samarkand and Panjakent, was closed. There is currently no discussion of it opening in the foreseeable future.

The Tursunzoda–Denau crossing west of Dushanbe remains open, and this is currently the best option if you are going to or from anywhere other than Tashkent and the northeast of Uzbekistan. It is well served by minibuses running in both directions, and providing you're not stuck behind a busload of returning migrant workers carrying all their worldly possessions, processing is fairly quick. The border guards are reportedly hyper-vigilant about searching through medications and your collection of digital photographs.

Travelling to or from Tashkent you need the Oybek crossing 60km north of Khujand. The closest settlement on the Tajik side is the town of Buston. This crossing is open 24/7 for foreigners (locals have to camp out at the gates if they arrive at night) and it is relatively well organised on the Tajik side. Uzbek customs are utterly paranoid, want to X-ray every last sock (we saw one elderly gentleman even having to remove his car bumper and mud flaps to put them through the machine) and allow their admittedly very cute sniffer dog (a spaniel) to jump over everything. It also got overly excited and peed on our picnic.

The border crossing at Bekhobod, just to the south of Oybek, is currently closed to foreigners.

You can cross to the Fergana Valley from Konibodom, northwest of Isfara. This border is little used by foreigners and onward transport is poor; try to arrange a taxi to meet you on the Uzbek side.

Until recently, the border crossing at the Kyzyl–Art pass south of Sary Tash was the only place where foreigners could easily enter Tajikistan from **Kyrgyzstan**. Though a photogenic spot, this necessitated a drive the whole length of the Pamir Highway if you wanted to reach Dushanbe or the west of the country.

If you are travelling to or from Sughd, it is also possible to cross the border between Isfara and Batken. This gets you neatly into Kyrgyzstan, but you are then more or less stuck unless you have an Uzbek visa too, as the road onwards to Osh skirts through an Uzbek enclave. The alternative is to find an amenable taxi driver to detour around the checkpoints. The border at Karamyk, sadly, is closed to anyone but citizens of Tajikistan and Kyrgyzstan, having opened for a few weeks in 2012 due to unrest in Khorog.

Tajikistan does share a border with **China**, and a road links Murghab with the incredible Karakoram Highway. This crossing is currently closed to foreigners, though many have tried. Reports of Chinese- and Kyrgyz-speaking travellers with UK or US passports talking their way across the border appear online, but this approach is strongly discouraged until the border becomes verifiably multilateral. We are keeping our fingers crossed.

HEALTH   *with Dr Felicity Nicholson*

BEFORE YOU GO Comprehensive travel insurance should be the first thing on your list when you contemplate travelling to Tajikistan. Choose a policy that includes medical evacuation (MEDEVAC) and make sure you fully understand any restrictions: it is not uncommon for insurance companies to exclude certain activities (including mountaineering) from cover. Leave a copy of the policy documents at home with someone you trust, and keep a copy of your policy number and the emergency contact number on you at all times. Prospekt Clinic (page 87) can assist with MEDEVAC arrangements.

Your GP or a specialised travel clinic (page 39) will be able to check your immunisation status and advise you on any additional inoculations you might need. It is wise to be up to date on **tetanus**, **polio** and **diphtheria** (now given as an all-in-one vaccine, Revaxis, that lasts for ten years), **typhoid** and **hepatitis A.** Immunisations against hepatitis B and rabies may also be recommended depending on the duration of your stay and the sort of activities you will be undertaking.

Hepatitis A vaccine (Havrix Monodose or Avaxim) comprises two injections given about a year apart, though you will have cover from the time of the first

PERSONAL FIRST AID KIT

It is highly advisable to prepare your own first aid kit and to carry it with you wherever you travel in Tajikistan. A minimal kit should contain:

- A good drying antiseptic, eg: iodine or potassium permanganate
- A few small dressings (Band-Aids)
- Suncream
- Insect repellent
- Ibuprofen or paracetamol
- Immodium and rehydration salts
- Ciprofloxacin or norfloxacin (for travellers' diarrhoea)
- A pair of fine-pointed tweezers (to remove thorns, splinters, ticks, etc)
- Alcohol-based hand sanitiser or bar of soap in plastic box
- Clingfilm or condoms for covering burns (for anyone with a camping stove)
- Sterile kit including needles, syringe and scalpel blade

injection. The course typically costs £100 and, once completed, gives you protection for 25 years. The vaccine is sometimes available on the NHS. **Hepatitis B** vaccination should be considered for longer trips (two months or more) and by those working in a medical setting or with children. The vaccine schedule comprises three doses taken over a six-month period, but for those aged 16 or over it can be given over a period of 21 days. A minimum period of eight weeks is needed for those under 16 for the three injections. The rapid course needs to be boosted after one year. A combined hepatitis A and B vaccine, Twinrix, is available, though at least three doses are needed for it to be fully effective.

The injectable **typhoid** vaccines (eg: Typhim Vi) last for three years and are about 75% effective. Oral capsules (such as Vivotif) may also be available for those aged six and over. Three capsules taken over five days last for approximately three years but may be less effective than the injectable version especially if they are not taken correctly. Typhoid vaccines are particularly advised for those travelling in rural areas and when there may be difficulty in ensuring safe water supplies and food.

Tajikistan is classified as a high-risk **rabies** country. Vaccination before travel is highly recommended as there is likely to be a shortage of the specific post-exposure treatment needed in Tajikistan.

There is a small risk of **tick-borne encephalitis**, a viral infection spread by infected ticks, which is more common between April and September. If you intend to go trekking in forested areas during these months, then it would be wise to get immunised. The vaccine (Ticovac) is readily available and is given as a two-dose course with a follow up booster 5–12 months later if the traveller is at continued risk. The two doses are given ideally a month apart, but can be given two weeks apart if time is short. Prevention of tick bites is paramount (see box, opposite).

There is a risk of **malaria**, predominantly vivax, but some falciparum too, from June to October in the southern part of the country bordering with Afghanistan. Anti-malarial prophylaxis will be suggested to travellers visiting those regions during those months. The most likely regime is chloroquine and proguanil, but Malarone, doxycycline or mefloquine can be used as alternatives. Seek medical advice to see which is best for you.

While pharmacies in Tajikistan are numerous, especially in the main cities, and some are well equipped, you should still pack a **first aid kit** (a comprehensive

Prevention is always better than cure, so if you are going to be walking in rural areas ensure that you are dressed appropriately with long sleeves, long trousers tucked into boots and a hat. At the end of the day check each other for ticks.

Ticks should ideally be removed as soon as possible as leaving them on the body increases the chance of infection. They should be removed with special tick tweezers that can be bought in good travel shops. Failing that you can use your finger nails: grasp the tick as close to your body as possible and pull steadily and firmly away at right angles to your skin. The tick will then come away complete, as long as you do not jerk or twist. If possible, douse the wound with alcohol (any spirit will do) or iodine. Irritants (eg: Olbas oil) or lit cigarettes are to be discouraged since they can cause the ticks to regurgitate and therefore increase the risk of disease. It is best to get a travelling companion to check you for ticks; if you are travelling with small children, remember to check their heads, and particularly behind the ears.

Spreading redness around the bite and/or fever and/or aching joints after a tick bite imply that you have an infection that requires antibiotic treatment, so seek advice.

kit is essential for trekkers and others visiting remote areas) and any prescription medicines you require.

Have a dental checkup before you arrive in Tajikistan. Dental services are very basic outside Dushanbe.

TRAVEL CLINICS AND HEALTH INFORMATION A full list of current travel clinic websites worldwide is available on w istm.org. For other journey preparation information, consult w travelhealthpro.org.uk (UK) or w wwwnc.cdc.gov/travel/ (US). Information about various medications may be found on w netdoctor.co.uk/travel. All advice found online should be used in conjunction with expert advice received prior to or during travel.

IN TAJIKISTAN The medical system in Tajikistan is seriously overstretched. The quality of medical training has fallen since the end of the USSR, many doctors have left to find work abroad, hospitals are run-down and equipment is out of date. Outside of the major cities there is also a shortage of drugs and other medical supplies. If you are ill or have an accident, you will be able to receive basic emergency treatment in Dushanbe, Kulob or Khujand but will then require evacuation (MEDEVAC) to a country with more developed medical infrastructure for ongoing care.

Most towns in Tajikistan have *aptekas*, small pharmacies selling a range of generic drugs. You do not need a prescription to purchase medication, but should read the instructions carefully or get someone else to explain them to you.

Water
DO NOT DRINK TAP WATER It can be a serious health hazard. Use bottled water, which is widely available, or even better, take a reusable water bottle and filter with you.

Common medical problems
Travellers' diarrhoea Diarrhoeal diseases and other gastro-intestinal infections are fairly common, and perhaps half of all visitors will suffer in this way. Travellers'

Although Tajikistan is not an area with a high risk of malaria, mosquitoes can carry diseases and their bites are, in any case, uncomfortable. As the sun is going down, don long clothes and apply repellent on any exposed flesh. Pack a DEET-based insect repellent (roll-ons or sticks are the least messy preparations for travelling). Repellents should contain between 50% and 55% DEET and can be used for children and pregnant women. Insect coils and fans reduce rather than eliminate bites. Travel clinics usually sell a good range of nets, treatment kits and repellents.

Mosquitoes and many other insects are attracted to light. If you are camping, never put a lamp near the opening of your tent, or you will have a swarm of biters waiting to join you when you retire. In hotel rooms, be aware that the longer your light is on, the greater the number of insects will be sharing your accommodation.

diarrhoea, as well as more serious conditions such as typhoid (of which there are not infrequent outbreaks, even in Dushanbe), comes from getting bacteria in your mouth. To avoid it you should ensure that you observe good hygiene practices, such as regular hand washing, using bottled water (including for cleaning teeth), and avoiding foods of doubtful provenance. Many travellers use the following maxim to remind them what is safe:

PEEL IT, BOIL IT, COOK IT OR FORGET IT

This means that fruit you have washed and peeled yourself, and hot foods, should be safe but raw foods, cold cooked foods, salads, ice cream and ice are all risky, and foods kept lukewarm in hotel buffets often harbour numerous bugs. That said, plenty of travellers and expatriates enjoy fruit and vegetables, so do keep a sense of perspective: food served in a fairly decent hotel in a large town or a place regularly frequented by expatriates is likely to be safest, but even this is not guaranteed.

If you are struck down with diarrhoea in spite of your precautions, remember that dehydration is your greatest concern. Drink lots of clear fluids. Sachets of oral rehydration salts give the perfect biochemical mix to replace all fluids you are losing. If you don't have rehydration salts, or can't stand the taste, any dilute mixture of sugar and salt in water will do you good: try Coke or orange squash with a three-finger pinch of salt added to each glass (if you are salt-depleted you won't taste the salt). Or add eight level teaspoons of sugar (18g) and one level teaspoon of salt (3g) to one litre (five cups) of safe water. A squeeze of lemon or orange juice improves the taste and adds potassium, which is also lost in diarrhoea. Drink two large glasses after every bowel action, and more if you are thirsty. These solutions are still absorbed well if you are vomiting, but you will need to take sips at a time. If you are not eating, you need to drink three litres a day plus whatever is pouring into the toilet. If you feel like eating, take a bland, high-carbohydrate diet. Plain rice, dry bread or digestive biscuits are ideal.

If the diarrhoea is bad, or you are passing blood or slime, or you have a fever, you will probably need antibiotics in addition to fluid replacement. Consult a doctor as soon as possible. A dose of norfloxacin or ciprofloxacin repeated twice a day until better may be appropriate (if you are planning to take an antibiotic with you, note that both norfloxacin and ciprofloxacin are available only on prescription in the UK).

Altitude sickness If you are heading into the Pamirs it is important to be aware of the possibility of altitude sickness. Acute mountain sickness (AMS) can affect everyone – even really fit people – during a rapid ascent and staying more than 12 hours above 2,500m (8,203ft). It regularly afflicts those travelling along the Pamir Highway from Sary Tash. Altitude sickness is caused by acute exposure to low partial pressure of oxygen: in layman's terms this means that the amount of available oxygen decreases as you ascend, to the point that the body has insufficient oxygen in the blood to continue functioning normally. Symptoms of mild altitude sickness include headaches, nausea, anorexia (lack or loss of appetite for food), insomnia and confusion, and can be minimised by taking time to acclimatise to the altitude. Many people recommend taking acetazolamide (Diamox) prophylactically to assist in acclimatising. Discuss this with your doctor or other health-care professional before you go. Even if you are taking Diamox, developing any symptoms which might be AMS means that you should descend at least 500 metres as soon as possible.

More serious forms of mountain sickness include pulmonary oedema (fluid on the lungs) and cerebral oedema (swelling of the brain). The first is characterised by a shortness of breath, dry cough and fever and the latter by a persistent headache, unsteady gait, confusion, delirium and loss of consciousness. These are both medical emergencies and need immediate evacuation and treatment by qualified professionals.

A useful free download on altitude sickness can be found at w medex.org.uk.

Prickly heat In Dushanbe and the lowlands, it can become exceptionally hot in summer: temperatures above 45°C are not unknown. A fine pimply rash on the chest or forearms is likely to be heat rash; it is caused by sweat becoming trapped beneath the skin and causing a histamine reaction. Cool showers, dabbing dry, and talc will help. Treat the problem by wearing only loose, 100%-cotton clothes and sleeping naked under a fan. An antihistamine tablet may help reduce the itching, as will hydrocortisone cream or Sudocrem.

Sunstroke and dehydration The sun in Tajikistan can be very harsh, even in the mountains where the lower temperatures may suggest otherwise. Sunstroke and dehydration are serious risks.

Wearing a hat, long loose sleeves and sunscreen helps to avoid sunburn. Prolonged unprotected exposure can result in heatstroke, which is potentially fatal. Stay out of the sun between noon and 15.00.

In the heat you sweat more, so dehydration is likely. Don't rely on feeling thirsty to tell you to drink – if your urine is anything other than colourless then you aren't drinking enough. Carry bottled water with you at all times and make sure you stop to drink it.

Rabies Rabies can be carried by all warm-blooded mammals and the disease is transmitted to humans through contact with an infected animal's saliva. If you are bitten, scratched or licked, you must assume that the animal has rabies. Scrub the wound with soap under a running tap for around 10–15 minutes or while pouring water from a bottle, then pour on antiseptic, or alcohol if none is available. This helps stop the rabies virus entering the body and will guard against wound infections, including tetanus.

As previously mentioned, Tajikistan is classified as a high-risk rabies country, and vaccination before travel is strongly recommended. If you are bitten and have not had a course of pre-exposure vaccine then you will require a blood product Rabies Immunoglobulin (RIG) and five doses of vaccine given over 30 days. The

Please note that the information below is an overview and self-treatment must only be carried out in emergency situations and after professional medical assistance has been sought. We strongly recommend that any visitors to remote parts of Tajikistan attend a first aid course before arrival.

In the event of a major accident or other emergency, don't panic. Call for help (phone a hospital, your insurance company or even flag down a passer-by) but don't wait for assistance to arrive before starting treatment. Keep note of what has happened, any changes in the patient's condition, and the type and quantity of any drugs you administer.

BLEEDING Applying pressure to a minor wound will stop it bleeding as the blood will begin to clot naturally. If the wound is on a limb, raising it above the heart will also help.

For larger wounds, pack the wound with a large, clear dressing and apply pressure for 10 minutes. This should slow or stop the bleeding. Wrap a bandage tightly around the original dressing to maintain the pressure. Stitches may be required. If the blood is pumping out fast and at high pressure, there may be damage to an artery. Put pressure on the wound and, if you know how, tie a tourniquet further up the limb. Seek medical help fast.

Internal bleeding is difficult to diagnose but symptoms include pain, external bruising, and bloody discharge from the ear, nose, mouth, anus or urethra. If this type of bleeding is suspected, get to A&E straight away and, in the meantime, treat the casualty for shock (see opposite).

BURNS Minor burns (first- and second-degree) can be superficial or slightly deeper, causing the skin to blister. Normally these will heal naturally if kept clean and dry, but if blisters cover more than 20% of the body (10% for children), they should be treated as severe burns (see below), as the fluid loss from the blisters can be fatal.

Severe or third-degree burns affect all layers of the skin and may burn nerve endings, preventing the casualty feeling pain. They include electrical and chemical burns. Casualties with severe burns often suffer from shock (see opposite) and need to be taken to hospital urgently. Infection is also highly likely.

Cool the burn by running it under cold water. If anything is stuck to the burn (such as clothing), cut it back but do not pull it off. Do not burst blisters or add any creams. Using clean plastic (ideally cling film but a plastic bag or condom will do), cover the burn to keep bacteria out. Tape the plastic in place, ensuring the tape is stuck to the plastic and not the skin.

To replace lost fluids, dissolve half a teaspoon of salt and a tablespoon of sugar in 500ml water and give it to the casualty to drink. However, if the burn may have to be operated on shortly, give only small sips of this liquid.

RIG and first dose of vaccine should be given as soon as possible and ideally within the first 24 hours. Neither RIG nor rabies vaccine were available at the time of writing in Tajikistan and so evacuation would be the only recourse. Having three doses of the vaccine before travel over a minimum of 21 days, but ideally 28 days, simplifies the post-exposure treatment by removing the need for RIG and reducing

FRACTURES If bones are broken a long way from help, you may need to set them temporarily to prevent further damage. Closed fractures (those where the skin is unbroken) may be diagnosed by the pain, swelling of the limb and even the feeling of bones grating together. If you expect help to arrive soon, immobilise the broken limb using a splint (anything from a stick to a rolled up newspaper will do). If help is further away, consider using traction (slowly pulling the limb until the ends of the bone fall back into the right place) before tying the splint.

If the bone pierces the skin (an open fracture) it will need urgent medical help. Clean the wound with antiseptic and dress it to reduce the risk of infection. Straighten the limb immediately (ideally before it becomes swollen) and splint it. If the patient is unconscious, splint the wound before bringing them round, as the pain will be excruciating.

HEAD INJURY Even a small bang to the head can cause brain injury but the amount of blood often makes head injuries look more severe than they actually are. If a casualty is unconscious or has signs of brain injury (closed eyes, blood or clear discharge from the facial orifices, failure to respond to questioning, or making incoherent noises), call for help immediately. Dress the wound and put the casualty in the recovery position. Carefully monitor their breathing, circulation and responses until help arrives.

HEART ATTACK A heart attack is usually caused by a clot or blockage that cuts off the blood supply to part of the heart. If the casualty has chest pain, a shooting pain in the arms, difficulty breathing, an irregular pulse, blue lips, dizziness and an impending sense of doom (a genuine symptom), seek immediate medical attention.

If the casualty is conscious, make them sit or lie down to reduce strain on the heart. Give them aspirin (300mg) to thin the blood. Keep checking their pulse and breathing, beginning CPR if either of these vital signs fails. If anyone has a GTN spray handy, then give two puffs under the tongue. Note that CPR guidance has changed over the years, check up-to-date advice before travelling.

SHOCK Shock is the inadequate circulation of blood and resulting deprivation of oxygen to vital organs. It results from extreme fluid loss, heat problems, spinal cord injury, hypothermia, major infections or severe allergic reactions. Shock can kill.

Initial symptoms of shock include a racing heartbeat, sweating and clamminess. The casualty may also start panting, feel dizzy and sick, and have a weak pulse. If the shock is extreme, the person may become aggressive, gasp and yawn and then fall unconscious. The heart will ultimately stop.

If someone is suffering from shock, get professional help fast. In the meantime, you need to get blood to the brain and the heart. Get the casualty to lie down with their feet raised. Keep them warm with a blanket.

the post-exposure treatment to two doses of vaccine given three days apart. While evacuation may still be necessary, it is less of an emergency. Three doses of vaccine cost around £170 in the UK and last for at least ten years unless you are planning to work as a vet abroad when boosters are recommended annually. Without the correct treatment for rabies following exposure the mortality is almost 100%.

Tetanus Tetanus is caused by the Clostridium tetani bacterium and though it can accumulate on a variety of surfaces, it is most commonly associated with rusty objects such as nails. Cutting yourself or otherwise puncturing the skin brings the bacteria inside the body, where they will thrive. Clean any cuts thoroughly with a strong antiseptic.

Immunisation against tetanus gives good protection for ten years, and it is standard care practice in many places to give a booster injection to any patient with a puncture wound. Symptoms of tetanus may include lockjaw, spasms in any part of the body, excessive sweating, drooling and incontinence and the disease results in death if left untreated. Mild cases of tetanus will be treated with the antibiotic metronidazole and tetanus immunoglobulin, while more severe cases will require admission to intensive care, tetanus immunoglobulin injected into the spinal cord, a tracheotomy and mechanical ventilation, intravenous magnesium and diazepam.

SAFETY

At the time of going to press, all travel restrictions to Tajikistan have been lifted by the UK's Foreign and Commonwealth Office (FCO); all parts of the country are accessible to foreigners. That said, localised violence in Dushanbe, the Romit Valley and along the border with Afghanistan in 2014 and 2015 has previously caused the FCO to suggest heightened vigilance when travelling in those areas of Tajikistan.

More seriously, in July and August 2012 foreigners were advised against all travel to GBAO, and in particular Khorog, following a security incident (see box, page 159). Twenty-two British and Commonwealth nationals had to be evacuated from the area.

Dushanbe is considered relatively safe, but there have been occasional muggings and petty crime against foreigners. Instances of sexual assault, including rape, have been reported to consular staff, included suspected use of 'date rape' drugs. Take care not to leave drinks unattended, nor accept drinks from strangers.

There is a general threat of terrorism in Tajikistan, though foreigners are not currently thought to be a principal target. Incidents in Tajikistan in recent years include an explosion outside a restaurant in Dushanbe in March 2011, and the discovery of three abandoned vehicles containing improvised explosive devices in Sughd two months earlier.

ROAD SAFETY Driving standards in Tajikistan are generally poor, and the state of the roads even worse. The wide variety of vehicles on the roads, from decrepit Soviet-era makes to large modern 4x4s, makes for traffic travelling at different speeds. Overtaking on the inside, and illegal U-turns, are among many common infringements in the cities. The poor state of repair of most roads, with pot-holes and often inadequate or non-existent street lighting, adds to the difficulties. In rural areas, animals and pedestrians wandering into the road present a considerable risk.

If you are driving in Tajikistan, you will need to display care and caution, always wear a seat belt, and never drink and drive. Try to avoid driving outside cities after dark, as roads are poorly lit and other vehicles may not have working lights. Bad driving also creates a risk to pedestrians.

When on foot, you should avoid the local practice of crossing busy roads by walking out to the centre of the road and waiting for a gap in the oncoming traffic, even if this means taking a detour to cross the road at the next set of traffic lights. Do not expect cars to stop for you, even if you are on a zebra crossing.

WOMEN TRAVELLERS

Tajikistan is generally a safe place to travel, whether you are male or female. That said, you should exercise the usual personal safety precautions and dress modestly, especially in conservative rural areas. It is not culturally acceptable to wear revealing clothing (including shorts, vest tops, or T-shirts which reveal your stomach) in Tajikistan. If in doubt, look at what ordinary women are wearing on the street, and dress with commensurate modesty.

If you are staying in a homestay, you will be the guest of a family, and will often be invited to take your meals with the mother and other family members. You may eat separately from the men, but this is not an affront: the women are welcoming you into their sisterhood and, if they speak a little English, will speak far more openly with you than they would if their male family members were present.

In guesthouses and cheap hotels, particularly those on the roadside, women travellers should be more careful than when staying in family-run accommodation options and more upmarket hotels. Guests in these places tend to be predominantly male, as are the staff, and although the majority of stays will be perfectly fine, we have experienced – and heard of other cases of – sexual harassment. If you are travelling alone, or with another woman, do not sit up late drinking and socialising with male guests or staff, as it may be viewed negatively, increasing your vulnerability. Check that there is a working lock on your door, and if you think that the lock is faulty (or that the staff have another key), consider also putting a chair or table behind the door to block it.

Unaccompanied women may receive unwanted attention in bars and clubs but this is usually deflected with a few terse words. If the harassment continues, alert the management or leave the premises and find a more pleasant alternative. Try to avoid physical confrontation, as alcohol-fuelled violence and being tailed home are not uncommon. There have been suspected cases where 'date rape' drugs have been used; keep a close eye on your drink, and do not accept drinks from strangers. Particular caution should be taken when hailing taxis: in Dushanbe phoning for a cab, or getting the establishment you are in to do this for you, is a safer option.

LGBTQ TRAVELLERS

Homosexuality has been decriminalised in Tajikistan but there is, to our knowledge, no open gay scene in Dushanbe. Many people in Tajikistan are deeply conservative, especially when it comes to the issue of sexuality, and homosexuality is still often seen as a mental illness (a hangover from the Soviet period).

If you are travelling with a same-sex partner, you would be wise to refrain from public displays of affection and be cautious when discussing your relationship with others: it is often simplest to allow others to assume you are simply travelling with a friend. Double rooms frequently have twin beds, so asking for one room is unlikely to raise eyebrows in any case.

TRAVELLERS OF COLOUR

Travellers of African descent, and those with red or blond hair and very pale skin, tend to stand out while travelling through Tajikistan, despite millennia of cultural mixing in the region. You may be stared at on the street, or approached to have your photograph taken, especially in smaller towns and rural areas. Many of these interactions are out of curiosity and easily, even humorously, managed. However, alcohol-fuelled aggression is not uncommon, so try to avoid physical confrontation if possible.

TRAVELLING WITH A DISABILITY

People with mobility problems will experience difficulty travelling in Tajikistan. Public transport is rarely able to carry wheelchairs, few buildings have disabled access, and streets are littered with trip hazards such as broken paving, uncovered manholes, and utility pipes. Hotel rooms are often spread over multiple floors without lifts and assistance from staff is not guaranteed. If you have a disability and are travelling to Tajikistan, you are advised to travel with a companion who can help you when the country's infrastructure and customer service fall short.

TRAVELLING WITH KIDS

This is relatively easy given Tajiks' focus on family life. Children are welcomed in restaurants and shops but you may have difficulty manoeuvring pushchairs in and out of buildings and along broken pavements. Nappies, baby food and other similar items are available in supermarkets and larger stores, but you are unlikely to find European brands. Journeys by car and public transport are often long and uncomfortable, and food supplies erratic, which may deter families with younger children travelling into the interior of the country.

WHAT TO TAKE

You may wish to consider taking the following with you, in addition to the usual holiday packing.

- **Plug adaptors** Sockets in Tajikistan are the twin round pin, continental European type. The voltage is 220V.
- **A torch** Many parts of Tajikistan, including city streets, are unlit at night, and pavements may conceal dangers such as uncovered manholes. Power cuts are not uncommon. If you are planning to camp, or use homestays in rural areas, you'll need a torch to navigate to the latrine at night.
- **Mosquito repellent** Tajikistan may not be a major malarial country, but the swarms of mosquitoes you may encounter in summer among its lakes and forests can still damage your enjoyment of your holiday. Make sure you also pack long-sleeved shirts (you'll also need these for visiting conservative areas and religious places).
- **Warm clothing** If you are planning a trip to Tajikistan in the winter months (which in the north of the country means November to April), or plan to head up into the mountains, you need to treat its cold temperatures with respect, with good warm clothing minimising areas of exposed skin. The locals wrap themselves in fur, but if you do not want to wear fur clothing, outdoor adventure shops are probably the best source of suitably warm garments. Dress in several layers, with particularly warm outer garments.
- **Good footwear** In winter, wear rubber-soled boots, preferably lined with fleece. If you are trekking, good hiking boots are essential.
- **Flip-flops** You'll need these inside homestay accommodation (shoes are left at the front door in Tajik homes). They can also come in useful in bathrooms.

- If you will be staying in bottom-range accommodation, a **sleeping bag** or **cotton sleeping bag liner**, of the kind used by youth hostellers, can help save you from unsavoury bedding. A **universal sink plug** is also worth packing.
- Good **suncream**, a **lip salve**, **sunglasses** and a spare set of any **prescription glasses**. Swiss army type **knife**, packed into hold luggage. A versatile knife can be a godsend in many situations.
- **Toilet paper**, **wet wipes** and **hand sanitiser gel** are highly advisable and will make staying clean infinitely easier.
- **Dental floss** and **a needle**, a roll of **gaffer tape** and a packet of **cable ties** will enable you to fix almost anything while you're on the go.
- **Small gift items** related to your home country make ideal presents for hosts
- **Pictures** of your family and your home area. People love to see these.
- **Sanitary towels and tampons** are not widely available outside larger cities.

MONEY

The unit of currency in Tajikistan is the Tajik somoni (TJS). Notes are printed in denominations of one, three, five, ten, 20, 50, 100, 200 and 500 somoni with coins of five, ten, 20 and 50 dirhams. You may occasionally get one-, three- and five-somoni coins. The somoni was introduced in 2000, replacing the Tajik rouble.

WHAT TO CARRY The standard advice for travellers in the developing world used to be to carry most of their money in travellers' cheques. These days, however, and especially in a country with an underdeveloped banking system like Tajikistan, it is almost impossible to change them outside the largest banks in Dushanbe, and even there you'll get an unfavourable rate.

You will need to carry most of your money in cash. US dollars are the easiest to exchange, though someone can usually be found to exchange euros, roubles or, at a push, sterling. Divide your money between multiple locations about your person and carry a dummy wallet with just a few dollars and some old supermarket loyalty cards as a decoy for pickpockets and anyone attempting to extract a bribe.

ATMs are increasingly common in Tajik cities, and you'll find them both at banks and in the lobbies of larger hotels. They often dispense both somoni and US dollars. If you run out of cash in a smaller town, banks will often advance you cash on a MasterCard or Visa card, or you can receive Western Union, MoneyGram and other money transfers.

Prices in this guidebook are given in either US dollars or Tajik somoni. The currency used in each instance is the one that the company or organisation advertises for itself.

CHANGING MONEY Banks are more or less everywhere in Tajikistan, even if they don't have an ATM, and, providing they have sufficient cash behind the counter, all of them will change US dollars and Russian roubles. It is usually possible also to change euros. If you have another currency it is still worth asking, for if they cannot do it they may still be able to summon someone from the bazaar to change it for you.

Dushanbe and the larger cities also have a number of money-changing booths: you'll recognise them by the boards outside advertising their current buy and sell rates for various currencies. Their rates may be incrementally better than in the banks, but there's not a great deal in it.

Tajikistan's money changers are less fussy than others in the region, but to avoid hassle at an inconvenient moment you should keep your foreign notes clean, unfolded and uncreased. Flattening them inside a book may help. If there are any marks on the notes, including ink stamps from where they have been counted in a bank, they may be rejected. High-denomination bills are preferred, as are US dollars printed since 2010.

BUDGETING

Tajikistan is, on the whole, a cheap country in which to travel. Yes, it is possible in Dushanbe to spend US$400 a night in a hotel, eat in expensive restaurants, and hire a car and driver to escort you to every last lamp post, but fortunately this is a lifestyle choice only, and in many parts of the country it would be an impossibility in any case as top-end facilities with top-end prices are simply not there.

In Dushanbe, it is possible to get a dormitory bed for US$10, a clean, budget double room for US$40, and a mid-range room with breakfast included will set you back around US$80. Upwards of US$200 a night is not uncommon for the top-end hotels. The price of meals is similarly varied: café snacks start at around US$1.50, and for a meal in a top-end hotel restaurant with wine you can easily be looking at US$70 per person.

Outside of Dushanbe your money will go noticeably further. Other than accommodation, transport and meals will be your greatest expenditures. If you are travelling on a budget you will survive on US$25 a day but this will restrict your sleeping options and require you to travel solely by public transport. A budget of US$50 would give you far greater flexibility.

Prices start rising dramatically when you make special arrangements. Car and driver hire is particularly expensive as it is generally charged by the kilometre and you will need to pay for both directions, even if you are only travelling one way. Trekking guides and pack animals are reasonably cheap by international standards, but the costs quickly add up if you are trekking for a protracted period or part of a very small group.

Museum and theatre tickets are an absolute steal in Tajikistan, so even budget travellers should be able to enjoy plenty of culture and entertainment. You will rarely pay more than US$1 to visit a museum or cultural site, and seats at theatrical performances, including the opera and ballet, typically start at US$2.

GETTING AROUND

Tajikistan is not an especially large country, but the lack of infrastructure is such that travelling from A to B will always take up a significant proportion of your time. The best approach is to consider the journey itself as part of the adventure and, however you choose to travel, look out of the window and try to enjoy the views.

BY AIR Tajik Air (w *tajikairlines.com*) and Somon Air (w *somonair.com*) have domestic flights covering various destinations in Tajikistan, but the only two routes that fly regularly are those between Dushanbe and Khujand, and Dushanbe and Khorog. The timetable is movable at best, and flights are liable to be changed or cancelled at short notice, especially if the weather is poor. The availability of tickets for the Khorog flight is particularly unreliable as there is a maximum of 16 passenger seats on each flight, and one trekking party or NGO delegation can easily book out the whole lot.

You should be aware that many of the planes in use are old and have not been maintained in accordance with international standards. The terrain and unpredictable weather conditions also make for challenging flying conditions. Weigh up the pros and cons of flying, sit next to the emergency exit if you have the choice, and if you are walking across the runway to the plane, do not walk in front of the propellers. Even at a distance of 20m it is possible for things to get sucked into the blades.

BY ROAD Wherever you want to go in Tajikistan, getting there will be half the fun. Riding around in the back of a truck is still a distinct possibility, but things are getting easier: the extent of sealed roads has greatly increased, new tunnels are cutting the number of nail-biting mountain passes, and road-clearance crews work to keep the main highways clear of rockfalls and other debris.

However close your destination, you should allow plenty of time to get there. Taxi and minibus drivers may appear to be in a rush, but they're also the most likely to get flat tyres or to break down entirely. Snowfall and avalanches stop even the most determined of drivers. The journey may take a while but you will get there eventually, *inshallah* (God willing – you will hear this a lot!). Bad roads and cramped buses can be physically very wearing, so make sure you factor in as much time as you can between long trips for recharging your batteries.

One thing to bear in mind when travelling by road is dust. Even on predominantly paved roads there is plenty of sand and grit. Keep a scarf or bandana handy to protect your nose and mouth and keep anything that might get damaged (specifically electronics) inside the vehicle with you, as any bags on the roof will look like they've been through a dust storm.

By bus Tajikistan's buses fall into two categories: relatively modern, usually Chinese-made buses that serve set, inner-city routes; and the *mashrutka*, overcrowded minibuses in varying stages of decay that are driven by devils on speed. Private bus company Asian Express (page 69) offers services in large,

(page 69)

HITCHHIKING IN TAJIKISTAN

With thanks to our hitchhiking guru, Steve Dew-Jones (@SteveDewJones)

It is never possible to recommend hitchhiking without a word of caution, due to the inherent risks involved, but I know from experience that it is both possible and a lot of fun, wherever you are in the world.

Tajikistan is no exception, although, as with much of central Asia, the Western concept of hitchhiking does not exist in quite the same way, as the bulk of vehicles double up as taxi services. As such, it is indeed important to proceed with caution, both in terms of choosing which driver/vehicle you trust to brave the winding (and in some cases death-defying) slopes of the Pamir Highway, and clarifying whether you are willing to pay a small sum for the privilege.

Beyond this, the same rules and advice apply to Tajikistan as to anywhere else in the world. Top tips include standing in a visible position (but not the middle of the road), making sure there is space for drivers to pull in on either side of where you are standing, and having a few words of the native language under your belt (20 words can get you a surprisingly long way) to ease negotiations over direction and any monetary contribution you do (or do not) wish to make.

Patience, as ever, is a virtue when hitchhiking, and this is not helped by the noticeably decreased volume of traffic in Tajikistan, especially in remote areas. Try to make sure your driver takes you to a helpful spot, although this may be hard to communicate. Where possible, aim for petrol stations or main roads leading out of town (in the direction you wish to travel), and make sure you have a map.

2

- Drive a car that is common in the local area: you won't stand out and, if you break down, the parts and expertise to repair it are more likely to be available.
- Check you have a spare tyre, jack, handle and wheel wrench. Spare oil and water, a tow rope, a jerrycan of fuel and a shovel are also highly advisable.
- If you have the option, get central locking, electric windows and air conditioning: they give you greater control over what (and, indeed, who) comes into the vehicle with you.
- Make sure you know the rules of the road and have a good idea about where you are going. Tell someone you trust your route and your expected time of arrival.
- Carry your driving licence and any vehicle documentation with you at all times. Photocopies are useful for handing to police and other interested parties.
- Ensure there is a first aid kit, food and plenty of drinking water in the boot in case of emergencies.
- A mobile phone (or a satellite phone in remote locations) is essential in the event of an accident or a breakdown you can't fix by the side of the road.

air-conditioned coaches throughout southern Tajikistan from its main hub in Dushanbe. Minibuses, however, are by far the most common, and if you are travelling between smaller cities in Tajikistan they'll be the most usual form of transport. You are not guaranteed to get a seat, and will likely spend much of your journey with someone else's shopping on your lap and their elbow in your face.

If you are going on a long journey, try to get a minibus that leaves early in the morning. There are two reasons for this. First, it will maximise the hours of daylight driving. Your minibus may or may not have all its lights working (the same goes for other vehicles on the road) and the driver will have a better chance of seeing where the bends are. Secondly, it is not uncommon for minibus drivers to have a cheeky drink (or three), so starting out early maximises your chances of a sober drive.

By taxi Most towns have taxis. Drivers instantly mark up their fares for a foreigner, so be prepared to haggle. There are two types of taxis: professional taxis which may even have a yellow taxi sign on the roof, and general motorists who are happy to pick up passengers and drop them to their destination for a few somoni. In both cases, you will need to agree a fare at the start of your journey and be prepared to stop and ask directions *en route*. Having a map and the name of any landmarks close to your destination will certainly help, as will writing down the address in Cyrillic script.

For longer drives it is often possible to hire a car and driver. Again, you will need to confirm the price in advance, though remember the final price may depend on the distance driven. Ordinary taxi drivers may consent to being hired for several days, otherwise approach a travel agent. The Safar Drivers' Association in Khorog (page 158) is the best bet if you want to hire a car and driver to take you up the Pamir Highway.

Self-drive Having your own vehicle gives you the ultimate freedom to travel where you want, and we would thoroughly recommend it. You need to be well prepared and do your research beforehand (the encyclopedic *Vehicle-dependent Expedition Guide* by Tom Sheppard (Desert Winds, 1998) and *The Adventure Motorcycling*

Handbook by Chris Scott (Trailblazer 2012) stand out) but Tajikistan has some of the most remarkable drives in the world, and it would be a pity to miss out just because of a lack of transport.

A 4x4 is highly advisable for overlanding in Tajikistan, particularly if you want to get away from the main roads. You can frequently find yourself driving over mud and rock and through riverbeds, particularly in the spring, and will need the extra power to keep yourself from getting stuck. The Land Rover is still the vehicle of choice for most overlanders, but getting parts in Tajikistan is nigh on impossible: you'll need to bring your own spares, or compromise and get a Toyota Hilux, which local mechanics will be more familiar with.

Whatever your vehicle, there are several important points to consider. Fuel and water are top of the list. Carry as much fuel as you can to increase your range. Away from the large towns, fuel can sometimes be hard to come by and the quality is often low. It's worth filtering fuel through a specialised filter or piece of gauze to prevent the crud blocking the fuel lines. Make sure your spare container is kept topped up.

Petrol (*benzene*) in Tajikistan is sold by the litre and is usually available as octane 91 or 92. The 95 is much harder to come by. Diesel (80) is significantly cheaper and has the added advantage that you can always siphon some off a truck (with the driver's permission) if you run low in the middle of nowhere. Along with fuel, carry as much water as possible, both for yourself and to cool your engine in case of overheating.

Other essentials to carry are a comprehensive toolkit and manual for your vehicle, key spare parts and tyres (the locals often carry two), and a first aid kit. If you plan on doing any off-road driving, sand mats or chicks and a tow rope are strongly recommended.

Road surfaces vary greatly. Throughout the book, we have attempted to give an indication of road quality, but local conditions can also vary greatly, with a gravel surface suddenly giving way to a kilometre of deeply rutted tracks. Mud and landslips present the greatest challenges in spring; rocks, pot-holes and random obstacles can blow a tyre at any time of year.

By bicycle Tajikistan is a popular destination for cyclists pitting themselves against the challenges of the Pamir Highway or passing through the country on a multi-country trip. It is not unusual to see Lycra-clad foreigners sweating their way up long and lonely hills, and they inspire both curiosity and confusion in the local population.

Tajikistan's roads are hard on both cyclists and their bikes. Replacement parts are not generally available locally, necessitating a wait in Dushanbe while DHL delivers whatever is needed from home. For an account of cycling the Pamir Highway, complete with practical tips, see box, pages 176–7.

MAPS Detailed, up-to-date maps of Tajikistan are best purchased before you leave home. Stanfords Maps in London (**w** *stanfords.co.uk*) has a reasonable collection of both political and topographic maps and also has a number of trekking maps for the Pamir and Fann ranges.

In Dushanbe, it is possible to buy the locally produced *Tajikistan Tourist Map*. It has a scale of 1:1,200,000 and is available in both English and Russian. It shows the main roads and tourist sites and has useful city plans of Dushanbe, Khujand, Kulob, Qurgonteppa and Khorog.

It is also possible to buy a reasonable city plan of Dushanbe (1:24,000, Russian only) and the excellent 1:400,000 scale map of the Zarafshan and Yagnob valleys, which is produced by the Zarafshan Tourism Development Association (ZTDA). They are available from the Bactria Centre (page 81).

You wake up in a tent, under a bridge or in a bush and think, 'Where shall I go today?' Mounting your steed, bags loaded behind you and only a map in front, all you have to do is choose. Overland travel by motorbike is quite possibly the most liberating form of travel: there's something about being able to reach out and touch what's around you.

Tajikistan is a serious place to bike, especially outside of Dushanbe and the bigger towns. Don't be fooled by the grand-sounding National or Pamir highways. Both roads are undertakings with large stretches of broken rock or dirt track. The seasons should also be taken into account as high passes are likely to be snowy (not very funny on four wheels, let alone on two) and riding conditions are often quite literally freezing. That said, the views along these routes are unsurpassed, with a rugged, harsh beauty, and that tingling feeling of being on roads a stone's throw from Afghanistan or China should bring some warmth back to your toes.

If you think you are ready for the challenge, source a suitable bike and fly it (or, even better, ride it) to Tajikistan. Look for something with long suspension, a front disc brake, a big front wheel and a rack or way of carrying your kit; keeping it on your back is far from advisable. Before you leave, make sure you check the lights and horn (louder the better), the front and back brakes (it's a long way down those precipices), the suspension (you're going to need it), and that the chain is in good condition with plenty of oil. Make sure the wheels are round (seriously) and the tyres have a good amount of tread left in them. If the bike looks too old, is making particularly odd noises or rattles on tarmac, find something better. Traffic is rare and mechanics are only to be found in big towns. There are more fulfilling things than finishing an epic journey with your bike in the back of a truck.

Before you go, ask yourself lots of questions. What's my fuel range? Do I know how to repair a puncture? How will I navigate? Do people know where I'm going and what time I'll check in with them? Do I have enough clothes to be warm and dry? Will I need a sleeping bag?

Dushanbe to Khorog is just 500km by the summer route, but the road conditions are such that the ride may take two to three days or more if the road has fallen into the river again. If that sort of thing excites you, get to it.

For the Pamirs, the best available map is *The Pamirs – a tourist map of Gorno-Badakhshan, Tajikistan, and background information on the region*, which has a scale of 1:500,000. The most recent edition was published in 2016 and is available from **w** geckomaps.com.

Other Gecko maps available include *Northern Tajikistan – a tourist map of Sughd, with adjacent areas of Uzbekistan and Kyrgyzstan* and *Southern Tajikistan - a tourist map of Khatlon and Direct Rule Districts, with adjacent areas of Uzbekistan and Afghanistan*. Both are published at a scale of 1:500,000.

TREKKING

Trekking is one of the main reasons that visitors come to Tajikistan: the mountains are exceptionally beautiful, and the more remote and higher reaches are accessible only on foot. There are suitable routes for everyone here, from those who fancy a

ESSENTIAL EQUIPMENT
- Spare key
- Puncture repair kit
- Engine oil
- Buggies for rack
- Basic tools (spanners, pliers, screwdrivers)
- Emergency food and water
- Reliable map (1:500,000 or less) and compass

EXCEPTIONALLY USEFUL EQUIPMENT
- Wire
- Duct tape
- WD40 and grease
- Spare throttle and clutch cables
- Spark plugs and spare bulbs

CLOTHING
- Helmet with visor, goggles or sunglasses (for dust)
- Thick bike gloves
- Hard-wearing jacket and jeans (or similar) with overtrousers
- Sturdy walking boots or biker boots
- Thermal layer and fleece jacket

The kit listed here is the absolute minimum for a short ride. Anyone wishing to go a long distance should read *The Adventure Motorcycling Handbook* by Chris Scott for practical information on bikes, preparations and maintenance, as well as known trips and overland adventure stories. The website w horizonsunlimited.com is an unparalleled resource for up-to-date overland information, and w advrider.com gives plenty of inspiration.

Don't drive after dark and keep it rubber side down.

Bryn Kewley travelled with us on our first trip across Tajikistan, caught the overland bug, then started motorcycling all of the way from the UK to Singapore.

day hike to a lake or waterfall to see the birds and have a picnic, to serious climbers who want to make a first ascent or trial new routes up peaks over 6,000m.

The main areas for trekking are the Fann and Zarafshan mountains in the northwest of Tajikistan, and the Great and Little Pamirs (collectively 'the Pamirs') in the east. Both areas have definite attractions: which you choose will depend on how long you have available, the time of year, and what you want to see. Specific trekking routes are described in the relevant chapters of this guide; however, we thought we would include a basic summary here to whet your appetite.

The Fann Mountains are at the western end of the Pamir-Alay range, on the border of Tajikistan and Uzbekistan. There are some substantial peaks here, including Chimtarga (5,487m) and Bodhkona (5,138m), and they remain snow-capped year-round. In their shadow, however, are considerably more accessible ridges and passes which even those of moderate fitness levels can trek. The aquamarine lakes in the Fann are some of the natural jewels of Tajikistan, and there are also picturesque meadows, waterfalls and woodlands. You are unlikely to see snow leopard here, but wild boar, hawk, eagle and fox are far more commonplace.

The Zarafshan and Yagnob valleys are both part of the Zarafshan Range, and if you trek here you will see a fascinating combination of ancient cultures and natural wonders. The trekking routes are numerous, and it's also a great spot for mountain biking and horseriding. Routes in the Yagnob Valley typically include homestays in Yagnobi villages, and consequently the chance to see first-hand the Yagnobis' ancient Sogdian culture (see box, page 99).

The Pamirs is a vast area, covering around two-thirds of Tajikistan's territory. Most treks are up on the high-altitude Murghab Plateau, though this is only accessible in the height of summer. Karakul Lake is a popular trekking destination, but the real reason to trek on the plateau is the opportunity to see, meet and stay with Kyrgyz families in their yurts. Trekking here, you also stand a chance of spotting snow leopard and Marco Polo sheep, albeit at a distance.

Still in the Pamirs, the Wakhan Corridor is split between Tajikistan and Afghanistan. Tajikistan is on the northern bank of the river, and you look across at the rugged peaks of the Hindu Kush. An ancient east–west trade route, the corridor is dotted with ruined forts and shrines. It is exceptionally remote, but that is part of the attraction.

Easier to reach is the Bartang Valley, not far from Khorog. This is the route you'll take if you want to trek on the Fedchenko Glacier, a vast expanse which is some 1,000m deep at its thickest point. Trekking around the natural reservoir, created by a landslide in the mid-20th century, is also highly recommended.

Tajikistan's mountains, though stunningly beautiful, are dangerous. The weather can be harsh, the rocks and scree are unstable, and the area is prone to earthquakes. If you do get into difficulty, there is no mountain rescue, and you will be a very long way from a hospital. If you want to trek (and we really do think you should – it's an incredible experience), you need to be properly prepared.

Buy the most detailed topographical maps available (pages 51–2) and plan your route with the help of an experienced local guide. Train thoroughly, and make sure you have all the necessary clothing and equipment. This includes a comprehensive first aid kit. Never, ever trek alone. Source a knowledgeable guide from a local tour operator – if in doubt ask PECTA (page 157) or META (page 175) and tell someone else who you trust where you are going and when you expect to be back. Remember to update them on your return.

ACCOMMODATION

Accommodation options in Tajikistan stretch from the absurd to the sublime, and sometimes are both at once.

At the **top end** of the market, Dushanbe has luxury hotels with marble bathrooms, quality restaurants and hot- and cold-running flunkies. Their private generators keep the power running whatever's happening in the city and your fellow guests will be well-heeled businessmen and expatriates. You will, however, pay well in excess of TJS1,500 (US$170 or so) a night for the privilege, and once through the door could be in more or less any city on earth.

Mid-range hotels are a mixed bag, with some charging excessive sums for fairly basic facilities. The Soviet-era hotels often fall into this bracket, but there are also pleasant surprises such as Hotel Mercury in Dushanbe and the gorgeous riverside Serena Hotel in Khorog.

Tajikistan has plenty of **budget** rooms. Whether you'd want to stay in them is a different matter. Family-run guesthouses are frequently the best option (and ideal

The price codes used in this guide indicate the approximate price of a standard double room with breakfast, per night. Note that many hotels in Tajikistan, especially the older, Soviet-built accommodation, offer a wide variety of room permutations and rates, so this can only serve as a rough guide. The number of rooms has been listed where possible, though there are some instances where an establishment either could not or would not confirm the number of rooms on offer. The price codes below exclude the cost of any booking fee and are based on the exchange rate in use at the time of research.

Luxury	$$$$$	US$200+	TJS1,760+
Upmarket	$$$$	US$100–200	TJS880–1,760
Mid-range	$$$	US$50–100	TJS440–880
Budget	$$	US$20–50	TJS176–440
Shoestring	$	up to US$20	up to TJS176

for meeting other travellers), but you'd probably best get used to shared bathrooms and a squat toilet in the garden.

Recent years have seen the development of **community-based tourism** (CBT) in Tajikistan, and this is a huge boon to travellers in the Fann and Zarafshan mountains and in the Pamirs. Not only are **homestays** affordable (usually US$10 per person plus meals) but they give you the opportunity to see inside a Tajik home, meet a family and fill up on home-cooked food.

Designated **campsites** are relatively uncommon in Tajikistan and those sites typically lack facilities: you will not, for example, find electricity hook-up points or drinking-water taps. It is permitted to camp in the national parks and, indeed, in many remote areas camping will be your only option, especially if you are trekking. Note that there are still unmarked minefields in Tajikistan, particularly in border areas and on the banks of the Panj River, so you should exercise utmost caution at all times. If you wish to put up a tent on private land you will need to ask the owner and will usually be expected to pay a few dollars for the privilege. If you are trekking with local tour operators, they will often provide camping equipment for you, otherwise you will have to bring everything you need with you from home. Reasonable quality tents and sleeping bags are not available to buy locally.

Within Tajikistan, a number of NGOs run **guesthouses** to accommodate their staff. Most of these are in rural areas or located along major highways where it would be convenient to stop for the night. The Mountain Societies Development Support Programme (MSDSP)'s guesthouse near Kalaikhum (page 151) is particularly convenient if you've been delayed by rockfalls or other incidents on the Pamir Highway.

It is not possible to pre-book these guesthouses because they understandably give priority to their own staff, who might need a bed at very short notice. Instead, you will need to call in in person to enquire for that night. If they have space, they will accommodate you for a small fee (**$**) and will usually be able to provide some form of simple supper as well.

EATING AND DRINKING

Tajikistan does not have a long tradition of eating in restaurants: it was nigh on impossible during the Soviet period due to food shortages and the fact that people

2

The price codes used in this guide indicate the average price of a meat-based main dish, excluding vegetables and the 10% service charge. The price of a full meal is likely to be several times higher.

Expensive	$$$$$	US$10+	TJS88+
Above average	$$$$	US$5–10	TJS44–88
Mid-range	$$$	US$3–5	TJS26–44
Cheap and cheerful	$$	US$1.50–3	TJS13–26
Rock bottom	$	up to US$1.50	up to TJS13

were encouraged to eat collectively in the work canteen. This has changed in urban centres, particularly as families choose to host wedding feasts and other large celebrations in restaurants rather than at home, but you will not find the density or diversity of restaurants typical in some other parts of Asia.

Restaurants in Tajikistan (particularly those situated outside of Dushanbe) typically have a limited menu of Russian and Tajik dishes. It is rare for everything listed to actually be available. If the restaurant is not fully booked for a celebration you won't need a reservation, nor to wait for a table. Service may be chaotic but it is generally good-natured.

Sit-down places to eat typically fall into three categories. There are large, often fairly ghastly, restaurants which only cater to groups, either private parties or tour groups. These serve a buffet or set menu, and they may or may not welcome independent guests.

Second, and infinitely preferable, are Western-style restaurants which have multiple tables, a menu, and cook to order. You can wander in off the street and sit down, as long as it's during opening hours. In larger cities you'll have a choice of different cuisines – Dushanbe's restaurant scene is looking decidedly cosmopolitan these days – and you can expect a reasonable level of customer service. You will be expected to leave a tip: 10% is standard.

Thirdly, you have local cafés, which are unpretentious and generally offer good value for money. These typically serve Tajik cuisine or other easily prepared snacks, and depending on the establishment you will either order from the counter and then take a seat, or wait for someone to come to you. There is unlikely to be a menu, and staff may well not speak English, so be prepared to look around at what other people are eating, point and smile. A tip, though not expected, is always appreciated.

More common than restaurants and cafés are street-side food stalls: from American fast-food stands with burgers and fries, to smoking grills and the vinegary smell of *shashlik* and onions wafting down the road, making your stomach rumble. Women with trays piled high with savoury pastries saunter through markets and the lobbies of office buildings; trestle-tables nearly buckle beneath the weight of freshly baked bread. The local fare tends to be tastier (and cheaper) than attempts at foreign food.

Tajikistan has very few clubs and bars: there is just a scattering of establishments in Dushanbe and Khujand. They tend to be frequented predominantly by businessmen (both locals and foreign nationals); it's unusual to see unaccompanied women in bars unless they're working. Champagne and expensive vodka brands such as Beluga are the status drinks of choice, and cocktails are increasingly popular. Drinking to excess is common, as is drink-driving home.

TAJIK CUISINE Tajikistan runs on bread and tea. Wherever you are, from a customs post to a shepherd's hut, there will always be a kettle on the boil and a few china tea bowls filled with a light, steaming tea.

Tajik cuisine is definitely central Asian (plenty of grilled meats and dairy products), but with an influence from Afghanistan and Russia too. The national dish, as far as there is one, is *plov* or *osh*, an oily rice-based dish with shredded carrot, meat and occasionally raisins, roasted garlic or nuts. Plov is eaten with the hands from a communal plate at the centre of the table.

Equally popular is *qurutob*. Balls of salted cheeses (*qurut*) are dissolved in water and poured over dry, flaky bread. The dish is then topped with onions fried in oil. It may be accompanied by *laghman* (noodle soup with mutton). Tajik restaurants tend to offer diners quite a limited menu.

Every meal is accompanied by round, flat bread called *non*. Non is treated almost reverentially: it should not be put on the floor, placed upside down or thrown away. If it has turned stale it should be given to the birds.

Common snacks include *manti* (steamed meat dumplings), *somsa* (triangular pastry with a meat and onion stuffing) and *belyash* (deep-fried dough stuffed with minced lamb).

Dairy products feature heavily in Tajik cuisine. In addition to the qurut are *chaka* (sour milk) and *kaymak* (clotted cream), both of which are eaten with bread. Western-style yoghurt, including bottled yoghurt drinks, is popular for breakfast.

If you are in Tajikistan in late summer and early autumn, the country is bursting with fresh fruits. Roadsides stalls sell watermelons the size of beach balls; the sweet, juicy pomegranates are a glorious shade of pink; and you can also enjoy grapes, apricots, apples, figs and peaches.

PUBLIC HOLIDAYS

Tajikistan's public holidays are a mixed blessing. While they'll be the bane of your existence if you need to cross the border, extend a visa or go to the bank, they are also an opportunity to join family feasts, see *buz kashi* and, if you're in Dushanbe for Independence Day, soak up the pomp and circumstance.

1 January	New Year's Day
8 March	International Women's Day
21–23 March	Navruz
1 May	International Labour Day
9 May	Victory Day
27 June	National Unity Day
9 September	Independence Day
6 November	Constitution Day

SHOPPING

In a land where the label 'Made in Turkey' is seen as a mark of the utmost quality, you shouldn't expect too much. Decades of centralised control made the Tajiks used to poor-quality manufactured goods and, with the fall of the Soviet Union, China has happily stepped in to supply shoddily made plastic goods and chemical-laden foodstuffs to the masses. Supply chains are wobbly at the best of times and, as we found to both our shock and delight, it is indeed possible for one person to hold a third of the country's supply of bacon in their fridge.

2

Tajikistan's larger towns tend to have at least one **supermarket**, typically with a meat counter, bakery section, a fridge of various dairy products, and fresh vegetables. The rest of the store will be stuffed with row after row of tinned fish, tinned vegetables, jam, fruit juice and unbelievably large plastic sachets of mayonnaise-style salad dressing. You may also find occasional treats such as Pringles, Kit Kats and caviar. Smaller shops akin to **convenience stores** are scattered along even the most unprepossessing of streets and sell a more limited range of bread, biscuits, carbonated drinks and dairy products. These shops all sell shampoo, soap and razors.

There is a **bazaar** in every town, and small **roadside stalls** everywhere in between. These are the best places to buy your fruit and vegetables; they'll be fresh and very cheap. Much of the produce is seasonal, and women often sit selling things they've grown themselves.

If you need to buy **electronics** (including computer parts or camera accessories) it's usually worth heading to the bazaar. Branded items are in short supply and very expensive, but it is usually possible to get a generic, Chinese-made version to do the same job. If a trader does not have what you need he will frequently phone a friend and a bystander will be dispatched to retrieve what you need from elsewhere in the market. Do not be surprised to see people soldering or cannibalising parts to order.

Souvenirs in Tajikistan fall into two categories: those made specifically for the tourist market, and the (often nicer) traditional items produced by individual artisans for local sale. Look out in particular for finely carved woodwork, painted pottery, embroidered textiles and jewellery made from local silver or Badakhshani lapis lazuli.

NGOs have encouraged a lot of artisans (particularly women) to produce quality items for sale in tourist-oriented shops. Keep an eye out for **Yak House** (page 178) and **De Pamiri** (pages 160–1), and feel good as you shop that you're supporting the craftsmen rather than middlemen.

PHOTOGRAPHY

Tajikistan is an exceptionally photogenic country, with magnificent landscapes, striking buildings and great opportunities for portraiture. The usual rules apply when you are taking photos: don't point your camera at military or police, or any kind of government building; and be sure to ask permission when you are taking photos of people. On the whole, you'll find the Tajiks are more than happy to have their photos taken, but it is always respectful and polite to ask. It is highly unlikely that anyone will ask for money to take their photo.

It is sometimes possible to get spare memory cards, batteries and chargers for cameras in the department stores in Dushanbe, but you should not rely on the right make and model being available when you need it. The locally available products tend to be cheap generic models from China and the quality is generally poor.

MEDIA AND COMMUNICATIONS

NEWSPAPERS Tajikistan has a number of weekly or tri-weekly newspapers, the majority of which are published in Tajik or Russian. They are typically either government-owned or linked closely to a particular political party. Daily newspapers are not considered viable because of their low circulation and low advertising revenues.

The newspapers with the greatest circulation are the government-backed *Jumhuriyat* (circulation 8,000), the loosely independent *Kurer Tajikistana* (circulation 40,000) and *Khalk Ovozi*, an Uzbek-language paper printed by parliament (circulation 8,600).

The 1994 Tajik constitution and 1991 Law on Press Freedom theoretically prohibit censorship and protect journalists. The reality is that those who disagree with government policy are frequently discouraged from speaking freely and the provision on libel of the 1991 legislation enables government officials to punish critical viewpoints for 'irresponsible journalism', which includes jail terms and fines.

TELEVISION AND RADIO State television and radio are financed from the national budget; revenues from advertising do not allow for financial independence. Politically, the government channels are biased and scrutiny of the authorities is entirely absent. According to sources, there are no independent broadcasters in Tajikistan. Generally, the regions can receive the national television channel, a local state-owned broadcaster and Russian ORT and RTR. Russian channels are transmitted by satellite.

Prior to 1992, cable television stations did exist, but they were then banned. The official explanation concerned alleged 'pornographic movies and other inadmissible programmes'. It is, however, generally accepted that the political advertising carried by the cable television stations prior to the elections caused their prohibition.

A greater breadth of opinion is distributed by radio stations, and the BBC World Service continues to broadcast in Tajik as well as regularly updating the w bbc. co.uk/tajik website with news footage and commentary (also in Tajik).

PHONE The country code for Tajikistan is +992; all city codes begin with 03.

Only a fraction of Tajikistan's businesses and homes have a landline phone, largely because the infrastructure does not reach out into the hinterland. This explains in large part why mobile phones have taken off in such a big way: there are more than four million cell phones in use in the country.

Tajikistan's most popular mobile service providers are Beeline, Tcell and Megafon. To get a SIM card you will need to take your passport to one of their offices or branded stores. You will need to give your current address (even if it is just your hotel), and filling out the various forms and processing them takes about 20 minutes. Expect to pay around US$3.

Topping up your phone is easy. You can do it in the store, anywhere showing your network's logo, and at any of the bill-pay machines on the street. The machines (which are frequently orange) allow you to type in your phone number, feed in bank notes and *voila*! You've topped up.

Practical Information MEDIA AND COMMUNICATIONS

2

SATELLITE PHONE

A reliable communication link is always a concern while travelling in Tajikistan, especially if you are likely to be travelling or trekking in the mountains and beyond the coverage of the cell phone networks.

The portable Thuraya satellite phone (w *thuraya.com*) is becoming cheaper and is the ideal option. The new version of the phone is as small as a normal GSM handset and you can even get a pay-as-you-go account; however, its battery life is not as long as the older versions – an important consideration in an environment with unreliable power supplies. A new feature is a facility where a credit card is linked to the account and when a secret code is SMS messaged to Thuraya, your account is topped up by a predetermined amount.

Though the coverage of phone networks is improving, it is still by no means universal and large sections of the country (particularly remote and mountainous areas) are black holes for reception. If you are travelling to such areas and may need to keep in contact, a satellite phone is the most reliable (and often only) option.

INTERNET Tajikistan is slowly getting online, and Wi-Fi is available in cafés in towns and cities across the country. Local SIM cards now include data packages, and it is also possible to buy an internet dongle for your laptop, enabling you to get online wherever there is 3G.

POST Tajikistan does have a domestic postal service – with a central post office in most large towns – but little if anything travels by it. Letters and parcels are transported internally by hand (often with the minibus drivers) and couriers and diplomatic bags are the preferred method to send and receive anything overseas. DHL and FedEx both have agents in Dushanbe, as do a number of smaller courier firms.

BUSINESS

The Tajik government is actively seeking foreign investment, particularly for projects in the energy and mining sectors and, to a lesser extent, in agriculture too. The country certainly needs money to develop, and there are undoubtedly large profits to be made by some, but the current combination of overzealous, virtually impenetrable bureaucracy and endemic corruption is a significant deterrent.

In 2017, **Doing Business** (w *doingbusiness.org*) ranked Tajikistan 128 out of 190 economies for ease of doing business. This ranking is slightly skewed, however, by the relative ease of enforcing contracts and the legal protection offered to investors. In other criteria, notably getting electricity, trading across borders and getting construction permits, Tajikistan ranks in the bottom five economies worldwide. It's not an enviable position to be in, and one that the government needs to take far-reaching steps to resolve if it is to make the country an attractive place to invest.

BUYING PROPERTY

Foreigners are permitted to buy property in Tajikistan, though as with many things in the country it can be a time-, money- and bureaucracy-intensive purpose for which you will require local assistance.

The vendor must obtain a certificate from the Bureau of Technical Inventory (BTI) listing the technical characteristics of the building or land and its inventory cost, as well as information on encumbrance. It is issued for three months. The property may be inspected.

In parallel to this, the vendor must get a tax clearance certificate from the Ministry of State Revenue and Duties showing that all property taxes have been paid. This theoretically protects the buyer from any unforeseen tax burdens related to the property, including payment of any taxes in arrears.

These two certificates must be notarised, along with the sale purchase agreement. Supporting documentation that is required includes:

- Identification documents of buyer and seller, including document confirming tax ID (either ID certificate or a passport with a tax ID stamp) of each of the parties involved
- Documents confirming the seller's ownership rights for the property

- Rights-confirming documents for the land plot where the building is located
- Original foundations documents of the agreement parties, ie: charters, foundation agreements and documents on registration
- Documents evidencing authorities of the agreement signatories such as Power of Attorney, Extract from the Minutes of the General Meeting of Shareholders or Order on Appointment of the CEO, etc.

The cost of notarising these documents is dependent on the size of the property. The sale purchase agreement must then be registered with the local Hukumat (equivalent to the local council). It puts a seal on the sale purchase agreement and formally records the new owner in its books. This part of the process is theoretically free, but you may be asked to pay a fee to speed the process along.

The purchaser then goes to the BTI in order to register the building and the property rights transfer. A note is made in the registry book and the inventory cards of BTI on the basis of the purchase agreement. If the property is land rather than a building, it is also necessary to make an application to the State Land Use Committee stating the current and intended land use. Registering with the State Land Use Committee can take up to one month, though land rights are automatically transferred with the rights to the building or land.

CULTURAL ETIQUETTE

On the whole, Tajiks are very welcoming of guests. Their culture has been shaped over thousands of years by different people and different ideas, and so much of what you see, hear and experience will seem familiar to you. If you look at what people around you are doing and do likewise, are friendly to those who you meet, and don't court controversy by discussing politics, religion or sexuality, you will be a model guest. Any inadvertent mistakes you do make with regard to cultural etiquette will be overlooked, or politely corrected.

Hospitality is very important in Tajikistan: this was historically a country of traders and nomads, after all, and with a relatively hostile climate, especially in the winter months, it was expected that you would welcome strangers into your home to keep them safe. If you meet someone during your travels, you might well be invited into their home to meet their family. Note that an invitation to go to someone's house for 'a cup of tea' invariably means something more substantial, often a full meal. If you take a small gift with you, it will be much appreciated. It doesn't have to be something expensive, or even particularly imaginative: a box of sweets or chocolate, or a cake from the bakery, is ideal. Your host might initially decline the gift, but persist: this denial and insistence, often repeated two or three times, is a Tajik tradition.

On **entering a home** in Tajikistan, step over the threshold, not on it, as otherwise you will bring bad luck on the household. The same is true if you hug or kiss your host in the doorway: instead, step into the room before you embrace. Whether you are visiting an ethnically Tajik family or a Russian one, you should remove your shoes at the door. There is usually a mixture of assorted slippers and flip-flops available to wear around the house, and they are there for you to borrow. Pick ones which are an approximation of your size, and if you have very large feet then just accept that your heels will be hanging off the back.

In **more traditional households** you may find that men and women are entertained in separate rooms. Although there is little concern about women being seen by non-family members – few if any families in Tajikistan still practise purdah – they

2

often feel more comfortable sitting and talking with their own sex. Foreign women might well be able to move between the male and female groups, especially if they are with a male partner or friend; men should remain with the other men.

Bread is the culinary staple in Tajikistan, and it is treated almost with reverence. It should ideally be torn rather than cut, should not be placed face-down on the table, and should be eaten up before it goes stale so that none is wasted. You can use both hands to tear it, but should then eat, serve yourself from a communal dish, and pass food to other people using only your right hand. As in other Muslim cultures, the left hand is generally considered unclean.

At the **end of the meal**, thanks are given by the act of bringing the hands together in front of the face, then moving them down in an action symbolising a washing gesture. If you are in a private home, it is your host who will lead this silent prayer. It is also the signal for everyone to get up from the table and leave: don't continue picking at the food in front of you after this sign has been given.

Mosques, **shrines** and **other holy places** often have their own sets of rules and you should endeavour to observe these. If in doubt, ask, as it is better to appear naive than disrespectful. Requirements are likely to include removing your shoes, covering your head (women only) and wearing long trousers or a skirt that covers the knees. Shorts and strapless T-shirts will get you strange looks anywhere in Tajikistan and should not be worn in conservative areas such as the Pamirs. At religious sites they really are unacceptable. You may be expected to wash your hands and face. In some places only one gender is permitted to enter. Whatever your personal opinion, you should respect the community's wishes.

TRAVELLING POSITIVELY

The single most important thing you can do for Tajikistan is to advertise the country's existence. Too many people still look at you with an utterly blank expression when you say 'Tajikistan', and one or two blinkered individuals have flatly contested that the country even exists. To develop economically, socially and politically Tajikistan needs foreign investment, foreign recognition and foreign scrutiny. Responsible tourists can contribute in all these areas by becoming both observers and ambassadors.

We endorse use of Tajikistan's community-based tourism initiatives as they ensure your money goes directly to the local community. The Zarafshan Tourism Development Association (ZTDA, page 111) does sterling work co-ordinating homestays, drivers, trekking guides and porters, as do the Pamirs Eco Tourism Association (PECTA) and Murghab Eco-Tourism Association (META).

If you want to volunteer in Tajikistan, Habitat for Humanity has one- and two-week projects in Tajikistan for groups of volunteers to build and renovate homes and construct water filters alongside families and local communities. For more information on setting up a volunteering trip contact Habitat for Humanity Great Britain (⟍ 01753 313539; e supporterservices@habitatforhumanity.org.uk; w habitatforhumanity.org.uk).

Part Two

THE GUIDE

HYATT

HYATT
REGENCY™
DUSHANBE

26/1, Ismoili Somoni Avenue,
Dushanbe, Tajikistan
Tel: +992 48 702 1234
www.dushanbe.regency.hyatt.com

3

Dushanbe and Environs

Telephone code: 0372

Laid back and lushly landscaped, Tajikistan's capital city feels more like a market town than a metropolis, its skyline scraped by a handful of mid-rises and accented by the world's now second-tallest flagpole. Without centuries of Silk Road wealth or the patronage of indulgent emperors, Dushanbe's façades have historically been far humbler than those of many of its central Asian rivals, though that is changing with the controversial push towards bigger, bolder buildings: the opulent Navruz Palace and immense National Museum of Tajikistan among them. But the geography of the valley, the paths of the rivers, and the acres of parkland and trees still define the shape of the city and give it a quietly bustling feel. Today, the city's population is 802,700, predominantly ethnic Tajik, but with significant numbers of Uzbeks, a steadily decreasing Russian community, students from India, and a smattering of European and American expats working in the international aid and development sectors.

In the heart of the Hisor Valley, at the confluence of the Varzob and Kofarnihon rivers, Dushanbe (meaning 'Monday') takes its name from the weekly market, which historically took place on this site. Though archaeological finds suggest an ancient heritage, the modern city is just 80 years old, and its former name of Stalinabad reveals its past is forever linked to that of the USSR.

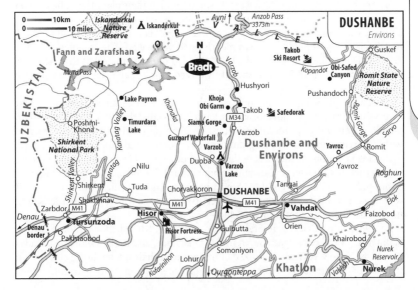

Dushanbe's geographical isolation may have contributed to its less starkly Soviet architecture, but many of the more notable buildings from the country's decades as a republic of the USSR – including the central post office and the much-loved Vladimir Mayakovsky Drama Theatre – have been demolished in recent years and replaced by even larger commercial structures financed by developers from across Asia. Still, many of the buildings in the centre of the city are predominantly low-rise, brightly painted, and hark back to an earlier Russian style. The tree-lined avenues, and the manicured parks and cafés in squares, create an almost continental feel, and the clutch of monuments and museums speak to Tajikistan's push for a post-independence architectural legacy.

At 812m above sea level, Dushanbe is undoubtedly a mountain capital, and it is therefore no surprise that easy day trips from the capital put you up close with an impressive landscape. The three gorges – Romit, Shirkent and Varzob – are all picturesque picnic spots with fine trekking opportunities, and the 19th-century Hisor Fortress confirms the importance of the mountains as a natural defence against attackers.

HISTORY

Little is known about Dushanbe's ancient past. Archaeological finds, including coin hoards, jewellery and a copper depiction of the Greek god Dionysus, confirm that the area came under the influence of the Graeco-Bactrian Empire (page 10) and its successors, and that local inhabitants were both skilled craftsmen and well connected with the outside world.

The earliest written account of a settlement in the vicinity of Dushanbe does not date until the mid 17th century, and it refers only to a small community situated at the crossroads of trading routes between Bukhara and Samarkand in the west, the Pamirs in the east, and Afghanistan in the south. The town would have changed little by the time Alim Khan, Khanate of Bukhara, fled the Red Army and sought refuge in this mountainous outpost in 1920, though the fall of the Bukharan Emirate to the Russians would change the fate of Dushanbe forever.

The old states of central Asia were dissolved, and in their place the Uzbek Soviet Socialist Republic was formed in 1924. Dushanbe was initially the capital of the autonomous Tajik territories and then, five years later, it became capital of the new Soviet Tajik Republic and was rechristened Stalinabad. The completion of the Termez–Dushanbe railway line, in 1929, enabled building materials to be shipped in from across the USSR, and the city we recognise today slowly began to take shape.

Dushanbe grew rapidly in the first half of the 20th century. Tajikistan's first hydro-electric power station, located at Varzob, provided the city with power, urban planning demanded modern amenities, and the population expanded fourfold with the arrival of economic migrants, prisoners of war and exiles from other parts of the Soviet Union. At the peak of this migration, ethnic Germans alone numbered 50,000 (nearly a quarter of Dushanbe's population). Dushanbe was becoming truly cosmopolitan – a poster child for Soviet planning and centralised control – and it was rewarded for its success with universities, a zoo and botanical gardens, and numerous statues of communism's elite.

In 1961, as part of his de-Stalinisation initiative, Khrushchev announced that Stalinabad would once again be known as Dushanbe, and in the following decades there was a slow revival of Tajik culture among urban intellectuals, centred on the capital. The renewed interest in the Tajik language in particular culminated

The 1988 massacre of ethnic Armenians in the Azerbaijan SSR was to have consequences far beyond its borders. Some Armenian refugees were temporarily resettled in Dushanbe but the PR was mishandled: rumours were rife that as many as 5,000 refugees were on their way and that they were to be given public housing in spite of already severe shortages. Assurances to the contrary were rejected, and demonstrations turned violent.

From 12 to 14 February 1990, Dushanbe was in turmoil. Twenty-two people were killed and more than 500 injured, many of them Armenian or other ethnic minorities. Buildings were looted and property was smashed. The protesters' demands were for radical economic and political reform, but they were to come to naught: Soviet troops were called in to quash the demonstrations. Calls for the resignation of the Tajik Communist Party's leaders were overruled.

in a peaceful demonstration in Dushanbe in February 1989, where students and intellectuals demanded that Tajik, not Russian, be considered the state language of Tajikistan. Protesters found their voice in the numerous independent papers that sprang up in the late 1980s, severe rioting rocked the city in 1990 (see box, above), and thousands of people flocked to Dushanbe to see Tajikistan declare independence from the Soviet Union on 9 September 1991. The Lenin statue on Lenin Avenue (now Rudaki) was the first Lenin monument in central Asia to be pulled down.

Optimism turned to pain almost overnight. Tajikistan's economy crashed and the country's first president, Rahmon Nabiev (page 15), had no real means of control. Mass demonstrations, some up to 15,000 people strong, took place on Rudaki; protesters from across Tajikistan camped outside the Presidential Palace and called for Nabiev's resignation. The government armed counter-demonstrators on Dusti Square, and people on both sides formed violent militias. The civil war had begun, and Dushanbe's population swelled with refugees.

Troops marched into Dushanbe in December 1992, seized the Presidential Palace and put Emomali Rahmon (see box, page 18), a little-known economics graduate with a support base in agrarian Kulob, in the seat of power. He remains in power today, and the vast new Palace of Nations, home to the president himself and numerous government ministries, is undoubtedly his architectural legacy to the city.

GETTING THERE AND AWAY

BY AIR The first commercial flight arrived in Dushanbe from Bukhara in 1924, and a proper airport opened just five years later. Today, the vast majority of Tajikistan's visitors arrive by air at Dushanbe's new terminal complex, built to serve 1.5 million passengers annually and opened in 2014, replacing the run-down 1960s-era terminal which lacked either a transit lounge or any pretence of comfort.

It should be noted that, due to weather conditions in the surrounding mountains, it is not always possible for flights to land in Dushanbe. Delays and cancellations are common, and it is also not unheard of for planes to route via Almaty and then return to Dushanbe once conditions improve. Allow plenty of time and keep your sense of humour.

Dushanbe airport [72 D5] (*Mirzo Mastongulov;* ✆ *(0474) 494 233;* w *airport.tj*) is within easy walking distance of the city centre, and in good weather (and without too much luggage) it is a pleasant stroll. Most hotels will arrange an airport pick-up for around US$15, unless you're staying at the Hyatt, in which case you'll pay an excessive US$40. The usual crowd of taxi drivers await outside the arrivals terminal and, after haggling, will usually deliver you to your destination of choice for TJS20–30. For those on a budget, buses 1, 8 and 12 run from the airport and along the length of Rudaki for TJS1.

Airlines The airlines listed here served Dushanbe at the time of going to press. Where the company has a Tajik office, the local address and phone number are given, otherwise you will need to call the international call-centre number provided or visit a general ticketing agent to make an enquiry. Most airline representatives arrive at their respective airport counter 3 to 4 hours before flight departure time.

✈ **Air Astana** 23 Druzhby Narodov; ✆ +7 727 244 4477; w airastana.com. Kazakhstan's excellent national airline operates 4 direct flights a week between Dushanbe & Almaty, with numerous onward connections to Europe & Asia.

✈ **China Southern Airlines** ✆ (0446) 16 888; w csair.com. Weekly departures to Ürümqi, with onward connections across China.

✈ **FlyDubai** 1 Bekhzod; ✆ (0446) 100 123; w flydubai.com. The UAE's low-cost carrier flies direct to Dubai thrice-weekly.

✈ **Kam Air** ✆ +93 799 974 422; w kamair.com. Twice-weekly flights to Kabul.

✈ **S7 Airlines** ✆ +7 495 783 0707; w s7.ru. Russia's largest domestic airline, part of the One World alliance, has flights to Novosibirsk with onward connections to Beijing, Dubai, Frankfurt, & Shanghai, as well as numerous Russian destinations.

✈ **Somon Air** 40 Mirzo Mastongulov; ✆ (0446) 404 040; w somonair.com. Tajik airline with international flights to Almaty, Bishkek, Dubai, Frankfurt, Irkutsk, Istanbul, Kazan, Kiev, Krasnodar, Krasnoyarsk, Moscow, Novosibirsk, Orenburg, St

Petersburg, Sochi, Ürümqi & Yekaterinburg, & a domestic flight to Khujand.

✈ **Tajik Air** 32/1 Mirzo Mastongulov; ✆ (0446) 015 050; w tajikair.tj. Tajikistan's national carrier flies to Almaty, Beijing, Bishkek, Delhi, Istanbul, Moscow, Novosibirsk, Samara, St Petersburg, Sochi, Surgut, Tehran, Ürümqi & Yekaterinburg. It also operates the domestic flight to Khorog.

✈ **Turkish Airlines** 13 Istaravshan; ✆ (0487) 017 570; w turkishairlines.com. Thrice-weekly flights to Istanbul with onward connections across Europe & to the USA.

✈ **Ural Airlines** 6A Lohuti; ✆ 14 520; w uralairlines.ru. Regular flights to Chelyabinsk, Kazan, Krasnodar, Moscow, St Petersburg, Samara, Ufa & Yekaterinburg, with reasonable onward connection to London via Riga (codeshare with Air Baltic).

✈ **UTair Aviation** ✆ +7 345 228 1054; w utair.ru. This Russia-based airline flies to Moscow daily with connections to other cities within Russia.

✈ **Yamal Airlines** ✆ +7 345 256 7077; w yamal.aero. Small Russian airline which offers thrice-weekly flights to Moscow.

BY RAIL Dushanbe's **main railway station** [ZZ5 F7] (*35 Rudaki;* ✆ *005*) is situated at the south end of Rudaki, just past the junction with Nazarshoev. There are only a few routes in regular operation and the equivalent bus journeys are typically faster, cheaper and more comfortable. Determined train lovers can reach Kulob (Thursday and Saturday), Qurgonteppa (Thursday) or Hisor (daily). The 330 train runs from Moscow to Dushanbe on Wednesdays and Saturdays (*from TJS1,700*), with the 319 train returning on Thursdays, but at four days and 6 hours in duration it is not a journey for the faint-hearted. You will require a visa for every country *en route*.

If you are passing by the railway station, do stop to take a look at the **stained-glass window,** which was made in the Soviet Realist style and depicts the great and glorious communist workers.

BY ROAD Dushanbe has a number of official and unofficial bus stations, and the one you require will depend on your destination.

The main bus station (*avtovokzal*) is 3km west of the city centre at the junction of Abuali ibn Sino and M Sheralizade. You can get here from Ismoili Somoni by taking bus 18 or 29 (*TJS1*). Long-distance buses leave here for destinations in southern Tajikistan including Qurgonteppa (*TJS30*) and Kulob (*TJS35*).

If you're travelling to Khorog or Kalaikhum (Darvaz), you need the **Badakhshan bus station** (*avtostansiya*) near the airport on the corner of Ayni and Ahmad Donish. Minibuses 1 and 8 will get you here from the town centre. Only minibuses and shared taxis operate this route, and all vehicles depart early in the morning to maximise the hours of daylight on the road. Try to reserve a seat the day beforehand. Getting to Kalaikhum takes around 12 hours and costs TJS140; the ride to Khorog is 16 hours and costs TJS250. This route is prone to rockfalls and resulting delays, particularly in the spring, and consequently many people prefer to fly.

Private bus company **Asian Express** provides regular services on large new coaches to cities and towns in southwestern Tajikistan, including Qurgonteppa, Nurek, Danghara, Kulob and Shahrtuz, departing from the company's own terminal [72 B3] (*110 Abuali Ibn Sino*).

Minibuses and shared taxis to Ayni (*TJS70; 2hrs*) Khujand (*TJS170; 5hrs*) and Panjakent (*TJS150; 5hrs*) depart from the **Cement Factory stand** [72 C1] (Tsementzavod avtostansiya) in the north of Dushanbe. Take bus 3 (*TJS1*) to get here from Rudaki. Minibuses making the short run to Varzob (*TJS4*) and Takob (*TJS3*) leave from **Varzob Bazaar stand**.

If you are planning to **self-drive** to Dushanbe, see box, page 50. Motorists coming from the Fann Mountains will be happy to know that the heretofore disastrous Anzob Tunnel has been cleaned up (page 105).

GETTING AROUND

Dushanbe is unusual among Soviet capitals in that it is small enough to explore almost everywhere on foot: only the remotest microdistricts genuinely justify a cab ride. Pavements are broad (though trip hazards are numerous; see box, page 70), most things are easy to find and you'll be able to properly appreciate the numerous green spaces, statues and intriguing pieces of architecture that punctuate the city.

BY TAXI If time is of the essence, most cars serve as impromptu taxis, so if you need a ride simply stand by the curb and put your hand out. If you prefer a pre-booked taxi, try **Taxi Service** (✆ 333 333) (Russian-speaking only) or **City Taxi** (✆ 0235 555; 0951 115 511 *after 19.00*). In both cases fares are typically around TJ30, but make sure you agree a price in advance. Do not, however, expect your driver to know where you are going: take your own map, write down the street address and any nearby monuments in Russian, and expect to have to stop and ask for directions.

BY BUS Dushanbe has a large number of buses and minibuses, some of which are Soviet relics and others which are brand-new gifts from China. These are cheaper than taxis (typically no more than TJS1 per ride) but it is likely you will have to stand. The destination and route number (if applicable) are written on the front of the bus or on a card in the window, though this is often in Cyrillic script. Most useful for tourists are bus 3, which travels continually up and down Rudaki; minibuses 8 and 22, which travel from Rudaki along Ismoili Somoni; and buses 1, 8 and 12 from Rudaki to the airport.

The streets of Dushanbe are a veritable assault course, and failure to keep your wits about you can result in an unwelcome visit to casualty. Health and safety, it seems, is something for the foreigners to worry about. To draw your attention to the numerous hazards on your doorstep (and hopefully to make you a little more aware of your surroundings) we've devised this special Dushanbe edition of I spy.

- Bare electricity cable – 2
- Black-haired pedestrian dressed in black (at night) – 1
- Legless beggar on skateboard – 5
- Missing manhole cover – 3
- Missing paving slab – 1
- Open drain/sewer – 1
- Shards of asbestos (tile or pipe) – 2
- Sawn-off signpost (ankle height) – 3
- Sawn-off signpost (shin height) – 4
- Unburied rebar – 2
- Underpass wheelchair ramp (one side of the road only) – 5
- Vehicle without headlights – 2

NB Points are awarded on the basis of the rarity of the hazard, not its severity!

BY CAR None of the international car-hire chains have offices in Dushanbe. However, the larger hotels can typically organise car hire (with or without driver). Rates vary depending on the type of vehicle and the distance to be travelled. It is advisable to get several quotes and be prepared to haggle hard. If you are driving yourself, expect to be stopped regularly by the Dushanbe traffic police. Always keep your documents handy, keep smiling, and pretend not to understand a word they say.

TOURIST INFORMATION

Although there is no official tourist information office in Dushanbe, the Open Society-backed **Tourism Development Centre** (*15 Ayni;* ✆ *14 873;* e *info@tdc.tj;* w *tdc. tj;* ⏶ *09.00–17.00 Mon–Fri, 09.00–noon Sat*) has a small apartment (#3, accessed from the rear of the building) from which it provides reliable tourist information and translation services and sells souvenirs. It is also responsible for co-ordinating training and marketing in Tajikistan's tourism sector.

The **Tajik Community-Based Tourism Association** (*12A Mirzo Tursunzoda, inside the Bactria Cultural Centre;* ✆ *12 558;* e *director@cbttajikistan.tj;* w *cbttajikistan. tj*), which works to ensure sustainable tourism practices and community-based hospitality development in Tajikistan, also provides tourist information and information regarding translation and other support services.

Even if you are visiting Dushanbe briefly, it is worth looking at *What's on in Dushanbe*. This is a weekly newsletter produced for the benefit of Dushanbe's English-speaking community. It covers upcoming events and things of interest. Particularly useful is information on walks each weekend in the Dushanbe area. To find, go to w mariansguesthouse.com, and click on 'WOID', or contact staff at e info@mariansguest house.com.

Since Tajik independence, almost all of Dushanbe's Soviet-era street names have been changed. Unfortunately for visitors, the city's inhabitants use the old and new names interchangeably, leading to much confusion. To help you find your way, here is a list of the renamed streets you're most likely to encounter.

OLD NAME	NEW NAME
Dzerjinsky	Maksim Gorky
Gorky	Tehran
Kommunisticheskaya	Shirinsho Shotemur
Krasnykh Partizan	Mirzo Tursunzoda
Kuybyshev	Akademik Radjapov
Lenin	Rudaki
Lenin Square	Dusti Square
Ordjonikidze	Bokhtar
Pobedy Square	Sipar Square
Profsoyuzov	Abuali Ibn Sino
Proletarskaya	Pulod Tolis
Putovsky	Ismoili Somoni
Rudaki	Said Nasyrov
Titova	Mirzo Mastongulov

Note that this book uses the new street names, as they are the ones written on street signs. This is particularly important to remember as the old and new Rudakis are, quite unhelpfully, two completely different streets.

LOCAL TOUR OPERATORS

Most hotels will be able to arrange guides, tours and airline tickets for you. However, it is often cheaper and more enjoyable to go with one of the specialist companies, a selection of which is listed below. If you only want to book an airline ticket, there are numerous ticketing agents at the south end of Rudaki and also along Lahuti. The staff at **Bunyod Air Travel** (*34 Rudaki;* m *(0918) 232 577;* e *bunyod@tajnet.com*) are particularly helpful.

Aziana Travel 23 Shamsi; (0446) 255 326; e info@azianatravel.com; w azianatravel.com. Tour expert *par excellence* Dmitri Melnichkov speaks both English & Russian & arranges tailor-made tours as well as the usual booking & support services. Highly recommended. See ad, page 96.

Hamsafar Travel 5/11 Pulod Tolis; 80 093; e hamsafarinfo@yahoo.com; w hamsafartravel. com. With both Russian- & English-speaking staff, Hamsafar Travel provides mountain treks with experienced guides, cultural tours, & can also arrange visas, permits & vehicle hire.

Muhammad Istamzad m (0992) 880 083 870, (0992) 501 292 532; e montaziretam@gmail.com.

Personable & knowledgeable, independent tour guide Muhammad Istamzad offers individualised guided day tours through Dushanbe & environs in many languages, including English.

Pamir Adventure 137 Rudaki; 11 812; e info@ pamir-adventure.com. Specialists in mountain tourism & tours, Pamir Adventure arranges trips across Tajikistan & the rest of central Asia. It is also able to make accommodation & transport bookings & assist with visas & other travel permits. In the office it sells a small selection of postcards, books, souvenirs & photographs. Reliable & helpful.

Pamir Peaks 191/44 Rudaki; (0487) 013 333; e info@pamirpeaks.com; w pamirpeaks.tj.

From its office inside the Ministry of Agriculture, Pamir Peaks offers a variety of mountaineering & trekking packages (including use of the Alpine International Base Camp), visa support (including visas on arrival) & hotel bookings. Contact it also for trekking maps, guides & porters.

Pamir Travel 154/8 Rudaki; ✆ 40 213; e pamir-travel@mail.ru; w pamir-travel.com. Established in 1992, Pamir Travel is the most experienced of Tajikistan's tour companies, arranging both

trekking & adventure packages as well as cultural tours. Highly recommended. See ad, page 96.

Tajikintourservice 46 Pushkin; ✆ 42 141; e tis@mkf.tj; w tis.tj. IATA-accredited ticketing agent able to book airline tickets, Tajik Air charter flights & helicopter hire. It is unable to take card payments online, but you can pay over the phone or by making a wire transfer. Tajikintourservice also has a ticketing desk at 14 Rudaki ✆ *(0433) 337 777; e kassa@tis.tj).*

 WHERE TO STAY

The last few years have seen a dramatic improvement in Dushanbe's accommodation options. Whereas in the past visitors were limited to a small selection of peeling Soviet façades with unpredictable utility supplies and scowling staff, a range of comfortable choices have now popped up, from hostels and homestays to lively guesthouses and international-brand hotels.

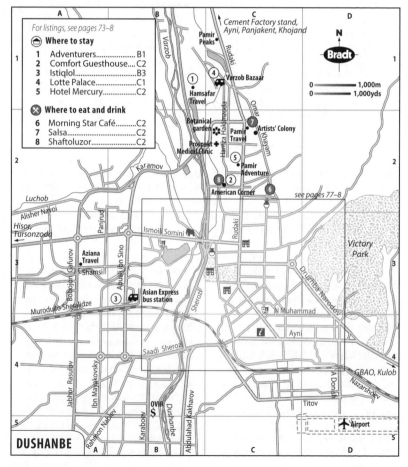

For listings, see pages 73–8

Where to stay
1 Adventurers............................ B1
2 Comfort Guesthouse.... C2
3 Istiqlol.................................... B3
4 Lotte Palace.......................... C1
5 Hotel Mercury.................... C2

Where to eat and drink
6 Morning Star Café.......... C2
7 Salsa.. C2
8 Shaftoluzor........................... C2

DUSHANBE

Accommodation prices in the capital are significantly higher than elsewhere in Tajikistan, largely due to the influx of business travellers and NGO workers travelling on expense accounts. However, most hotel managers will compromise on price, particularly if you are visiting in low season or staying for a protracted period, so it is always worth asking for a discount. You will usually get a better deal if you speak a few words of Russian, or ask a Russian/Tajik-speaker to bargain on your behalf.

LUXURY

🏠 **Hotel Serena** [77 F6] (85 rooms) 14 Rudaki; 📞 (0487) 024 000; e reservations.dsh@ serena.com.tj; w serenahotels.com. A stone's throw from the junction of Ayni & Rudaki, this beautifully presented hotel is owned by the Aga Khan. Service is attentive & understated; the building's exterior decoration & many of the textiles are influenced by traditional design. In particular, look out for the elaborately painted ceiling panels, carved wooden window screens, & the huge brass lanterns that light up the entrance-way & public spaces. The suites & serviced apts are available for long-term let. Wi-Fi is free. Highly recommended. **$$$$$**

🏠 **Hotel Tojikiston** [76 D3] (140 rooms) 22 Shotemur; 📞 (0446) 009 933; e hotel@tojikiston. com; w hoteltojikiston.tj. Also spelled Hotel Tajikistan. Situated on the edge of Central Park & with views across its numerous monuments, this hotel has become a monument in itself. The décor & furnishings are well maintained, & it has all the facilities you'd expect of a top-end hotel, including Tajikistan's largest (& newly renovated) swimming pool & 2 well-equipped conference rooms. Suites & apts also available. Wi-Fi is free. Cash payments are accepted in TJS only. **$$$$$**

🏠 **Hyatt Regency** [76 B3] (202 rooms) 26/1 Ismoili Somoni; 📞 (0487) 021 234; e dushanbe. regency@hyatt.com; w dushanbe.regency.hyatt. com. This international hotel has a superb location overlooking Komsomol Lake & with panoramic views across the city. The hotel is immaculate & the staff are superb. The bar & café are among the most tranquil havens in the city, & the facilities are second to none. Highly recommended for business travellers. See ad, page 64. **$$$$$**

🏠 **Sheraton** [77 H6] (148 rooms) 48 Ayni; 📞 (0487) 030 000; w sheratondushanbe.com. Situated near to the airport, this local branch of the international hotel chain offers business travellers spacious rooms & upmarket amenities. **$$$$$**

UPMARKET

🏠 **Asia Grand** [YY F4] (20 rooms) 21A M Tursunzoda; 📞 (0446) 007 777; e asiagh@mail. ru; www.asiagh.tj. Large, glass edifice replete with its own bowling alley, slot machines & the Jumanji children's play maze. Beds are comfortable & décor is neutral. B/fast is basic but included. AC sometimes works. Not to be confused with the Taj Palace, which shares the same building but is a preferable option. **$$$$**

🏠 **Hotel Atlas** [77 H6] (60 rooms) 32 Nisor Muhammad; 📞 (0446) 251 818; w atlashoteldushanbe.com. New, upmarket hotel by the owners of the Atlas B&B, featuring comfortable rooms with central Asian-inspired decorative flourishes & friendly, efficient staff with impeccable English. The indoor pool is especially enticing. Buffet b/fast & Wi-Fi inc. **$$$$**

🏠 **Hotel Mercury** [72 C2] (20 rooms) 9 Lev Tolstoy; 📞 44 491; e info@hotel-mercury.tj. Well-run hotel with friendly staff in a quiet location a few mins' walk from Rudaki. The hotel overlooks a large garden where b/fast is served. All rooms have immaculate bathrooms & are equipped with AC & a computer. There's no gym but the table tennis table provides hours of entertainment. Secure parking available within the hotel compound. **$$$$**

🏠 **Istiqlol** [72 B3] (64 rooms) 12 Spativnaya; 📞 (0446) 008 151; e info@istiqlol.tj; w istiqlol. tj. Reasonably maintained, if somewhat tasteless, rooms in an ugly building opposite the bus station. There is a small conference centre & a good-size gym, as well as an in-house restaurant. **$$$$**

🏠 **Kayon** [77 E4] (6 rooms) 7 Bahtar; 📞 16 229; e hotelkayon@mail.ru. Well-run guesthouse with attractive gardens & reasonable facilities. Two additional guesthouses nearby also available. B/fast & Wi-Fi inc. Cash payments only. **$$$$**

🏠 **Lotte Palace** [72 C1] (20 rooms) 19A Gagarina; 📞 224 3030; e info@lottepalace.tj; w lottepalace.tj. Brand new & centrally located, Lotte Palace is an upmarket boutique hotel. There's an attractive garden, rooms are large & the staff

3

are very well trained. It offers good value for money in this price bracket. **$$$$**

🏠 **Lotus** [77 F5] (32 rooms) 1 Proezd Lokhuti 5; 📞 (0487) 018 800; w hotel-lotustj.com. Tucked away in a quiet residential neighbourhood & guarded by a security wall, the Lotus features spacious rooms with high ceilings & large bathrooms. The tasty b/fast buffet & Wi-Fi are included, as is use of the fitness centre, swimming pool & bicycles you can take out for a spin around the city. **$$$$**

🏠 **Marian's Guesthouse** [77 F5] (7 rooms) 67/1 Shotemur; m (0935) 050 089; e info@mariansguesthouse.com; w mariansguesthouse.com. Exceptionally popular guesthouse owned by an Australian, Marian. The large, white house with its attractive balcony is situated within a verdant garden. Staff are remarkably friendly, & it's a great place to get information & find travelling companions. B/fast, laundry & Wi-Fi inc. **$$$$**

🏠 **Taj Palace** [77 F4] (38 rooms) 21B M Tursunzoda; 📞 (0487) 017 171; e sipar21@gmail.com; w taj-palace.tj. Clean but fairly soulless hotel in the same building as the Asia Grand. Though a significant improvement on its neighbour, there are still better options in this price bracket. **$$$$**

🏠 **Twins** [77 G5] (21 rooms) 1/21 Adkhamova; 📞 (0372) 214 414; w hoteltwins.tj. Situated in a central residential quarter of the city, Twins occupies a pair of mansion-like buildings, set in an ornate courtyard. The rooms are homely, with comfortable beds & lounge areas, & the staff are courteous & efficient. B/fast & Wi-Fi inc. **$$$$**

MID-RANGE

🏠 **Almos** [77 G6] (15 rooms) 6 Mirzo Rizo; m (0938) 177 272; info@almos.tj; w almos.tj. Opened in 2010, this lavishly decorated property resembles a baroque mansion. The garden is a great place to relax in the evening, & other facilities include a 'disco-bar', sauna & swimming pool, & Wi-Fi. Airport pick-up is free. A good mid-range option. **$$$**

🏠 **Atlas B&B** [77 H6] (29 rooms) 63 Mirzo Rizo; 📞 64 628; e info@atlasguesthouse.com; w atlasguesthouse.com. Comfortable guesthouse a short distance from the city centre. Kitchen facilities are available & bathrooms are immaculate. The staff speak English & will also arrange airport pick-up & car hire. B/fast, Wi-Fi & use of the fitness centre included. **$$$**

🏠 **Comfort Guesthouse** [72 C2] (8 rooms) 61 Khamza Khakimzade; 📞 89 465. Friendly, well-run guesthouse in a quiet location 20mins' walk from the town centre. Most guests are expats who come to socialise & enjoy the home-cooked meals. Free Wi-Fi. Book early. **$$$**

🏠 **Hotel Meridian** [77 G5] (27 rooms) 28 Repina; 📞 (0446) 203 399; e info@meridian.tj; w meridian.tj. A little away from the centre, this guesthouse has clean, fresh bedrooms with AC & Wi-Fi. Suites also available. Quality is comparable to that in hotels charging twice the price. **$$$**

🏠 **Hotel Poytakht** [77 F6] (127 rooms) 7 Rudaki; 📞 19 655; e info@hotelpoytakht.tj; w hotelpoytakht.tj. Another Soviet relic, the Poytakht (also commonly referred to as Hotel Dushanbe) has a great position at the corner of Ayni & Rudaki. Sadly, it's not only the architecture that reminds one of the USSR: the plumbing, rock-hard beds & hawk-eyed *babushkas* on every floor all suggest that you are trapped in an unnerving time warp. The b/fast, even by Tajik standards, is inedible & price-gouging is a problem if you arrive late at night. **$$–$$$**

BUDGET

🏠 **Hello, Dushanbe!** [77 H6] (13 rooms) Passage 4/1, Nisor Muhammad 5; 📞 (0502) 000 005; w hellodushanbe.com. With a very homely atmosphere & welcoming staff, this private residence-turned-hostel attracts travellers from around the world who seek comfort & high-pressure showers when going to or coming from the Pamirs. Private rooms available. Free Wi-Fi & simple b/fast inc. **$–$$**

🏠 **META Homestay** [77 G4] (3 rooms) 11 Zehni; 📞 12 083. Get to know Tajik life a little better by staying with someone in their home. Each spotlessly clean room sleeps 5–6 people, & the shared bathroom & toilet are also pristine. We came down in the morning to find our car had been washed & a bag of fresh bread & fruit from the garden was ready & waiting for our journey. To find it, get to Taik Sodirot Bank on Bekhzod, walk straight down Adhamov (formerly Popova) & Zehni is the first street on the left. The homestay is situated behind the grey metal gates immediately to the left of the #11 sign. If you get lost, phone & a family member will be swiftly dispatched to rescue you. US$20 pp inc b/fast. **$$**

SHOESTRING

🏠 **Adventurers** [72 B1] (4 rooms) 35 Vodonasos Putolis; 📞 20 093. Owned & run by

Hamsafar Travel, this small hostel caters mostly to backpackers stopping in Dushanbe *en route* to the mountains. Facilities are basic but English is spoken & the staff do try to be helpful. **$**

🏠 **Green House** [77 H6] (32 rooms) 98A Khusravi Dekhlavi; 📞 (0880) 082 725; **w** greenhousedushanbe.com. One of the most popular hostels in town, Green House offers the type of creature comforts trekkers & backpackers crave before or after excursions into the mountains. Free Wi-Fi & b/fast inc. **$**

🏠 **Yeti** [77 H6] (4 rooms) 4th driveway, Nisor Muhammad 16; **m** (0987) 360 004; **w** yetihostel. com. Situated in a spacious & ornate manse near the airport, the recently relocated Yeti offers a welcoming atmosphere with shared dorms, private rooms, a tent in the garden & a tour desk that can organise excursions. Free Wi-Fi & b/fast inc. **$**

✖ WHERE TO EAT AND DRINK

Dushanbe may be quite small for a capital city, but the legacy of Soviet relocation policies (and the subsequent influx of expatriates) is an ethnically diverse population with wide-ranging tastes. Whereas elsewhere in Tajikistan your dining options may be limited to mutton, mutton or mutton, here you can choose from Indian, Korean, Italian, Georgian, Middle Eastern and Chinese, as well as the occasional hamburger. Unusually for central Asia, even vegetarians stand a chance of a decent meal.

If you are desperate for a **fast-food** fix, your best options are burgers from **Chief Burger** [77 F6] (*21 Mirzo Tursunzoda*) and the charmingly misspelled **Max Biff Burger** [77 E4] (*40 Rudaki*) where you can munch away under the watchful eye of a 2m-tall plastic Tyrannosaurus Rex. The pizza is good at **Gulistan Pizzeria** [77 E4] (*74A Bukhoro*) and you won't be disappointed by anything deep fried in batter at **Southern Fried Chicken** [77 E1] (*30 Rudaki*), Dushanbe's own take on KFC. Frankfurter hot dogs and doner kebabs are available at **Tabaka** [77 E1] (*also 30 Rudaki*). All these options fall in the **$–$$** price bracket.

Unless alternative opening times are given, the restaurants listed below are open for both lunch and dinner. Telephone numbers are given only where there is a landline and likelihood the phone may be picked up.

RESTAURANTS
Expensive
✖ **Focaccia Grill** [76 B3] 26/1 Ismoili Somoni; 📞 (0487) 021 234; ⏱ 06.00–23.00. Light, airy restaurant inside the Hyatt Regency serving high-quality Mediterranean & international cuisine. Service is meticulous & there is a fair selection of imported wines on the wine list. If you are having an intimate dinner with friends, it is also possible to book the 14-seat private dining room. **$$$$$**

✖ **InAzia** [77 H6] 48 Ayni; 📞 (0487) 030 000; ⏱ 18.00–23.00 Tue–Sun. Situated off the main lobby of the Sheraton Hotel, this pan-Asian powerhouse is almost always near the top of the Dushanbe's best-of restaurant lists. Swathed in an elegant, intimate ambience & first-class service, diners choose from Chinese, Japanese, Indonesian, Thai & Vietnamese specialities. **$$$$$**

✖ **Kuhsor** [77 F6] 14 Rudaki; 📞 (0487) 014 000; ⏱ 18.00–23.00. Perched on the rooftop of the Serena Hotel, the Kuhsor has the best dinnertime views of the city. Staff are attentive without fussing, & the ambience is sophisticated. Ideal choice for a romantic dinner. **$$$$$**

Above average
✖ **Delhi Darbar** [76 D2] 55/1 Rudaki; **m** (0917) 340 488; ⏱ noon–23.00. With evocative décor & pleasant waiting staff, this Indian restaurant offers excellent curries, thalis & tikkas. Friday nights feature an all-you-can-eat buffet. **$$$$**

✖ **Kutaisi** [77 F5] 2 Behzod. Regularly proclaimed as the best Georgian food outside of Georgia, Kutaisi – formerly called Tiflis & named for Georgia's second-largest city – feeds a never-ending stream of contented expats. The traditionally prepared *khachapuri* (cheese bread) & numerous vegetarian dishes prepared only with seasonal ingredients are particularly good. **$$$$**

✖ **Morning Star Café** [72 C2] 164 M Tursunzoda; 📞 89 464; ⏱ 8.00–18.00 Mon–Sat.

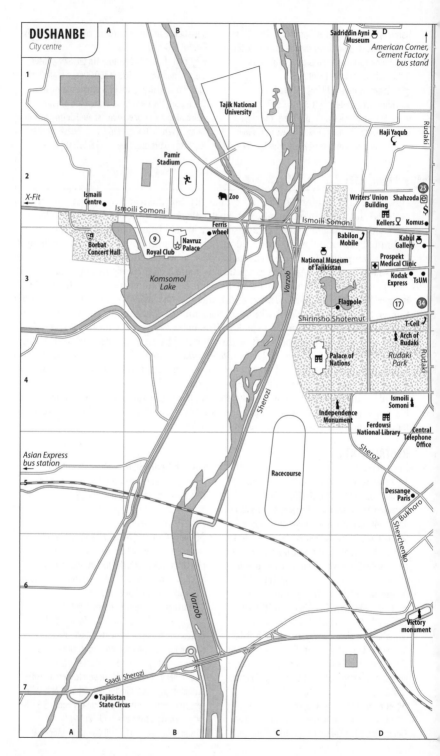

DUSHANBE
City centre

Sadriddin Ayni Museum

American Corner, Cement Factory bus stand

Tajik National University

Rudaki

Haji Yaqub

X-Fit

Pamir Stadium

Zoo

Ismaili Centre

Ismoili Somoni

Writers' Union Building

Shahzoda

25

Kellers

Komus

Babilon Mobile

Kabul Gallery

Borbat Concert Hall

9

Royal Club

Navruz Palace

Ferris wheel

National Museum of Tajikistan

Prospekt Medical Clinic

Komsomol Lake

Varzob

Flagpole

Kodak Express

TsUM

Shirinsho Shotemut

17

34

T-Cell

Sherozi

Palace of Nations

Arch of Rudaki

Rudaki Park

Rudaki

Asian Express bus station

Independence Monument

Ferdowsi National Library

Ismoili Somoni

Central Telephone Office

Sheroz

Racecourse

Dessange Paris

Bukhoro

Shevchenko

Varzob

Victory monument

Saadi Sherozi

Tajikistan State Circus

76

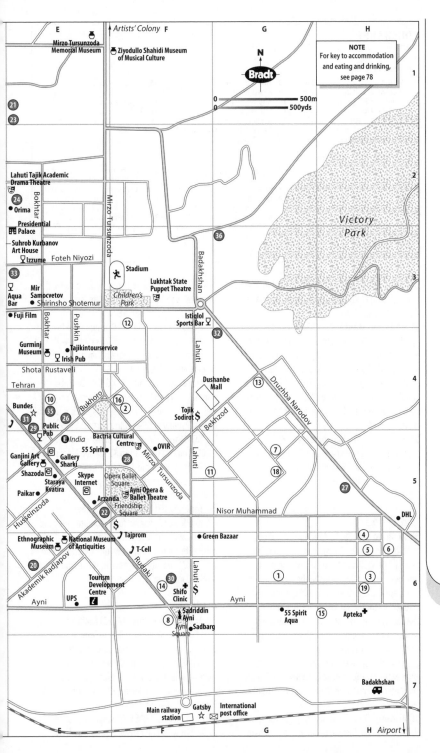

E | Mirzo Tursunzoda Memorial Museum

↑ Artists' Colony **F**

Ziyodullo Shahidi Museum of Musical Culture

G

N

Bradt

NOTE For key to accommodation and eating and drinking, see page 78

H

1

0 _____ 500m
0 _____ 500yds

2

21
23

Lahuti Tajik Academic Drama Theatre
24 ● Orima

Presidential Palace
Suhrob Kurbanov Art House
Izzume ● Foteh Niyozi

Bokhtar

Mirzo Tursunzoda

Badakhshan

36

Victory Park

2

3

33
Aqua Bar
Mir Samocvetov
● Shirinsho Shotemur
● Fuji Film

Stadium
Children's Park
Lukhtak State Puppet Theatre

12
Gurminj Museum
Tajikintourservice
Irish Pub
Shota Rustaveli
Tehran

Bokhtar
Pushkin

Istiqlol Sports Bar
32

Lahuti

Dushanbe Mall

13

Druzhba Narodov

4

Bundes
10
35 26
31 29 Public Pub

Bukhoro

16
2

Tojik Sodirot $

Bekhzod

Lahuti

7

India
Ganjini Art Gallery
Shazoda
Paikar ●
Staraya Kvatira
Skype Internet

55 Spirit
Bactria Cultural Centre
28
OVIR
Opera Ballet Square
Ayni Opera & Ballet Theatre
Arzanda
22 Friendship Square

Mirzo Tursunzoda

11

18

Nisor Muhammad

27

DHL

5

Husseinzoda

Ethnographic Museum
National Museum of Antiquities

Tajprom
T-Cell

● Green Bazaar

4
5 6

Akademik Radjapov

20

Tourism Development Centre
UPS

Rudaki

14 30
Shifo Clinic $

Lahuti

1

Ayni

3
19

6

Ayni

8
Sadriddin Ayni
Ayni Square
Sadbarg

● 55 Spirit Aqua

15 Apteka

Badakhshan

7

Main railway station
Gatsby
International post office

E   **F**   **G**   **H** *Airport*↓

DUSHANBE *City centre*
For listings, see pages 73–9

Lively restaurant serving unsophisticated American fare including Philly beefsteaks, barbecue chicken & pizza. Non-smoking. $$$$

✖ **Rudaki Restaurant** [77 F6] 14 Rudaki; ☎ (0487) 014 000. The Serena's main restaurant serves international fare. A buffet is available at b/fast, lunch & dinner, & à la carte options are available throughout the day. The restaurant is popular for business lunches. Sit at the back for views across the garden, & enjoy the good choice of wines. $$$$

✖ **Salsa** [72 C2] 1 Karamova; ☎ 48 857. This popular spot offers up pan-Latin American fare, including Mexican & Ecuadorian favourites. Also does a good line in cocktails, pizzas & desserts. $$$$

Mid-range

✖ **Al Sham** [77 E6] 11 Akademik Radjapov; ☎ 71 200; ⏰ noon–23.00. Every large city in central Asia seems to have at least one good Lebanese restaurant, & Dushanbe is fortunately no exception. Meats are properly marinated & tastily cooked; the salads are fresh & varied. The courtyard garden is particularly pleasant on a summer's evening, though the music can be rather loud. The mixed cold meze (*TJS25*) go perfectly with a chilled Baltica beer or fresh juice, & the erratic snatches of belly dancing are guaranteed to put a smile on your face. Highly recommended. $$$

✖ **Arirang** [77 E1] 96 Rudaki; ☎ 224 4343; ⏰ 11.00–23.00. Dishing up an excellent spread

of Korean mains & sides in generous portions, this intimate, wood-panelled restaurant is a favourite for locals & expats alike. $$$

✖ **Hojion** [77 H5] 11–13 Druzhba Narodov; ⏰ 08.00–23.00. Fun, casual Tajik dining with excellent grilled meats & salads. Dining in the magic cavern costs extra. $$$

✖ **Merve Restaurant** [77 G4] 47 Druzhba Narodov; ☎ 18 002; ⏰ 09.00–midnight. Large & well-established restaurant serving Tajik & Turkish dishes. Popular with wedding parties. $$$

✖ **Tajj Mahal** [76 D3] 81 Rudaki; ⏰ 10.00–23.00. Don't let the blaring Bollywood videos keep you from enjoying the delicious curries & main dishes from around India at this popular curry house. Accepts cash only. $$$

✖ **Toqi** [77 G3] 29 Kurbon Rakhimov; ⏰ 10.00–22.00. Named for the ornate men's cap worn throughout central Asia & offering local Tajik cuisine, this fun, slightly over-the-top *chaykhona* serves quite possibly the best, most succulent lamb & grilled meats in Tajikistan. $$$

Budget

✖ **Azadi Square Café** [77 E5] Azadi Sq; ⏰ 11.00–21.00. Immediately in front of the Ayni Opera & Ballet Theatre is this outdoor café where the waitresses run frantically from one parasol-shaded table to the next. Fast food, salads & *shashlik* are washed down with beer or soft drinks. Popular with families. $$

✖ **Café Merve** [77 E1] 92 Rudaki; ⏰ 09.00–22.00. Lively Turkish café with tasty kebabs &

flatbreads. Layout is more like a canteen than a restaurant, but service is fast & there is a constant turnover of tables. $$

✗ Shaftoluzor [72 C2] 25 Said Nosir; ⏱ 11.00–16.00 Mon–Fri. Kebabs, flatbreads & other cheap eats. $$

CAFÉS AND TEA HOUSES

Drinking tea is a central part of Tajikistan's Persian heritage, and the tradition of taking tea and talking business continues in Dushanbe unabated, even if today it is as likely to take place in the air-conditioned lobby of an upmarket hotel as in the open air of a street-side *chaykhona* (tea house). Coffee lovers will find an increasing number of places to get their caffeine fix, and the accompanying cakes and snacks will surely stave off starvation until dinner.

As well as those listed below there are **three outdoor cafés** situated around the fountain outside the Opera House. There is little to choose between them; they all serve the same selection of *shashlik* and salads, soft drinks and beer. Do as the locals do and enjoy a pot of green tea while snacking on a plate of sunflower seeds, watching the world go by. A can of soft drink costs TJS4.

⌨ Chaykhona Rokhat [77 E2] 84 Rudaki; ⏱ 18.00–midnight. This Soviet interpretation of a traditional Persian tea house is a Dushanbe institution popular with locals & expats alike. The Tajik food is simple but tasty, & you'll spend a fair amount of time staring up at the beautifully decorated ceiling. The *laghman* (noodle soups with mutton & vegetables) are particularly good, & an imported beer costs just US$2.

⌨ Lavazza [77 E4] 40 Rudaki; ⏱ 08.00–23.00. Squeezed amid the nondescript storefronts of Rudaki, this tiny branch of the Italian coffee purveyor serves delicious coffee & cakes, with free Wi-Fi if you can score a seat. The outlet also sells imported coffees & teas by the box.

⌨ The Lounge [76 B3] 26/1 Ismoili Somoni; ⏱ 09.00–01.00. This outdoor terrace at the Hyatt Regency is one of the most tranquil spots in Dushanbe. Different teas, coffees & soft drinks are served along with cakes & other light snacks. The terrace is closed in winter. Also try the pastry shop in the hotel lobby.

⌨ Mashrabiyya Chaykhona [77 F6] 14 Rudaki; ⏱ 07.00–midnight. Inspired by a traditional Tajik tea house & complete with wooden lattice screens, embroidered cushions & low tables, this cleverly arranged café has views across the Serena's gardens. High tea (*served

daily 15.00–17.30*) is reasonable value at TJS39 & Wi-Fi is free if you ask for the access details nicely.

⌨ Segafredo [77 E3] 70 Rudaki. Italian-style café with real espresso (*TJS7*) & reasonably priced food. Wi-Fi is free, & it's a good place to meet expats, particularly over lunch. The outdoor tables are the best (if you can get one), as indoors can get a little smokey. The raspberry cake (*TJS20*) is our favourite, especially when washed down with a pot of jasmine tea (*TJS8*). Note that a 7% service charge is automatically added to your bill.

⌨ Suzani Lounge [77 F6] 14 Rudaki; ⏱ 07.00–midnight. The relaxed café & bar in the lobby of the Serena is a popular place to meet & is beautifully decorated with *ikat* fabrics. Tea, coffee, sandwiches & other snacks are available throughout the day. Homemade cakes & confectionery from the patisserie in the hotel lobby make an ideal mid-afternoon treat.

⌨ Tapioca Hut [77 E4] 3 Bokhtar; m (0934) 626 969; ⏱ 08.00–23.00. This cosy, Brazilian-inspired café, with indoor and outdoor seating & a soulful music selection, serves tasty coffees, fruit juices & bubble teas, along with sandwiches, desserts & other light snacks. Fire up a hookah as well.

BARS AND CLUBS

Dushanbe has no shortage of places to drink vodka, as an evening stroll along any street will show, but it's not exactly a party town. A few nightclubs have opened in recent years, with heavy-drinking and enthusiastic clientele, but they often feel somewhat seedy and the large number of commercial sex workers does nothing to improve their image.

3

That said, if you're with a group of friends and can prearrange how to get home, try out Kellers or the Irish Pub, and then, once inebriated to the point you no longer care, pull on your dancing shoes and dance the night away to the accompaniment of pounding bass and panting, sweaty clubbers. Keep your wallet well hidden and make it clear whether or not you're happy to pay for company. Check out w dushanbe-post.com or w tonight.tj for the latest nightlife suggestions.

Bars

♀ Aqua Bar [77 E3] 68 Rudaki; ⊕ 10.00–23.00. Lively bar with indoor & outdoor space. Excellent drinks menu & cocktails start from TJS24. If you're recovering from the night before, they also do a good b/fast menu, mostly involving omelettes in various guises.

♀ The Bar [76 B3] 26/1 Ismoili Somoni; ⊕ 18.00–02.00. Inside the Hyatt Regency, The Bar serves a wide range of imported liquors & champagne, & also does a good line in cocktails. In the summer months, The Bar is closed, but The Lounge & garden terrace are open & serve the same drinks list. Prices are expensive by Tajik standards, but not incomparable to bars in London or New York.

♀ Irish Pub [77 E4] 21 Bokhtar; ⊕ noon–23.00. One of only a handful of places to get Guinness (albeit in a can) in Dushanbe. Expect to pay a whopping TJS40 for the privilege.

♀ Istiqlol Sports Bar [77 F3] 47 Druzhby Narodov; w sportbar.tj; ⊕ 10.00–02.00. If there's a major football match or other sporting event on, this is the place to watch it. Entry is free, the screen is huge, & in addition to beer they claim to have the largest cocktail menu in Dushanbe. Beers & cocktails both start from TJS8.

♀ Izzume [77 E3] 44 Foteh Niyez; ⊕ 10.00–02.00. This popular Egyptian hookah bar also serves up coffee & Middle Eastern dishes, as well as sushi, in a casbah-like environment. Don't miss the 5-tier chocolate fountain.

♀ Kellers [76 D2] 6 Ismoili Somoni; ⊕ 11.00–23.00. Dushanbe's only German beer hall brews its own beer (TJS3 but not unpalatable) & attracts an ever-happy crowd of expats & locals. The garden is packed on summer evenings.

♀ Public Pub [77 E5] 2 Bokhtar; ⊕ 11.30–23.00, til midnight Fri, Sat. Mere staggering distance from Irish Pub, Public Pub also serves canned Guinness, along with local & regional beers & other spirits. The food menu is heavy on the fried items &, being an expat paradise, the items aren't cheap. Live music, game nights & comedy shows round out the weekly entertainment offerings, when footy isn't on the telly.

Nightclubs

☆ **Bundes** [77 E4] 60 Shotemur; Where all the cool kids supposedly hang out, Bundes is a resto-bar with a revolving DJ roster & an unwelcoming door policy. They sell Guinness in bottles, though.

☆ **Choco** [76 D3] 22 Shotemur; ⊕ 22.00–04.00. Buried in the bowels of Hotel Tojikiston, Choco has held on as other entrants to Dushanbe's nightclub scene have come & gone.

☆ **Gatsby** [77 F7] Rudaki at Nazarshoev, just east of the Dushanbe Railway Station entrance; ⊕ 18.00–04.00, til midnight Sun. Located down a carpeted staircase on a vast underground level in the railway station complex, entering Gatsby – pronounced & sometimes spelt 'Getsby' – is like entering a speakeasy. Once inside, the flashing lights, white leather banquettes & pulsing pop & techno music are more 2020s than 1920s.

☆ **Royal Club** [76 B3] Ismoili Somoni, inside Navruz Palace; m (0989) 988 888; w royalclub.tj; ⊕ 21.00–04.00, til midnight Sun. Appropriately situated inside the opulent Navruz Palace, this equally opulent 'luxury-luxury nightclub' features elaborate interiors, state-of-the-art lighting & sound systems, a well-heeled crowd & hefty drink prices. Frequently hosts live concerts & international DJs.

ENTERTAINMENT

Dushanbe is not known for being an entertainment hub, even by local standards. The absence of a developed middle class with disposable income has severely limited the growth of the entertainment sector, such that those options that are available are either the legacy of Soviet policies to introduce high culture to the masses (such as the ballet and Russian-language drama theatres), or more recent initiatives spearheaded by NGOs.

That said, if you are prepared to engage with the city's cultural offerings with a sense of humour, or to make your own entertainment with friends, there are places to go and things to be seen. Many things do indeed become more entertaining with the lubrication of a small amount of vodka (pages 79–80) and many expatriates and short-term visitors find themselves developing an unexpected fondness for Dushanbe's less sophisticated diversions.

CULTURAL VENUES The **theatre season** in Dushanbe runs roughly from October until June and during this time you'll be able to catch occasional performances at the city's theatres, as well as at the **Bactria Cultural Centre**. There are two good online sources for event information, **w** dushanbe-post.com and **w** tonight.tj.

Ayni Opera and Ballet Theatre [77 F5] (*28 Rudaki*; \ *14 422; ticket office* ⊕ *08.00–20.00*) Widely agreed to have the finest interior in the city, the Ayni Opera and Ballet Theatre is a white Neoclassical building established in 1940s to host folk dances and ballet. Many of the early ballerinas and singers trained at prestigious conservatoires in Moscow and the standard of performance was consequently high. The first Tajik ballet was performed here, though Russian and classical productions tended (as they do today) to receive a better reception from the audience.

Opera and ballet performances continue to take place at the theatre, with the accompaniment of a substantially sized orchestra, and are well worth the TJS10 ticket fee. The quality may not be as high as it once was, but it is still a memorable experience and, if you happen to catch *Swan Lake*, you'll no doubt be as confused as we were by the alternative Soviet ending. Regardless of whether or not a performance is scheduled, be sure to take a look inside the building: the central marble staircase is particularly impressive, as is the gilt-laden auditorium.

Bactria Cultural Centre [77 F5] (*12A Mirzo Tursunzoda*; \ *12 558; e* bactria@ acted.org; **w** bactriacc.org; ⊕ *09.00–18.00*) With the support of French NGO ACTED (**w** www.acted.org), the centre hosts a lively programme of concerts and music workshops and encourages musical collaboration between Tajik artists. It also has a visual-arts display space and supports arts education, language teaching and conservation. Runs an annual film festival. Recent highlights have included European Week and a musical festival. Concert tickets cost TJS10.

Borbat Concert Hall [76 A3] (*26 Ismoili Somoni*) Close to Komosol Lake, this venue hosts occasional performances of Tajik music. Tickets cost from TJS5.

Lahuti Tajik Academic Drama Theatre [77 E2] (*86 Rudaki*; \ *13 751*) Established in parallel with the now-demolished but much-loved Mayakovsky Drama Theatre in the early 20th century, this theatre is named in honour of A Lahuti, the Tajik writer and dramatist who was the first to translate Shakespeare's plays into Tajik. The Red Army Theatre was evacuated here during World War II, and in the decades that followed, the theatre's company toured across the Soviet Union and even to Afghanistan. The company continues to premiere new works in Tajik, as well as to perform Tajik and Russian classics. Tickets cost TJS10–12.

Lukhtak State Puppet Theatre [77 F3] (*54/1 Shotemur*) Established in 1985, this professional theatre, which has toured globally, has a repertoire of more than 40 productions, including a large number of contemporary works. Although some performances are specifically geared towards children, others are designed for an adult audience. The theatre's façade is a wonderful mosaic of riotous colours and is alone sufficient justification for a visit.

Tajikistan State Circus [76 A7] (*2 N Karabaeva*) Shows at Dushanbe's permanent circus building, opened in 1976, are lively affairs and particularly popular with local children due to the presence of both acrobats and animals. Although there is a resident circus troupe here (including a circus school), some of the best performances come from visiting companies from Russia and China. Free demonstrations are given on Tuesday and Wednesday afternoons; tickets for standard performances cost TJS10.

CINEMAS Most of Dushanbe's cinema halls screen films in Russian only, though you can generally still follow the plot of the blockbuster action films. **Kayhon Cinema** [77 F4] (*47 Bekhzod;* w *kayhon.tj*) at Dushanbe Mall and **Tamosho Cinema Navruz** [76 B3] (*14 Ismoili Somoni;* w *tamosho.tj*), inside Navruz Palace, screen the latest movies in their original languages at least once a week. The **Bactria Cultural Centre** [77 F5] (page 81) also has occasional film showings in other languages, including English, some of which are part of its annual film festival. Cinema tickets are more expensive than theatre tickets: expect to pay around TJS20 for a 3D show.

The **Djhavonon Cinema** (*112 Rudaki;* w *sinamo.tj*) shows a range of 2D and 3D movies in an attractive, Neoclassical building.

For a smaller selection of Russian films, you can also try **Dom Kino** (*43 Bukhoro*).

SHOPPING

In the civil war years there was next to nothing to buy in Dushanbe and, without a large middle class, consumer goods are not always in great supply. The influx of expatriates has caused some improvement, and most goods are now available somewhere, providing you don't want a particular brand. A few artisans do continue producing traditional, handmade products and, with the help of NGOs, have brought their goods to market in Dushanbe.

There are two basic rules to remember when shopping in Dushanbe: if you want something, buy it there and then as there is no guarantee it will be in stock tomorrow; and be sure to haggle on price.

SOUVENIRS Tajikistan has a long history of producing gifted artists, and one of the best souvenirs from the country is undoubtedly an original artwork. Professional artists work and exhibit their paintings at the **Artists' Colony** [72 C2] (*khudojnik colonia*) at 13 Omar Khayam, and their virtual gallery is online at w tajikart.com. In a rather more formal setting, you can view works for sale at **Suhrob Kurbanov Art House** [76 D3] (formerly the Tajik Painters' Union Exhibition Hall) on the corner of Rudaki and Ismoili Somoni, and the small **Art Gallery Tajikistan** is located at 54/9 Shotemur. At the **MINO Miniature Art Centre** (*16 Gani Abdullo;* m *0919 009 669*), Tajik miniaturist Olim Kamalov sells paintings and carved chess sets.

You'll find bric-a-brac and the occasional antique at **Green Bazaar** [77 F6] (see opposite), and inside the old **TsUM** [76 D3] department store (*83 Rudaki*). The latter is also a good source for household goods, electronics and crafts. **Staraya Kvatira** [77 E5] (*35 Rudaki*), a veritable Tardis of Soviet memorabilia (including uniforms, medals and hats), offers portraits of former dictators and a large number of old, Russian-made cameras.

For handicrafts and gift items, including jewellery, weaving and embroidery, scarves and wall hangings, the following stores tend to have a good range of items of reasonable quality.

Gallery of Modern Art of Tajikistan [77 F4] 47 Bekhzod, Dushanbe Mall, 3rd Fl; ⊕ 10.00–20.00 daily. Large, impressive collection of 20th- & 21st-century Tajik painting, sculpture & handicrafts.

Gallery Sharki [77 E5] 30 Rudaki; ⊕ 09.00–21.00 Mon–Fri. Fixed-price souvenir shop with a reasonable selection of hand-painted ceramics (large plates cost TJS85), colourful chess sets, Pamiri socks & exceptionally ugly figurines of squat Tajik men in supposedly traditional dress. The miniature trees decorated with semi-precious stones must take hours to make but, sadly, also fall rather outside the parameters of good taste.

Ganjini Art Gallery [77 E5] 37 Rudaki; ⊕ 10.00–18.00 Mon–Sat. Large shop stuffed with textiles from floor to ceiling. The traditional clothing & *suzani* embroidered wall coverings are particularly good. Staff are friendly & keen to talk about the older pieces. Most of the customers seem to have just gone in for a chat.

Kabul Gallery [76 D3] 1 Ismoili Somoni; ⊕ 09.00–18.00 Mon–Fri. Hardly more than a hole in the wall, this tiny shop has piles of low-grade Afghan carpets (various sizes) & a small amount of jewellery.

Mir Samocvetov [77 E3] 32 Shotemur; ⊕ 09.00–18.00 Mon–Fri. Literally 'world of semi-precious stones'. Jewellery, vases & artworks made from a variety of minerals, many of which have been mined in Badakhshan.

Noor Art Gallery [76 B3] 26/1 Ismoili Somoni; ⊕ 10.00–20.00 daily. Small but well stocked with paintings, handicrafts, housewares & souvenirs. Inside Hyatt Regency.

Suhrob Kurbanov Art House [76 D3] 87 Rudaki; ⊕ 09.30–18.00 Mon–Sat. The double-window display of this unit looks somewhere between a museum display case & a shopfront. Coarse pottery vessels that may or may not be antiques are displayed in front of large, bright paintings of eye-catching geometric designs. Inside it is often possible to see an artist at work & to ask him about his craft.

Tillo Teppe [77 F5] 12A Mirzo Tursunzoda; ⊕ 09.00–18.00 Mon–Fri. Inside the Bactria Cultural Centre. Predominantly sells textiles (including felt & woven carpets) & accessories, but also has a few maps & books for sale in English. If the shop is closed, ask inside the main building & someone will open it for you.

MARKETS The largest and best-stocked market in Dushanbe is **Green Bazaar** [77 F6] (*cnr Chekhov & Lahuti*). Also known as Shah Mansur or Zilloni Bazaar, this is the city's wholesale fruit and vegetable market. Whether you actually want 10kg of spoiled apricots or have simply got carried away with the atmosphere is neither here nor there, but a few hours here gives real insight into commercial life and the people-watching is second to none. Chinese household goods, cheap clothing and chickens you can slaughter yourself are also widely available.

Smaller and slightly quieter is the **Barakat Bazaar** immediately behind TsUM (*83 Rudaki*) [76 D3]. The choice of fresh produce is not as wide as elsewhere, but the quality is certainly comparable and it's on the way to almost everywhere.

For clothing, try **Sadbarg** [77 F6], the indoor market at the intersection of Rudaki and Ayni. Ready-made clothes, shoes and fabrics are all on sale, and there are several tailoring workshops on the upper floors if you want something altered or made to measure. Anchored by the **Auchan** hypermarket, **Dushanbe Mall** [77 F4] (*47 Bekhzod;* ⊕ *08.00–23.00 daily*) has American-style clothing boutiques, a food court and a cinema.

SUPERMARKETS Dushanbe's supermarkets are always remarkably well stocked with vodka, tinned fish and imitation cognac, but supplies of what others might regard as staples are somewhat more erratic. The following shops tend to keep a reasonable supply of fresh produce, meats and dried goods, as well as brand-name confectionery and soft drinks, and a few other imported goods. They also sell cleaning products and basic household items.

Arzanda [77 E5] 30 Rudaki; ⊕ 07.00–midnight. Well-stocked shop with a reasonable range of fresh produce, breads & meats. The tinned foods aisle is impressive (though one wonders who exactly needs a dozen different brands of tinned fish), as is the selection of teabags & coffee. Foreign brands such as HP, Heinz & Nescafé are all in evidence. There is an ATM by the entrance.

Auchan [77 F4] 47 Bekhzod, inside Dushanbe Mall; ⊕ 08.00–22.00. Large hypermarket with vast selection of groceries & household products. **Orima** [77 E2] 92 Rudaki; ⊕ 07.00–21.00. Turkish supermarket chain with a number of stores in Dushanbe. Look out for the yellow-&-red signs. Also at 30 Rudaki & 126 Ismoili Somoni. **Paikar** 20 Husseinzoda; ⊕ 08.00–20.00. Probably the best selection of meat & dairy products.

ELECTRONICS AND PHOTOGRAPHY There are a large number of computer shops selling everything from laptops to printer cables, all situated cheek by jowl along Rudaki 56–64. If you can't find what you're looking for here, the ground floor of **TsUM** [76 D3] (*83 Rudaki*) has stalls selling computer parts old and new, cables, chargers, batteries, memory cards and the like. Branded items tend to be expensive, but Chinese copies are a fraction of the price and usually work just fine.

For passport photos and printing, go to **Kodak Express** [76 D3] (*83 Rudaki; ⊕ 08.00–19.00*) or **Fuji Film** [77 E3] (*cnr Shotemur & Rudaki*).

BOOKS AND MAPS There is no English-language bookshop in Dushanbe, though the **American Corner** cultural centre [72 C2] (*66 Tolstoy;* ☏ *(0363) 729 878*) may have English-language books to loan. The **Tajik National University** [76 B1] has its own bookshop, and there is also a daily stall outside the **Firdausi National Library** [76 D4].

For maps, the easiest option is **Komus** [76 D2] (*91 Rudaki; ⊕ 09.00–19.00*), a stationery store that stocks fold-out maps of both Dushanbe and Tajikistan as well as wall maps. The Dushanbe street map costs TJS20 and is simple to read even for non-Russian speakers.

SPORTS/FITNESS

Dushanbe's top-end hotels typically have their own pools and fitness facilities, and indeed these are the highest-quality sports venues in the city. However, they are not always open to non-guests (enquire at reception), so the following options may also be of use.

BOWLING
Taj Bowling [77 F4] 21 Mirzo Tursunzoda; ⊕ 14.00–02.00 daily. Inside the Asia Grand Hotel complex.

GYM
55 Spirit [77 E5] 34 Husseinzoda; w 55spirit. tj; ⊕ 06.30–midnight daily. Fully functional fitness centre with weight training, cardio, boxing, personal training, fitness classes & massage. **55 Spirit Aqua** [77 G6] 48 Ayni; w 55spirit.tj; ⊕ 07.00–23.00 daily. Full-service fitness centre with indoor swimming pool. Inside Sozidanie Business Centre. **Fitness Club** [77 F4] 21 Mirzo Tursunzoda; ⊕ 08.00–22.00 Mon–Sat. Inside the Taj Palace Hotel.

Taekwondo Centre 25 Bokhtar; ⏰ 08.00–20.30 Mon–Sat. Fitness centre with kickboxing & tae kwon do classes available on request.

X-Fit [76 A2] 7/2 Bagautdinova; w xfit.ru; ⏰ 07.00–23.00 daily. Branch of upmarket Russian fitness centre chain with weightlifting equipment, cardio, swimming, personal training & massage services.

RUNNING

Hash House Harriers Search for 'Dushanbe Hash House Harriers' on ■. Meet every Sat for a session of running & drinking.

TENNIS

Kasri Tennis [76 B3] 45 Ismoili Somoni; ⏰ 08.00–21.00 daily. Indoor tennis courts opposite the Hyatt Regency.

YOGA

India Cultural Centre [77 E5] 45 Bukhoro; ✆ 17 172; www.indianembassytj.com; ⏰ 10.00–18.00 Mon–Fri. Yoga classes, as well as Katha dance & tabla drumming classes. Inside the Embassy of India.

OTHER PRACTICALITIES

EMERGENCIES For medical emergencies, see box on pages 42–3.

In an emergency, call the following numbers for assistance. It is unlikely, however, that the operator will speak any English, and help is not guaranteed to arrive.

Ambulance ✆ 03
Fire ✆ 02
Police ✆ 01

COMMUNICATIONS

Post Dushanbe's Soviet-era central post office was demolished in 2015 as part of the recent purge of Tajikistan's architectural legacy, but its interim replacement is at 47 Bukhoro (⏰ *08.00–18.00 Mon–Sat, 08.00–15.00 Sun*). It is advised, however, that letters and parcels destined for addresses abroad be sent directly from the government-run **international post office** [77 F7] (*35 Nazarshoev, adjacent the Dushanbe Railway Station;* ⏰ 08.00–18.00 *Mon–Fri, 08.00–13.00 Sat*). Theoretically the office operates as a poste restante, but there is no guarantee that post bearing your name will ever reach there. If you want to increase the likelihood of your post arriving (regardless of whether you are sending or receiving), using a courier is your most reliable option. The two major international companies both have agents in the city, and there's little to choose between them.

DHL [77 H5] 52 Druzhba Narodov; ✆ 21 999; e reception@dunyo-llc.com; ⏰ 09.00–18.00

UPS [77 E6] 13 Ayni; ✆ 72 376; e messengertj@mail.ru; ⏰ 09.00–17.00

You will be required to present your passport when sending an item. For larger packages and high-value items you will also need all relevant customs paperwork, including purchase receipts.

Phone Most of Dushanbe's **internet cafés** (page 86) now offer Skype and other VoIP services, which are the cheapest ways to call internationally. If you prefer a landline, the **Central Telephone Office** [77 E4] (*55 Rudaki*) is open 24/7 and is staffed with an operator to assist you.

Every other shop sells SIM cards for the various telecom companies, though buying one requires a certain amount of patience (pages 59–60). The main providers all have shops and customer service centres in Dushanbe: try **Babilon**

3

Mobile [76 D3] (*5 Ismoili Somoni*), **T-Cell** (*37/1 Bokhtar, 6A Rudaki* [76 D3], *77 Rudaki & 269 Ayni*) [77 F6], **Beeline** (*29/9 Ayni & 55 Rudaki*), and **Megafon** (*73/2 Huvaydulloev*). Beeline also has a store inside **TsUM** [76 D3] (*83 Rudaki*) where service is faster than most. A SIM card here costs US$3 and includes US$3 of talk time.

To top up your phone, either pop into a shop or use one of the colourful self-service machines on the street. These look like a cross between a public telephone and an ATM and are relatively easy to use if you can work out the requisite words of Russian, or have someone show you what to do.

Internet The use of internet dongles is increasingly common in Dushanbe, and they can be bought from the above-mentioned mobile-phone providers. Many restaurants and hotels now provide Wi-Fi, much of which is free, and this is how the vast majority of people choose to get online.

If you prefer to go to a café, however, there are plenty of centrally located options which will give you free Wi-Fi if you buy a coffee. The suggestions below also have computer terminals you can use if you don't have your own device, for which you'd expect to pay TJS5 per hour.

⊟ **Diplomat** 1 Ismoili Somoni; ⊕ 08.00–22.00. Centrally located
⊟ **Shahzoda** [77 E5] 37 Rudaki; ⊕ 08.00–23.00. Fast connection speeds & VoIP availability.

⊟ **Skype Internet** [77 E5] 30 Rudaki; ⊕ 08.00–22.00. Probably not authorised by the daddy of all VoIP providers, this cybercafé nevertheless has a good connection speed & helpful staff. VoIP calls are, of course, available.

HAIR AND BEAUTY There are numerous small hair salons, barbers and beauty parlours scattered across Dushanbe, with a few European-style *coifferies* here and there. Still, there is little to choose between most of them, though be warned they tend to have more in common with a Soviet-era sanatorium than places of peace and relaxation. French chain **Dessange Paris** [76 D5] (*27 Bukhoro;* \(0488) 880 000; ⊕ 09.00–19.00 Tue–Sun), sets the standard with its full range of hair styling and beauty services. We've also used **Shabnam Salon** near TsUM [76 D3] (*66 Rudaki*). Like Dessange, the rather upmarket **Almos** (*1 Ismoili Somoni*) is immaculately clean and caters to a slightly wealthier clientele.

If you prefer to relax at the same time as being primped and preened, **Sayohat Spa** [76 B3] (*26/1 Ismoili Somoni;* \(0487) 021 234) is located inside the Hyatt Regency. It offers a wide range of massages and facials as well as exfoliation and body wraps. Expect to pay around TJS250 for a 1-hour treatment. There is also a steam room, sauna and a reasonably proficient hairdresser on site. The mid-range **Spa-Hayot** (*45/3 A Jomi;* \(0446) 302 222) and plush **Maisha Spa** [77 F6] (*14 Rudaki;* \(0487) 014 000) at the Serena Hotel also come highly recommended. In addition to treatment rooms at Maisha, there are two saunas, two steam rooms and a rooftop pool.

If you want to buy imported fragrances and cosmetics, try **Yves Rocher** (*66 Rudaki*) and **La Cité** (*32 Rudaki & 70 Rudaki*). **Arzanda supermarket** [77 E5] (page 84) also has a surprisingly wide selection of foreign-brand shampoos and other bath products.

MEDICAL Dushanbe's medical facilities are exceptionally basic and, in the event that you do have an accident or become seriously ill, you should contact your embassy for assistance. It is likely in that case that you will need to arrange MEDEVAC home or to a neighbouring country and, for that reason, medical insurance is essential. In the case of more minor incidents, the options below provide a reasonable level of service.

✚ **Prospekt Medical Clinic** [72 C2] 34 Foteh Niyozi; ☏ (0487) 024 400; e prospekt-clinik@ tajnet.tj; w prospektclinic.tj; ⏰ 08.30–16.30. General medical service offered by English-speaking staff. A single consultation costs US$100. The clinic can help organise MEDEVAC, if necessary.

✚ **Shifo Clinic** [77 F6] 106 Druzhby Narodov; ☏ 71 814; e farma_dushanbe@mail.ru; ⏰ 08.00–16.00. Efficient clinic with a range of diagnostic equipment. Some staff speak English, & there is a pharmacy on site. An appointment costs TJS59.

MONEY It often seems that two currencies are in use in Dushanbe: US dollars and Tajik somoni. The larger hotels typically quote prices in dollars, as do many of the travel agents. You are advised to keep a stack of both currencies, as few companies have the ability to take card payments, and you will not have the option to change travellers' cheques.

Almost any hotel in Dushanbe will offer a money-changing service, though you are likely to get a better rate on the street. There are a number of banks to choose from (though none of the big international names you're likely to recognise) and they can generally arrange Western Union as well as having a bureau de change.

Be aware that not all ATMs take foreign bank cards. If you get stuck, the ATMs in the foyers at **Hotel Poytakht** (page 74), the **Sheraton** (page 73) and the **Hyatt Regency** (page 73) can issue both USD and TJS to foreign bank card holders and are accessible round the clock.

$ **Agroinvest Bank** 1 Rudaki; ☏ (0446) 006 868; w agroinvestbank.tj; ⏰ 08.00–17.00 Mon–Fri
$ **Eskhata Bank** 49 Bukhoro; ☏ (0446) 000 600; w eskhata.com; ⏰ 08.00–16.00 Mon–Fri, 08.00–14.00 Sat. Also processes MoneyGram transactions.
$ **Orien Bank** 28 Shotemur; ☏ 10 568; w orienbank.com; ⏰ 08.30–16.00. Also at 15 Lokhuti (⏰ *08.00–16.00 Mon–Sat, 08.00–noon Sun*), 269 Ayni (⏰ *08.00–16.00 Mon–Fri, 08.00–noon Sat*) & 15 Druzhby Narodov (⏰ *08.00–16.00*

Mon–Fri, 08.00–noon Sat). Able to send & receive Western Union.
$ **Tajprom Bank** [77 F6] 22A Rudaki; ☏ 12 720 ⏰ 08.00–17.00 Mon–Fri. Willing to change GBP, though you may have to wait while they find out the rate & someone is summoned to check the notes.
$ **Tojik Sodirot Bank** [77 F4] 47 Bekhzod; ☏ (0446) 004 017; w tsb.tj; ⏰ 08.00–17.00 Mon–Fri. Able to send & receive Western Union.

REGISTRATION The **Office of Visas and Registration** (OVIR) [77 F5] is located at 5 M Tursonzade (⏰ *08.00–17.00 Mon–Fri, 08.00–noon Sat*) and registration takes three days. English is not spoken so you are advised to get your hotel or a travel agency to arrange the registration on your behalf (pages 30–1).

WHAT TO SEE AND DO

If Rudaki is Dushanbe's Greenwich Meridian, then Ismoili Somoni is its Equator. For ease of navigation, we've divided the city's sights into four quadrants (northeast, southeast, southwest and northwest) based on these two lines. Each quadrant is best explored on foot and can be either treated in isolation, or as part of a citywide tour, starting and finishing towards the northern end of Rudaki.

NORTHEAST Dushanbe's quiet, northeasterly quadrant is predominantly composed of residential streets lined with apartment blocks, and a scattering of low-rise embassy buildings. Well hidden among this is the **Mirzo Tursunzoda Memorial**

Museum [77 E1] (*59 Loiq Sherali;* ☉ *10.00–16.00 Tue–Sat; local/foreigner TJS1/2*), the house-museum of Mirzo Tursunzoda, a Tajik poet and prominent political figure in the mid 20th century. It is laid out as it was at the time of his death in 1977, and exhibits include his furniture and personal library.

Just a few minutes' walk away is the **Ziyadullo Shahidi Museum of Musical Culture** [77 F1] (*108 Loiq Sherali;* ☉ *09.00–17.00 Mon–Fri; TJS3*). Another house-museum, it belonged to Soviet-era composer and musician Ziyadullo Shahidi and is now run by his daughter, Munira, a leading light of Dushanbe's cultural scene. The museum regularly organises musical performances through the Shahidi Cultural Foundation (w *shahidifoundation.com*), and its extensive archives include letters and photographs charting Shahidi's career and those of his contemporaries.

At the southern end of this quarter, at the junction of Rudaki and Ismoili Somoni, is the historic **Presidential Palace** [77 E3] (President Rahmon's residence is the newer Palace of Nations; see page 90). This attractive building has an Italianate feel, helped in part by the fountains in the front courtyard. It is not possible to go inside the building, but certainly worth a look through the gates and a subtly taken photograph or two. Next door, the attractive **Chaykhona Rokhat** [77 E2] (pages 78–9), built in a traditional Persian style, is a good place to stop for tea and a snack.

SOUTHEAST Five minutes' walk from the junction of Rudaki and Ismoili Somoni is the intriguing **Gurminj Museum** [77 E4] (*23 Bokhtar;* w *gurminj.tj;* ☉ *11.00–16.00 Mon–Sun; local/foreigner TJS1/5*). Gurminj Zavkibekov was a Soviet film star and a keen collector of musical instruments. This small museum, run by his son Iqbol, not only exhibits his collection of traditional instruments from Tajikistan and neighbouring countries but also serves as a venue for musical performances. There is a small recording studio on site where traditional musicians can often be heard practising. An hour or two here is highly recommended for those with an interest in ethnomusicology, particularly if you understand Russian and can chat with the exceptionally knowledgeable Iqbol.

Back on Rudaki, walk past the unusual mosaic of dancers and musicians, made from different coloured stones. Be sure to stop at the **Firdausi National Library** [76 D4] (*36 Rudaki*) with its distinctive busts of prominent figures in science and the arts. Also known as the Academy of Sciences, this attractive whitewashed building incorporates aspects of both Stalinist and Islamic architecture. Since its foundation in 1933, it has expanded to house more than 2.5 million books in a variety of languages, as well as an important collection of ancient manuscripts that includes one of the earliest copies of Firdausi's famous work, the *Shahnama* (Book of Kings). There is also a small craft shop on site, and a bookstall outside most days.

Just past the library is **Friendship Square** [77 F5] (Maydoni Dusti), formerly known as Freedom Square (Maydoni Azadi), on which you'll find the **Ayni Opera and Ballet Theatre** [77 F5] (page 81) and, behind it, the small but pleasant park, **Opera Ballet Square** [77 F5]. It's a popular spot to stop and take a coffee in one of the open-air cafés, and plenty of people are sat happily watching the world go by.

Suitably refreshed, and with an optional diversion via **Green/Shah Mansur Bazaar** [77 F6] (page 83), walk to **Ayni Square** [77 F6] (Maydoni Ayni) and its imposing statue of Sadriddin Ayni who gives the square his name. Alongside it are two other statues: a fairly standard war memorial, and another rather more unusual sculpture in which at least one of the figures appears to be rolling on his back. Climbing inside the statue alongside him can make for some entertaining holiday snaps.

A short taxi ride to the east is **Victory Park** [72 D3], one of the largest green spaces in Dushanbe and site of a massive monument to the heroes of the Great Patriotic War, as the Soviets called World War II. A creaking, Soviet-era funicular (*TJS1*) transports lazier/braver individuals to the top of the hill, though it is probably safer to walk. From the top you get good views across Dushanbe, and an enterprising café owner capitalises on this in the summer months by setting out a few tables with parasols and serving cheap (but not particularly palatable) wines.

SOUTHWEST Dushanbe's cultural highlight is the **National Museum of Antiquities** [77 E6] (*7 Academics Rajabov;* \71 350; w *www.afc.ryukoku.ac.jp/tj;* ⊕ *09.00–17.00 Tue–Sun; local/foreigner TJS2.50/10*). The largest and most important museum in Dushanbe, it houses artefacts covering 3,000 years of Tajik history. Recently renovated, the museum is laid out according to a mixture of geography and chronology. Some of the more important items are labelled in English, and the staff are keen to tell you about the items on show.

Entering the building through its Neoclassical portico brings you into the main lobby, where some of the most impressive statuary and stonework is displayed. Take special note of the Oxus Temple altar from Takht-i Sangin, the site where the Oxus Treasure (now housed in the British Museum) was discovered in the late 19th century. Other artefacts excavated from the site, including weaponry, carved ivory, sculptures and fine metalwork, are in the two smaller rooms immediately between the lobby and the courtyard garden.

In the two rooms covering the Kushanian Period are a number of small but exquisitely carved pieces of statuary from the 3rd–5th centuries AD. If you look carefully at the hairstyles and dress in the figurative works you'll clearly see the Greek influence. Our favourite piece here is the terracotta tile with a relief entitled 'Man Deity with the Baton'. This figure is depicted wearing a kaftan and a Sassanid headdress and waving a baton to command the movements of seven stars.

Tajikistan's richest archaeological finds come from the area around Panjakent, and they are displayed in two rooms, one on each floor of the museum. Tajikistan's position as a melting pot of Silk Road ideas and art is reinforced with the (sadly decapitated) statue of the Hindu god Shiva and his wife, Parvati. The frescoes of archers and other battle scenes are remarkably well preserved for their age.

The museum's greatest draw, the Sleeping Buddha, takes pride of place on the second floor. Since the destruction of the Bamiyan Buddhas in 2001, this 16m-long statue is the largest remaining Buddha in central Asia. Dating from around AD500 and sculpted from local clay, it was discovered at the Buddhist monastery of Ajina Tepa in 1966 and had to be moved to Dushanbe in sections. If you are interested in this artefact, the museum staff will enthusiastically tell you about it and also show you photographs from the original excavation.

Also on this floor are the museum's collections of coins, gold, and a room given over to ancient manuscripts. The coins are an accessible way to chart the changing rulers of the region but also their international ties: in addition to depictions of the rulers themselves, there are numerous designs featuring Hindu and Greek gods.

The National Museum of Antiquities is the best available introduction to Tajikistan's rich history, particularly if you plan to travel to some of the archaeological sites in other parts of the county. The most important archaeological finds are here, not in the provinces, and the displays will help you contextualise them. It is permitted to take photographs providing you do not use a flash.

Right next door is the **Ethnographic Museum** [77 E6] (*7 Academics Rajabov;* \78 751; ⊕ *10.00–17.00 Mon–Sat; local/foreigner TJS2.50/10*), a smaller collection of ethnographic items including musical instruments, costume, carpets and jewellery. The museum stores more than 15,000 artefacts from all parts of Tajikistan, though only a fraction of these are on display at any one time.

Continuing southwest down Academics Rajabov, away from Rudaki, you reach the **Victory monument** [72 D6], another tribute to those who fought for the USSR during the Great Patriotic War (World War II). As well as a large arch, there is also an original tank, restored and repainted, which makes an ideal climbing frame for children and others so inclined.

Five minutes' walk along Tehran from Rudaki brings you to sprawling, manicured **Rudaki Park** [76 D4] (Bag-i Rudaki) and the side of the **Palace of Nations** [76 C4]. This imposing structure, with its golden dome, can be seen from across the city and it is home to both President Rahmon and many of the government ministries. Though photogenic, the palace guards are a little jumpy about foreigners wielding cameras, so if you wish to take a photo then do so subtly. This is not the place to set up your long lens on a tripod.

The park itself is a well-maintained space with numerous flower beds that come into bloom in early summer and are a colourful addition to the landscape right through to autumn. In September, the beds are a riot of red and orange. Whichever path you take through the park you'll be unable to miss the world's second-tallest flagpole. Rising 165m above the park, this controversial structure cost US$3.5 million to build and was erected as the world's tallest in May 2011 as part of celebrations to commemorate 20 years of Tajik independence. Three years later, the city of Jeddah erected a 170m pole, snatching the flag for Saudi Arabia.

Other photo opportunities in this area are the ostentatious golden statue of **Ismoili Somoni** [76 D4] with its two uniformed guards, the elegant, marble **Independence monument** [76 D4] (aka Stele), and the rather more tasteful **Arch of Rudaki** [76 D4]. The statue of Rudaki stands beneath a colourful mosaic arch and is reflected in the pool of water below. Don't miss the immense artificial waterfall built into the side of a hill overlooking the racetrack and the river.

Cutting through behind the **TsUM department store** [76 D3] (pages 82–3) and **Barakat Bazaar** (page 83) from Rudaki brings you up to Ismoili Somoni and the vast and modern **National Museum of Tajikistan** [76 C3] (*Ismoili Somoni;* \ *78 561;* w *newnmt.tj;* ⏱ *10.00–17.00 Tue–Sat, 11.00–16.00 Sun; local/foreigner TJS5/25, English-speaking guide TJS30*). Guarding the northern edge of Rudaki Park and replacing the much smaller Bekhzod National Museum as host to many of the country's national treasures, this purpose-built structure features 22 exhibition halls and 15,000m² of total exhibition space. The collection of some 50,000 artefacts encompasses items from the advent of Zoroastrianism through the Middle Ages and into the post-Soviet era. The 20th-century portraiture and sculptures from Soviet Tajikistan are notably impressive, as are the ornate 12th-century Islamic pottery and the convincing, life-sized copy of the Sleeping Buddha (page 89).

Continuing down Ismoili Somoni, you reach the beautifully ostentatious **Navruz Palace** [76 B3] (*Kokhi Navruz; 14/2 Ismoili Somoni;* m *(0938) 800 137;* w *kohinavruz. com;* ⏱ *08.30–17.00 Mon–Fri*), originally billed as the 'world's largest tea house' when it opened in 2013. Containing a *chaykhona*, billiards hall, bowling alley, multiscreen cinema, plush nightclub (page 80) and supermarket, the venue also plays host to high-level political summits and upmarket social events. Tours of the complex, which features intricately carved wooden doors, sparkly chandeliers, and folkloric mosaics made by artisans from northern Tajikistan, cost TJS25, with a TJS25 surcharge for an English-speaking guide. Just behind the palace is **Komsomol Lake** [76 B3]. This artificial reservoir, fed by the Varzob River, is a popular recreation spot for local people. On hot days small children shriek and splash in the slightly murky waters, while their families stand on the lakeside eating ice cream and other sticky snacks on sale. The park contains a rather rickety Ferris wheel, though we'd be exceptionally cautious about taking a ride.

NORTHWEST Crossing now to the northern side of Ismoili Somoni, you'll see one of Dushanbe's most unusual but striking constructions: the **Writers' Union Building** [76 D2]. It dates from the Soviet period but its façade is covered with life-sized statues of Tajik poets and other cultural heroes whose lives and work span the last millennium. With the notable exception of Firdausi, few of the names are easily recognisable to foreigners, but this monument does show the high esteem in which the Tajik people hold their vernacular literary figures.

A little back from Ismoili Somoni, next to the **Pamir Stadium** [76 B2], is the zoo [76 B2]. Once home to over a thousand animals (including elephants), the zoo, its staff and animals have been hard hit by Tajikistan's economic problems. Cages are small and the condition of the surviving animals is generally poor.

Further west beyond the stadium along Ismoili Somoni is the impressive Dushanbe branch of the **Ismaili Centre** [76 A2] (*entrance on Sportivnaya;* w *theismaili.org;* ⊕ *09.00–16.00 Sun*), part of a network of Islamic cultural and educational centres sponsored by the Aga Khan. The striking tan-and-turquoise façade is constructed of some three million bricks, and reflects a modern take on central Asian and Islamic architectural traditions, with state-of-the-art energy efficiency and technology improvements.

Situated behind the Hotel Avesto on Rudaki is another of the few signs that Tajikistan is in fact a nominally Muslim country: the mosque and *madrasa* **of Haji Yaqub** [76 D2]. This beautiful building, with its colourfully tiled portico, is Dushanbe's most important place of worship and is particularly busy on Fridays when up to 3,000 Muslims come to pray. Women are allowed in the courtyard only, but visitors are generally welcome providing they are respectfully attired. There is often a heavy police presence around the mosque, as the government is rightly or wrongly concerned about rising fundamentalism.

To the north of the mosque is Dushanbe's final house-museum, the **Sadriddin Ayni Museum** [76 D1] (*1 Kh Khakimzade;* ⊕ *10.00–15.00 Mon–Fri*). This small exhibition is dedicated to the life and work of the Tajik intellectual Sadriddin Ayni (page 23). Entry is free but there is a charge of US$3 if you take the guided tour (Russian and Turkish only).

The final site of interest in northwestern Dushanbe is the **botanical gardens** [72 C2] (*Samad Gani;* ⊕ *08.00–18.00; entry TJS1*). The garden covers 34ha and contains over 2,000 species of plant. It has been cared for by the academy of science since the early 1930s and miraculously seems to have survived the civil war without too much damage. The garden is particularly popular, with wedding parties coming here to have their pictures taken among the trees, pools and attractive wooden pergolas.

AROUND DUSHANBE

Once you've had your fill of Dushanbe's charms, it's time to get out into the great outdoors and experience Tajikistan's natural beauty first-hand. The following sites are all within a short distance of the capital and make either for a pleasant day trip, or a stop *en route* to other destinations.

HISOR There has been a settlement at Hisor, also spelt Gissar, since the Stone Age, and it has to rate as one of the unluckiest sites in Tajikistan. Due to its important strategic location and commanding views along the valley, it has been destroyed no fewer than 21 times: everyone from Cyrus the Great and Alexander the Great (neither of whom would have gained those monikers had Hisor's residents had anything to do with it) to Genghis Khan, Timur and, finally, the Red Army, razed

3

the town to the ground. Each time it had to be rebuilt almost entirely from scratch. As you might expect, only fragments of architecture remain from each of these painful periods in history.

Getting there By car, take the M41 west of Dushanbe and then take the left fork in the road to Hisor. The total distance is just 27km and should take you no more than half an hour.

If you are using public transport, take bus 8 from Ismoili Somoni to Zarnisar Bazaar on the western outskirts of Dushanbe, then the minibus to Hisor (*TJS2; 30mins*). Hisor bus station is on the eastern edge of the town, 5km from the fort, so you will need a shared taxi (*TJS1 per seat; 10mins*). Alternatively, there is a daily train service from Dushanbe to Hisor. Hisor train station is on the northern side of the town.

✕ Where to eat Though Hisor has no formal restaurants, there is an atmospheric *chaykhona* next to the museum serving *laghman*, *shashlik* and other small snacks as well, of course, as tea. There are also a number of food and tea stalls in **Hisor Bazaar**.

What to see and do The reason for Hisor's existence, and its recurrent destruction, is **Hisor Fort** (☉ *08.00–18.00; TJS1*), which is depicted on the TJS20 bank note. Flattened most recently by the Red Army when it drove out Ibrahim Bek and his Basmachi followers in 1924, all that remains of the original fort is the **Darvaza-i Ark**, an imposing stone gateway strongly reminiscent of the one marking the start of the Khyber Pass at Peshawar. The fort has been rebuilt with modern materials, Disney-style, in the design of the original and features period-inspired market stalls hawking souvenirs. There are fantastic views of the surrounding area from atop the front wall.

In front of this gate is a **mulberry tree** which, legend has it, was bent by Ali, son-in-law of the Prophet Muhammad, during a fight with a local magician. Alongside the tree is a **holy spring**, dedicated to an early Islamic missionary.

Facing the fortress are two *madrasas* (Islamic schools), the older of which, the **Madrasa-i Kuhna**, dates from the 16th century. Inside this madrasa is the Hisor Museum (☉ *08.00–18.00; TJS3*). Exhibits are displayed inside each former *hujra* (student cell) and include an archaeological map of Tajikistan, a Bactrian column, jewellery and numerous pottery finds. Unusually, some information is available in English.

The second madrasa, the **Madrasa-i Nau** (New Madrasa) is kept locked, but if you ask in the museum they will get you the key. Though the 19th-century building is not terribly interesting, you can get up on to the roof relatively easily and from there enjoy the view. Look out for the remains of the town's caravanserai (next to the museum), dating from 1808, and also the **mausoleum of Mahdumi Azam**, a Sufi preacher whose grave still attracts local pilgrims.

SHIRKENT AND KARATAG VALLEYS If you stay on the M41 rather than turning south to Hisor, you reach the town of **Tursunzoda**, named in honour of Mirzo Tursunzoda (see box, opposite) and home of the **Tajik Aluminium Company**, a smoke-belching industrial complex that still uses the Soviet technology installed in the 1970s.

You are most likely to find yourself in Tursunzoda *en route* to or from the Uzbek border crossing to Denau. Minibuses and shared taxis (*TJS20*) from Dushanbe ply the 60km, 90-minute route to Tursunzoda and the border, but a car must be hired for onward adventures into the Shirkent Valley.

Once a great silk-weaving centre, **Karatag** produced fine textiles for export to Afghanistan, Iran and Turkey. Mirzo Tursunzoda was born here in 1911, but today the small town, 10km north of Tursunzoda and reached only by shared taxi or hired car, is really only used as a stepping-off point for treks into the **Karatag Valley**. Popular day hikes include the steep climb to the glacier-fed **Timurdara Lake** (1,970m above sea level), or the slightly longer route to **Lake Payron**. Both sites offer excellent opportunities for camping. Like most of the water in Tajikistan, the lakes are a spectacular shade of turquoise, reflecting the alternating greens and browns of the surrounding mountains.

Continuing north, the Shirkent Valley forms the backbone of the **Shirkent National Park**. Founded in 1991 to protect areas of special scientific interest, the park has three sets of known **dinosaur footprints** (the largest of which contains more than 300 prints from Upper Jurassic-period sauropods and theropods), ancient **copper and tin mines** and a **Medieval necropolis**. You will, however, need a knowledgeable guide to find these sites.

If you prefer to wander the park alone, there are excellent trekking routes through the **gorge**, impressive **waterfalls** and a large number of **caves**. The park's **juniper forest** is thriving in spite of heavy logging in the mid 20th century, and it is hoped that ibex and Marco Polo sheep can be reintroduced once livestock grazing is restricted to certain areas. However, wildlife-spotting is impressive in the park, with bears, snow leopards, griffons, marten cats, falcons and Siberian wild goats among the diverse fauna. Among the natural wonders are archaeological monuments, studded with Stone Age and Medieval artefacts from local settlements and suggesting a developed agricultural and artisanal culture in the region from the 5th to the 7th centuries AD.

Guided tours to the valleys and accommodation at the **Abdurazok guesthouse** (**$**) in the village of Shirkent can be arranged by any of the local tour operators in Dushanbe (pages 71–2).

ALUMINIUM PRODUCTION IN TAJIKISTAN

The Tajik Aluminium Company's aluminium smelter at Tursunzoda is Tajikistan's only large-scale aluminium production facility. It has a production capacity of around 520,000 tonnes a year (making it one of the largest primary aluminium producers in the former Soviet Union), and when running at full capacity consumes some 40% of the current electricity-generating capacity of Tajikistan. It depends entirely on imported alumina for its feedstock.

The Tursunzoda smelter is vitally important to Tajikistan's economy: in 2010 its production of 348,850 tonnes of primary aluminium generated US$735.7 million, or 56.4% of all national export revenues. Income has risen in recent years as a result of increasing world aluminium prices, but physical production is in fact falling as a result of ageing equipment and the loss of skilled personnel. In 2010, a TALCO metallurgist earned just US$400 a month, a substantial salary in Tajikistan but a fraction of what they can earn elsewhere. Although in the past most Tajik-produced aluminium was exported to Russia and Europe, as of 2010 it heads to manufacturing centres in China and Turkey. A prospective deal with Russian investors recently soured, with the consequence that the plant still awaits much-needed upgrading. At the end of 2016, TALCO remained embroiled in a scandal involving alleged high-dollar deposits to a shell corporation based in the British Virgin Islands.

The production of this supremely versatile metal has always placed large energy demands on Tajikistan and necessitated the building of several hydro-electric plants on the Vakhsh River. While there was a centrally planned economy this was more easily achievable, especially as the experts were not allowed to leave the site without risking the sanction of spending a spot of time in a gulag.

VARZOB VALLEY Some 30km north of Dushanbe is the Varzob Valley, through which the Varzob River later flows on to the capital. At weekends, certain spots, particularly around the **Varzob Lake**, are crowded with Dushanbe families having a picnic or taking a stroll from their *dacha*, but walking even a few kilometres up into the surrounding hills will guarantee you peace and quiet.

Of the numerous short treks starting in this valley, two are particularly picturesque. The path to the **Guzgarf Waterfall** is 8km in length and will take someone with a reasonable level of fitness around 2 hours. The waterfall itself is a vertical torrent crashing down 30m from the rock above and in late spring the route is further enhanced with a carpet of blood-red tulips. Alternatively, an hour's walk from the main Varzob road brings you to the **Siama Gorge**, where the crystal blue waters rush steeply downhill from glaciers 3,300m above sea level, and through thickets of birch trees and fruit bushes, before joining the Varzob below.

Other things of interest in the upper reaches of the valley are the somewhat forlorn **Takob Ski Resort**, sadly in decline after its Soviet heyday, and the small **botanical garden** in the Kandara Gorge, an outpost of the Academy of Sciences. Though lacking in investment in recent years, the garden is thought to contain 10% of the species of flora native to central Asia, many of which can no longer be seen anywhere else.

Regular buses run to the valley from the **Varzob Bazaar** bus station in the north of Dushanbe. Tickets cost TJS2–3 depending on how far up the valley you wish to travel. For those travelling by car, there is a TJS3 road toll.

If you wish to stay in the valley, there is a Soviet-style **sanatorium ($)** at Khoja Obi Garm, though the focus is very much on health and cleansing rather than relaxation. It can be booked through tour operators in Dushanbe (pages 71–2). If you are trekking, you will probably prefer to camp.

ROMIT GORGE Leaving Dushanbe on the M41 east and taking the left fork in the road at Vahdat will bring you to the **Romit State Nature Reserve**. The reserve's mountain slopes, thickly forested with birch, mulberry, wild fruit and nut trees, are home to more than a hundred species of birds and, in their upper reaches, there are alpine meadows with a gorgeous carpet of springtime bulbs. Should you wish to try your hand at **fishing**, there are significant numbers of trout in the **Kafirnigan River**.

In the summer months, it is possible to trek from Romit to the Takob Ski Resort (see above) in two days. The route includes one pass and goes through the picturesque **Obi-Safed Canyon** with its traditional *aylok* (shepherds' camps). **Golden eagles** are a relatively common sight, and so are **Tugai deer** and fat, fluffy **marmots**.

MIRZO TURSUNZODA

Born in 1911, Mirzo Tursunzoda came from a family of artisans in the Karatag Valley. He studied initially with the local mullah and then at schools in Karatag and Dushanbe, ultimately graduating from the Tajik Institute of Education in 1930.

Tursunzoda was a gifted poet, and his poems glorified both his homeland and its people. He won numerous prizes, including the prestigious title 'Hero of Socialist Work'. While many literary figures from the Soviet period have fallen from favour, Tursunzoda has been elevated to a national hero of independent Tajikistan, too. His face appears on the TJS1 note, the city of Regar has been renamed in his honour, and in 2001 his 90th anniversary was celebrated with great zeal.

THE NUREK DAM

Rising 300m above the Vakhsh River, and stretching a remarkable 704m across, the Nurek Dam is one of the largest ever constructed. Built between 1961 and 1980, it consists of a cement shell filled with locally sourced rock, gravel and earth that have been compacted.

Nine hydro-electric turbines are installed in the dam, several of which were in use long before the dam's completion. The turbines originally each had a capacity of 300MW, but they have subsequently been retrofitted, increasing their joint capacity to 3GW, three-quarters of the country's total hydro-electric output.

It is possible to visit the Nurek power plant providing you get prior approval from the Ministry of Internal Affairs in Dushanbe (*29 Jalol Ikromi;* \ *(037) 221 2121;* e *info@vkd.tj*).

Though not quite spoilt for choice, you have two accommodation choices in the valley. The friendly **Islom Guesthouse** (m *(0992) 905 003 030;* **$**) is in Yavroz village, or you can go to the **Yavroz Sanatorium** (**$**), a rather more impersonal choice where healing waters from the local spring are still used to treat diseases of the musculoskeletal and nervous systems, as well as skin complaints. It is advisable to make transport and lodging arrangements prior to going via a local tour operator in Dushanbe.

NUREK An hour's drive southeast of Dushanbe, on the banks of the River Vakhsh, is the **Nurek Dam**, a surprisingly popular holiday destination with Tajiks. The dam supports the **Nurek Hydro-electric Plant**, and has created the 70km-long **Nurek Reservoir**. Construction of this epic building scheme took 19 years, finishing only in 1980, and it was thought to be such a marvel of engineering that busloads of tourists were brought here from other parts of the Soviet Union to gaze upon it in wonder.

The reservoir's waters are an attractive shade of aquamarine, and since the water is relatively clean it is a popular place to swim or hire a boat (*TJS8–10/hr*). Among the slightly peeling sanatoriums is the very pleasant **new hotel** with bargain-priced rooms (**$**). Shared taxis and minibuses make the 80km journey from Dushanbe several times daily (*TJS30–50; 2hrs*).

FOLLOW BRADT

For the latest news, special offers and competitions, subscribe to the Bradt newsletter via the website w bradtguides.com and follow Bradt on:

- 🇫 BradtTravelGuides
- 🐦 @BradtGuides
- 📷 @bradtguides
- 𝓟 bradtguides

In **TAJIKISTAN**

at the **PAMIR, FUN MOUNTAINS**

Trekking, Hiking, Jeep Tours, Transportation

WILD NATURE, CULTURE & ADVENTURE
See it, Feel it, Enjoy it

For details please contact:

AZIANA TRAVEL LLC
23, Shamsi Str., "Saodat" Trading Center
Building, office 193

734064 - Dushanbe, Tajikistan

ph: + 992/37/237-71-35, +992/44/625-53-26

mob: +992/918/84-34/03

e-mail: dmelnichkov@hotmail.com

WEB: www.azianatravel.com

LLC **"Pamir & Mountain Travel"** Your reliable partner in Tajikistan

CONTACTS:	SERVICES:
Head office	Adventure tours: trekking, rafting, mountaineering
Rudaki str 24, Penjikent	Jeep tours
735502, Tajikistan	Historical/Cultural tours
I.Somoni str. 14-61, Tajikistan	Excursion programs,city tours
734001, Tajikistan	Conference/Visa/hotel reservation
+992928450540	Local air tickets
+992935993737	Guide's service
+992938963505	Transportation service, transfers

www.pamir-travel.com   sadoullo@mail.ru
www.pamirtourservice.com   pamir-travel@list.ru

4

Fann and Zarafshan Mountains

Steeped in a cultural history as profound and rich as its geological history, few parts of Tajikistan are more beautiful than this northwest corner of the country. Snow-melt from the region's frozen peaks runs icy blue through verdant valleys and canyons, pooling in sparkling lakes and irrigating idyllic smallholdings and tiny, rustic mountain villages. If the Pamirs narrowly steal the award for most impressive mountainscapes, they lose out on accessibility. The Fann and Zarafshan mountains have it all: culture vultures can tromp to their heart's content among the ruins of Sarazm and Panjakent, or try out their ancient Sogdian with villagers in the Yagnob Valley; and trekkers, climbers and mountaineers have a seemingly infinite number of routes at their disposal, from the turquoise lakes of Iskanderkul and Haftkul to the strenuous passes of the Chimtarga Loop.

The Fann and Zarafshan mountains also score high for sustainable tourism. The Zarafshan Tourism Development Association co-ordinates information and services in the region, ensuring that your money goes straight into the communities who provide the services and rely on this income to survive.

YAGNOB VALLEY

Until the Russians blasted the road through the mountains, the Yagnob Valley was almost entirely cut off from the outside world, accessible only on foot when the weather would allow. It remains one of Tajikistan's most wild, unspoilt spots and a fascinating anthropological microcosm. The valley's singularity of language, traditions and landscape was first noticed by Europeans in the late 19th century, but the inhabitants of the region themselves consider their ancestral line to go back some 2,500 years into the past, to the era of the ancient Sogdiana civilisation. At almost 3,000m above sea level, the valley houses a mere 500 people year-round spread among some ten small settlements. The low population is due mostly to forced resettlement of the villagers to cotton-growing regions by the Soviets in the mid 20th century. The Yagnobis' stone houses are typically clustered in the relatively wide areas along the Yagnob River, surrounded by spectacular mountain peaks and incredible trekking trails. The valley is also home to striking petrified forests dating back to the Jurassic period, when the region was much more humid and fertile. The ferrous vines and hardened tree trunks stand up to 5m high, a reminder of the valley's timelessness and the resilience of nature.

GETTING THERE AND AWAY Access to the Yagnob Valley is 4km south of the village of Anzob, which necessitates leaving the main road at Takfon, a village 2 hours north of Dushanbe and 3½ hours south of Khujand, and driving east for around 20km. Shared taxis from Dushanbe stop at the turn-off to the valley, which is at the foot of

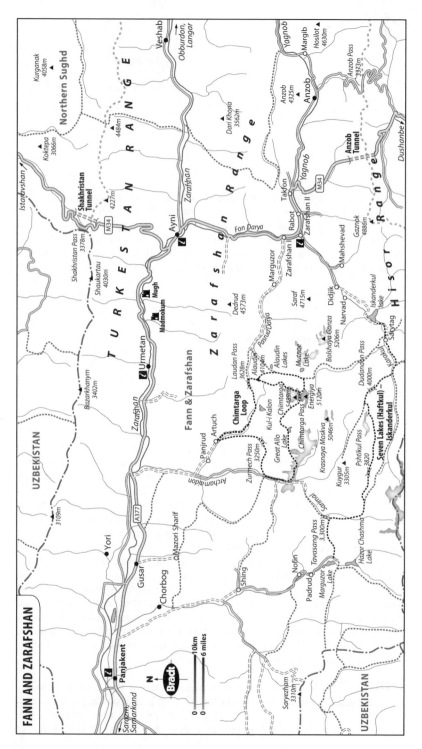

the descent from the Anzob Pass. From there, it may be possible to hire a taxi from Takfon east to Anzob and into the valley, including to the village of Margib. One or two shared taxis also run directly from Dushanbe to Margib, daily (*TJS50*). There is a road (of sorts) between Anzob and Margib, but it then peters out before you get to the village of Bedev, about 20km further to the east. If you plan to travel further into the valley, such as to the easternmost settlement of Kirionte, it has to be done on foot.

The upper parts of the valley are inaccessible for six months a year due to snow and rockfalls. It is best to visit between June and September.

WHERE TO STAY AND EAT ZTDA (page 111) has three homestays in Margib, all of which cost US$10, with an additional US$5 for meals. There is also a modest guesthouse in Margib called Malikov (⟍ *550 577*; **$**). Between Margib and Kirionte, trekking guides can usually arrange an informal homestay with families (for which you should offer a similar amount of remuneration, plus basic food supplies if you have them), but should you continue east of Kirionte you will need to camp and carry everything with you.

OTHER PRACTICALITIES ZTDA (page 111) can arrange trekking guides, pack animals and handlers. It also hires out camping equipment, including lightweight sleeping bags. These are best secured before setting off for the Yagnob Valley.

WHAT TO SEE AND DO Go to the Yagnob Valley to trek. The valley paths can be vigorous, sometimes requiring a wade across multiple river crossings, but travellers of a reasonable level of fitness and a willingness to sweat a bit can enjoy some of

THE YAGNOBIS

The Yagnobi people of the Yagnob, Kul and Varzob river valleys are thought to be the last remaining speakers of the ancient Sogdian language, and the Sogdians' genetic descendants. They fled to the mountains following the Arab invasion in 772, continuing to practise aspects of their Zoroastrian religion in addition to Islam. It is thought that as many as 25,000 Yagnobis may still survive in Tajikistan, though many of them have now abandoned their traditional way of life or intermarried with other groups.

Until the 1930s the Yagnobi lived untouched by the modern world, continuing their traditional agriculture as they had done for millennia. Their first interaction with the Soviets was the Stalinist purges, then forced resettlement in Tajikistan's lowlands in the 1950s and 1970s. Red Army helicopters evacuated entire villages, ostensibly to protect them from avalanches, but then forced the Yagnobi to work in searing heat on the collective cotton plantations. Villages were razed to prevent their inhabitants from returning, religious books were destroyed and, as a final ignominious act, Yagnobian ethnicity was officially abolished. Hundreds of Yagnobi families died in exile.

Since 1983 a small number of Yagnobis have returned to the Yagnob Valley, though many of their villages are still home to only a handful of families. The total permanent Yagnobi population in the valley is about 300 people, rising to 1,000 in the summer months. They live in basic mud-brick dwellings, without electricity, scrape a living from subsistence farming and, to the delight of linguists and historians, still speak in the Sogdian tongue.

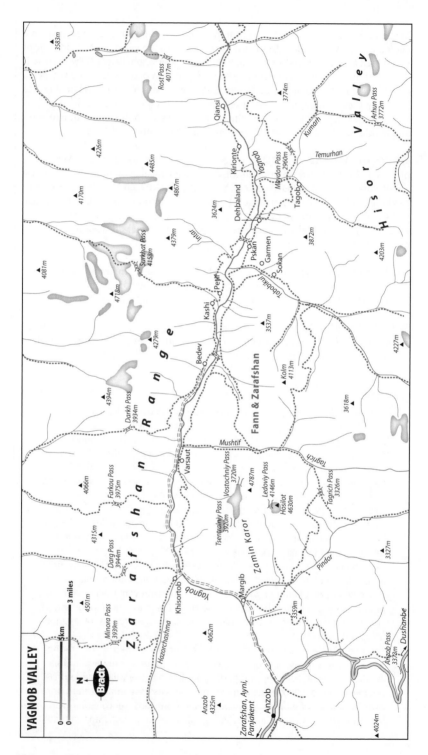

YAGNOB VALLEY

Bradt

0 5km
0 3 miles

YAGNOB VALLEY – EASY TREK

With thanks to Paramount Journey (w paramountjourney.com)

If you are relatively new to trekking and want to experience the pleasures of Tajikistan's mountains without excessive physical exertion, this easy-going multi-day trek is the route for you.

DAY 1 The starting point for this trek is Margib, a village pinned against the rock wall of Zamin Karor, and with jagged peaks looming all around. You'll hike east along the bottom of the river valley to Bedev – the first Yagnobi village – which typically takes around 4 hours (*18km*). Even this close to 'civilisation', the people are cut off by ice and snowfall for six months of the year, and the road along the valley floor is little more than a track. You will camp for the night in a meadow bordering the village's fruit orchards; a pleasant, shady spot.

DAY 2 The first part of the second day is an easy stroll along the Yagnob River. The path winds its way through three villages and over a couple of small bridges, and by early afternoon you will reach Pskan (about 10km from Bedev), where you can stay in the local guesthouse. The villagers here are friendly, keen to talk and introduce you to their traditions, even if you only share a handful of words in common.

DAY 3 The next day begins by continuing along the valley to Qiansi (12km), before leaving the human settlements behind and ascending the side of the valley into the wilderness. You'll climb to Langar (not to be confused with the village of the same name in the Wakhan Corridor), a summer pasture where Yagnobi shepherds graze their flocks. Marmot, popping up from their burrows to sun themselves, will be your most frequent companions, though you might also spot deer and birds.

DAY 4 It's a long but leisurely descent of 18km down to Langar on the final day of trekking. Look around to appreciate the beauty of the mountains and the meadows, but also to note the retreat of the glaciers. Reduced meltwater will undoubtedly be a problem here in future years. The way is lined with juniper bushes and then, as you approach the village, dozens of fruit trees. The villagers grow apples, mulberries, apricots and nuts in their orchards, and so at harvest time you can be guaranteed an organic fruit feast to celebrate your arrival.

In Langar you can stay at charming Kholov's Guesthouse (**$**) and also get a meal. There is no public transport link to or from Langar, so you will need to arrange a car, either with a company in Dushanbe or through Kholov himself.

As with all treks in Tajikistan, the path for this trek is unmarked and not always easy to follow. It is highly recommended that you engage a local guide who knows the area. Ask Paramount Journey (page 120) for a name and contact details.

central Asia's most beautiful landscapes. It takes four days each way to trek the full length of the valley, but just two if you stop at Kirionte, the last settlement. Most treks start from Margib, the largest of the valley's villages, which is overshadowed by dramatic rock formations. You can collect your guide and pack animals here, and be seen off with a cup of tea and a handful of *naan* or fruit.

YAGNOB VALLEY – AN ADVANCED TREK

With thanks to Paramount Journey (w paramountjourney.com)

This extensive trek showcases northwestern Tajikistan at its best, taking you well beyond the Yagnob Valley and into the remotest reaches of the Zarafshan Mountains. Follow the trek in the box on page 101 as far as Qiansi (3 days' trekking), then divert on to this longer route.

DAY 4 Settlements in this region are now fewer and further between, and as you climb the valley side from Pskan through Qiansi you enter into a rugged and little-explored wilderness. There are few signs of human habitation here; you'll see only occasional Yagnobi men shepherding their flocks to fresh pasture. Spend the night in one of their summer camps, at the foot of the Rost Pass (4,020m). It should take you around 5 hours of trekking to reach this point.

DAY 5 The way to the top of the Rost Pass is through small glaciers, though no technical climbing skills are required. The magnificent panorama of the Zarafshan range is spread out about you, and remains visible even as you descend through the foothills into the river valley. Your campsite for the night is at Sari Pul (2,350m), some 12km (*5hrs*) on from your previous night's stop.

DAY 6 On the final day, descend along the Ghuzn River to the village of the same name. Here, you'll see the interplay between the natural world and man's impact, as it is an area for small-scale manual coal mines, an industry that employs many local people. A 4x4 will be able to cover some, if not all, of the way to Ghuzn, depending on the current state of the road, so it's a good place to arrange a pick-up for your onward journey.

As with other treks in Tajikistan, it is recommended that you trek with a local guide. Ask Paramount Journey (page 120) for a name and contact details.

At Khisortob, 4km north of Margib and a short detour off the main track, is the **shrine of Khoja Guliston**, a local woman who turned herself to stone to escape inevitable rape at the hands of an advancing army. The Guliston rock is inside a simple stone hut, and only women may enter. You are expected to make a small donation towards the shrine's upkeep.

Continuing east, the path sticks to the northern bank of the river. Your guide will be able to point out the former **Basmachi den**, several more **shrines** and a village razed by the Soviets that is still unoccupied. As you pass by people's homes you are likely to be invited in for tea, and this will be one of the highlights of your trek. Despite being Muslim, Yagnobi women go uncovered, even in the presence of strangers, so you'll likely meet the whole family. During the spring and summer, villagers herd yak, harvest tobacco and make butter in accordance with age-old traditions, so visitors to the valley are afforded a glimpse of pre-Soviet life in the region.

The largest Sogdian-speaking village is **Pskan** on the south side of the river by the bridge. It is home to several Sogdian scholars, though they will also be able to converse with you in either Tajik or Russian. The road divides at Pskan: you can either take the left fork straight to Kirionte or turn right towards Tagob where there are more **Sogdian villages** and the 2,960m (4,735ft) **Maydon Pass**.

From the end of the valley determined trekkers continue on to **Romit** (pages 94–5) or head north via **Lake Sari Pul** to the Zarafshan Valley. Lake Sari Pul (not to be confused with the more famous lake of the same name in Afghanistan) is a haven for birdlife, in particular lammergeier and eagle. There is a village of the same name (though often written Saripool) nearby.

ISKANDERKUL   *Telephone code: 03479*

If you stare into the waters of the lake here at midnight, you'll see Alexander the Great, resplendent in golden armour, ride forth on the back of his horse, Bucephalus. Or so the locals say. We may have been a little sceptical, but it's never stopped us looking out into the inky blackness just in case. Conversely, during the new moon if the sky is cloudless, it shimmers with flickering stars. Just another reason to stay up past bedtime.

GETTING THERE AND AWAY Iskanderkul is accessed by following the largely unmade road (which, unusually for Tajikistan, is actually signposted) just north of Zarafshan village. The large Soviet-era mural on the end of a now virtually derelict mining complex is another useful landmark for the turning. Take the rusted suspension bridge across the river, then go straight.

The road winds its way for 25km, first through villages and then along increasingly steep tracks with some rather tight hairpin bends. A 4x4 is advisable here, particularly given that some stretches are littered with avalanche rubble, though you do see the occasional Lada bravely making the trip. Occasionally, winter snow and unexpected avalanches can make roads impassable, so check with filling station attendants and other drivers for conditions on the road ahead.

There is no public transport between the main road and the lake, so if you are travelling by minibus or shared taxi you will need to get off at the junction and hitch the rest of the way (see box, page 49). Iskanderkul is situated 134km from Dushanbe, a journey of less than 3 hours now that the Anzob Tunnel has been cleaned up, while Khujand is 221km to the northeast along the M34 motorway (*4hrs*), and Panjakent lies 152km to the northwest (*2hrs*).

WHERE TO STAY A row of newish 'luxury' **cabins** has been built along the lake, featuring en-suite bathrooms and hot water. You can enquire about the cabins at the fairly grim and run-down **holiday camp** on the edge of the lake with 30 'chalets' that have rather more in common with garden sheds than anything alpine. Both options are, however, cheap (**$–$$**). There is also a tiny three-room **lodge** just before the bridge to the camp (Sherzod; **$**), though the outdoor privy leaves much to be desired.

If you have a tent and warm clothing, there is also space for **camping**. The lake's warden will sometimes allow you to pitch your tent on his garden (immediately behind the office as you reach the lake); or, for greater privacy, continue along the road, past the president's *dacha* (summer house), and into the groves of trees. You can then camp right on the lakeshore, and there's even a sort of beach. Expect to pay TJS10 per person for camping.

Some 5km above the lake is the settlement of Narvad, followed by the village of Sarytag, another 4km beyond, where ZTDA or Pamir Travel (page 111) can arrange **homestays**. Among the two villages, four families currently host guests, all charging US$10 per person.

WHERE TO EAT AND DRINK There is a small **restaurant** at the holiday camp that is open to non-residents, replete with Russian soap operas and reality programmes blaring from the flat-screen TV in the corner. However, it is nothing to write home about, so you are better off bringing what you need for a barbecue or a picnic. You should also bring enough bottled water for the duration of your stay, as although the lake is clean enough for swimming, it's not safe enough to drink.

OTHER PRACTICALITIES It is possible to hire **canoes** and **mountain bikes** from the holiday camp. They cost US$2 per hour or US$10 for the day.

WHAT TO SEE AND DO The **lake** itself is Iskanderkul's main attraction. The water is an amazingly bright shade of turquoise, and with the snow-capped mountains in the background it looks picturesque from any angle. For those whose Persian is a little rusty, Iskanderkul means 'Alexander's Lake'.

With a surface area of 3.40km² and situated some 2,190m above sea level, Iskanderkul was formed by a rockfall, and if you head downstream (east of the lake) you'll see the impressive **waterfall** where the water finally overflows the rocks and cascades into the river. The falls are 40m high and there is a small (if somewhat precarious) viewing platform. The falls are also a local place of pilgrimage: look out for the coloured ribbons tied on to the bushes. Each one denotes a prayer or request.

A steep climb up the slope to the north of the lake gives you views down on to the **presidential** *dacha* and also brings you to **Snakes' Lake**. Its comparatively dark waters and marshes provide a haven for fish and birds, including the mountain geese and partridges ubiquitous in the area. Snakes' Lake is far quieter than Iskanderkul, as few locals bother to make the climb. A modest Soviet-era cemetery at the top of the slope, guarded by the surrounding mountain peaks and overlooking both lakes, can't help but inspire reflection in even the most hard-hearted of visitors.

AROUND ISKANDERKUL Well hidden in a cave above the village of Mahshevad is a **holy shrine** containing an ancient mummy, possibly the preserved remains of the Sogdian general Spitamenes. As this is a holy site, visitors are expected to wash themselves before going inside, and must be dressed respectfully. Women should ask before entering, and photography is forbidden.

While the mummy itself might be less than spectacular, the trek to the cave is one of the most beautiful in the region, with impressive vistas of mountain peaks and overhanging glaciers to inspire you. To reach the cave, cross the river at Khayronbed village 15km northeast of Iskanderkul, and then follow the track south to Mahshevad. You will need to ask in the village for the mullah, and he will guide you onwards to the cave. The walk takes around 3 hours and requires a reasonable level of fitness and a certain amount of scrambling. You should make a donation to the shrine to thank the mullah for his assistance.

Driving along the main road south of Iskanderkul, shortly before Zarafshan, you pass through the small village of **Rabat**. If you look closely up at the steep cliffs you will see that they are smoking, and at night you may even see the flames. These naturally occurring underground coal fires have been burning for so long that they were even mentioned by Pliny the Elder in the 1st century AD.

AYNI *Telephone code: 03479*

Ayni sits at the crossroads between Dushanbe, Panjakent and Khujand, and so almost all journeys in the north of Tajikistan pass through. It's an underwhelming town (albeit with some attractive views along the Zarafshan River), but it's a convenient spot if you need to break your journey.

GETTING THERE AND AWAY The road from Dushanbe, including the recently tidied-up Anzob Tunnel, is well surfaced and winds an attractive route through the Varzob Valley before climbing into the mountains. There are three toll booths (*TJS3/6.30/14.20*), so make sure you have sufficient small change. The drive takes a little under 3 hours. If you are travelling by public transport, the minibus departs from Dushanbe's Cement Factory stand several times daily and costs TJS60.

The road west from Ayni takes you to Panjakent. Until 2010 this was also the best route to Uzbekistan, entering not far from Samarkand, but the border is currently closed and the road sees little traffic. Its repair, therefore, is not a priority and the 5-hour drive is fairly rough, often on unmade road. The minibus to Panjakent, which departs several times daily, costs TJS60 and takes the same amount of time as travelling by car.

The opening of the new Shakhristan Tunnel in the autumn of 2012 has revolutionised the drive from Ayni to Khujand, cutting the 167km trip to about 3 hours. Jackknifed lorries on unmade mountain roads are (hopefully) now a thing of the past, and the handful of road tolls (*TJS23/6/2/4*) are a small price to pay for the dramatically improved conditions. Be sure to fill up with fuel before entering the mountains. The steeper hairpin bends are a little nerve-wracking, particularly given the speed at which the drivers take them, and the warnings proffered by the carcasses of less fortunate vehicles that have gone before seem to fall on deaf ears. A minibus ride, with several daily departures, costs TJS90.

WHERE TO STAY AND EAT Ayni has a small, clean self-catering hotel on Rudaki called **Varz** (m *092 852 8686;* **$**). There are a handful of cafés, an internet café, and several small shops and food stalls, all of which are along Rudaki.

WHAT TO SEE AND DO Ayni is a linear settlement stretched along the M34 motorway. Predictably there is a **monument to Ayni** (page 23) and a memorial to those who died in World War II. Rather more interesting, however, is the **Jamaladin Mosque**, a modern structure in the town centre that incorporates some architectural salvage from the 10th century. Alongside the mosque is a 13th-century **mud-brick minaret**, the protective casing of which has the unfortunate side effect of making it resemble an elongated Dalek. Called Varz-i-Minor, the minaret is representative of the region's conversion from the Zoroastrianism of the ancient Sogdians to Islam after the Arab conquests of the 7th century, and testament to the town's historical influence as a religious centre.

ZARAFSHAN VALLEY (EAST)

Rising to nearly 5,500m, the Zarafshan Mountains are an extension of the Pamirs that cut east to west across Tajikistan and into Uzbekistan. Coursed by glacier-fed rivers, the many verdant valleys of the range have, throughout the centuries, provided shelter for nomadic tribes and avenues of conquest for warring nations. The Zarafshan River at the bottom of the valley that bears its name irrigates an emerald-green strip of land, the vibrant colour of which stands in stark contrast to the crumbling, brownish-grey scree of the steep mountain slopes either side. Along with the parallel Yagnob Valley, the 200km Zarafshan Valley is a popular area for trekking, and within easy reach of Dushanbe, Khujand and Panjakent.

GETTING THERE AND AROUND The entrance to the eastern part of the valley is a mere 2km to the south of Ayni, itself just under 3 hours from Dushanbe and

4 hours from Khujand. From Dushanbe, shared taxis to the north of the country depart from the Stoyanka Khujanda at the north end of Rudaki, near Vodonasos, and taxis to the town of Sarvoda (also called Zaravshan-II), 30km south of Ayni – from which transport can be arranged to various points in the valley – cost TJS60, about half of the fare to Khujand. Be aware, however, that drivers are not usually keen on dropping passengers *en route* to the car's final destination, as those seats will often remain unoccupied (and unpaid-for) for the rest of their journey. Shared taxis from Khujand cost TJS60–80, with the same reluctance on the part of drivers to drop passengers midway.

From Ayni, there are shared taxis to Veshab, about a quarter of the way along the valley's length. The journey takes an hour and costs TJS30.

There is a rough road past Veshab to the head of the valley and, though it is passable in most vehicles, it is infinitely more comfortable in a 4x4. There are no minibuses in this end of the valley but most motorists are happy to pick up additional passengers providing they have room. Allow two full days to drive the full 200km length of the valley.

WHERE TO STAY AND EAT The ZTDA (page 111) has **homestays** in the villages of Veshab and Langar (**$**). In Obburdon, the very basic **Gozari Mir guesthouse** is near the mosque, which is free but gratefully receives donations. The last **homestay** in the valley is just past Dehisar, not long before the glacier. All homestays can arrange meals, and the trekking guides know exactly where to find them.

OTHER PRACTICALITIES The ZTDA produces an excellent 1:400,000 scale topographic map of the valley called *Zarafshan Valley*, which is available from its office in Panjakent (page 111), and we were also able to pick up a copy from the Bactria Cultural Centre in Dushanbe (page 81).

WHAT TO SEE AND DO The major appeal of the Zarafshan Valley is its magnificent landscape: deep gorges and cliffs, the Zarafshan River itself, groves of fruit and nut trees, and ribbons of irrigated land.

The valley has a number of **fortifications**; its inhabitants have constantly warred with one another or needed to see off invaders. The ruined **tower of Hazrati Burq** in Rarz, a town about 24km east of Ayni, dates from the 10th century and was once part of a far larger military complex. In Obburdon, immediately before the turn-off to the Obburdon Pass, is another **fortress**, built by the local bek in the 18th century. This site has been partially restored and is surrounded by pleasant orchards.

To the south side of the valley are several impressive peaks including **Samarkand Peak** (5,086m) and **Sery Utes** (4,434m), and potential routes for mountaineers are numerous. It is also possible to continue east to the surprisingly narrow and rapidly receding **Zarafshan Glacier**, though you require permission from the military commander in Dehisar to do so. Currently, the glacier extends over an area of about 133km^2, with an ice volume of some 15km^3, but surveys by the national hydrographical service indicate that it has receded up to 100m a year in recent times.

The villages along the valley, the largest of which are **Veshab** and **Langar**, are certainly picturesque. There are no tourist sights, per se, as they are simple rural communities, but you can enjoy wandering through the orchards, meeting local children, watching the shepherds herd their flocks and the labourers tend their fields. The scenes correspond with the rural idyll of the past, though the reality is that life is hard for those living here.

Travelling west from Ayni to Panjakent and, formerly, to Samarkand, you are retracing a leg of the Silk Road. Forts, mausoleums and mosques confirm this was a route much travelled as far back as 200BC and in which significant sums of money were invested. Historically, this was also a major route to and from Uzbekistan – a country with nearly 1.5 million ethnic Tajiks, according to the last official census, taken in 1996 – but since the border crossing was closed in 2010, the economy of the area has been in serious decline.

GETTING THERE AND AROUND Minibuses between Ayni and Panjakent drive the length of the valley in 4–5 hours and cost TJS70, and connect with buses travelling onward to Khujand or Dushanbe (a further TJS50). The road quality has improved in recent years, though not infrequently you will, as in much of the country, be sharing the road with herds of cattle.

Travelling off the main road generally requires you to have your own 4x4 transport or to hitch a ride with a passing vehicle. The notable exception is Panjrud, the location of Rudaki's mausoleum, which can reached by minibus from Panjakent (*TJS5*), and *en route* to Panjrud and Shing. The roads are unmade and consequently exceptionally bumpy. Remember that the border with Uzbekistan is currently closed; there is very little for visitors west of Sarazm.

WHERE TO STAY AND EAT Both ZTDA (page 111) and Pamir Travel (page 111) can arrange **homestays** in the remote and very scenic villages of Zimtud, Marguzor, Padrud, Nofin and Shing. There is also a **guesthouse** at Panjrud. All of these properties charge US$10 per person and will arrange meals on request.

Trekkers and climbers frequently use the **Artuch mountaineering base** (\ 56 661; e *artuch@bk.ru;* **$$**). Originally built for a trade union, this is a fairly grim option that must be pre-booked. Rather better is the Artuch homestay, which can be booked through Pamir Travel and is a rather more affordable US$10 per person.

OTHER PRACTICALITIES The Tajik government has begun to charge climbers who wish to ascend peaks over 4,000m. Permits cost US$50 for peaks of 4,000–7,000m, and US$100 for those over 7,000m. These can be arranged through Pamir Travel in Panjakent (page 111).

WHAT TO SEE AND DO The Zarafshan Valley was the site of the Sogdians' final retreat from Panjakent, and there are remains of their **fortresses** at Kum, Mount Mugh and Madm. Though the fortresses are in ruins, with often little more to see than the remains of mud-brick walls, locals can regale you with tales of battles against the Arabs, and will happily do so over tea. You will need a basic understanding of Tajik, or a guide who can translate.

Leaving the main road at Gusar and driving 10km south brings you to the **mausoleum of Khoja Muhammad Majorah** in the village of Mazori Sharif. Majorah was an Iraq-born missionary who came to Tajikistan in the 8th century, and pilgrims still come to pray at his shrine. The structure itself is contemporary with his death (8th–9th century), features incredibly fine wood carving including an elaborate *mihrab*, and is topped with an attractive tiled dome.

Rudaki, the so-called father of Tajik literature (see box, page 23) is purportedly buried in Panjrud, some 45km east of Panjakent. His **mausoleum**, a lovely and intricately designed brick structure topped by a turquoise dome and with ornate

Fann and Zarafshan Mountains   ZARAFSHAN VALLEY (WEST)

4

TREKKING IN THE FANN MOUNTAINS

More easily accessible than the Pamirs, the Fann Mountains (Fansky Gory) offer trekkers, climbers, mountaineers and even the occasional day tripper a bewildering array of routes and the opportunity to quickly escape all signs of habitation, getting in the midst of some awe-inspiring scenery. They can be accessed either via Iskanderkul (also part of the Fann; see pages 103–5), or travelling south from the valley road between Panjakent and Ayni, and the best time to visit is between June and September.

The majority of routes centre on Seven Lakes or Artuch. The **Seven Lakes**, or 'Haftkul' in Tajik, are a necklace-like string of turquoise lakes stretched out through the mountains to the south of Panjakent. There are numerous photogenic picnic spots and short walks along the various lakeshores, the best of which is at the seventh and final lake, Hazor Chashma.

Trekking from Seven Lakes to Iskanderkul takes five days. Starting at Marguzor you cross the Tavasang Pass (3,300m) into the Archa Maidan Valley, from where the trail splits to either the northern Zurmech Pass (3,250m) and Artuch (page 107), or to the Sarimal Valley and the Pshtikul Pass (3,820m) into the Archamaidon Valley. The best camping spot in the valley is at Duobai Sarimat, the confluence of the Archa Maidan and Duoba rivers, where you are likely to meet local shepherds.

Keeping to the left side of the Archamaidon River, cross the bridge and climb the Dukdon Pass (3,810m), which has impressive views of Mount Pushnovat (4,637m) to the northwest and Mount Dudandon (4,300m) to the east. You descend to the junction with the Karakul River, and follow the north bank along to Sarytag, from where it is just 5km to the western end of Iskanderkul.

For a more demanding six-day route, try the Chimtarga Loop starting from **Artuch**, where there is both a campsite and a camping hut with bunks (**$**). Trek southeast to Kul-i Kalon Lake, then climb either the Laudan Pass (3,628m) or the steeper Alaudin Pass (4,104m) to the Alaudin Lakes and thence south to Mutnoe Lake. There are homestays and places to camp (**$**) at both lakes. Climb the icy moraine of the Chimtarga Pass (4,740m) between Mount Chimtarga and Mount Energiya, both of which are considerably over 5,000m. The path descends to Great Allo Lake. Continue northwest into the Archamaidon Valley, following the river as far as Gaza before taking on the Zurmech Pass (3,250m), which neatly leads you back to Artuch.

There are a number of well-run homestays in villages in this part of the Fann. There are formal homestays (**$**) at Shing, Nofin and Padrud, and informal ones in the villages along the shore of Marguzor and also in Guytan. Trekking guides know which families are happy to host trekkers in their homes, and you can also stop in any of the villages and ask for a recommendation.

If you plan to trek in the Fann Mountains, we recommend *Fann Mountains Map and Guide* (ISBN 0 906227 56 0, available from w maps.ewpnet.com/fannmap.asp). Although it was first published in 1994, it is still an accurate and very useful map at a scale of 1:100,000.

Tajik woodwork on the inside, dates from 1956. It is situated within a peaceful, well-maintained garden, with a **small museum** adjacent displaying artefacts related to his life. The museum has no formal opening hours, but if you turn up and ask politely, someone with a key will likely be found to open it up for you.

There are some excellent hikes and climbing routes in the western part of the Zarafshan Valley. The two best routes here are the **Seven Lakes** and **Chimtarga Loop** routes through the Fann Mountains (see box, opposite).

PANJAKENT *Telephone code: 03475*

A bustling, prosperous city until recently, Panjakent was the gateway between Tajikistan and Uzbekistan, and indeed it should probably be part of Uzbekistan given that 70% of the population is ethnically Uzbek. The superb archaeological sites of ancient Panjakent and Sarazm have earned it the moniker 'the Pompeii of central Asia' and are potent reminders of its historical importance and erstwhile wealth.

For the time being, however, modern Panjakent is a virtual ghost town, its lifeblood choked off by the closure of the border in 2010. The flow of tourists has slowed to a trickle, and businesses are only just clinging on. Only if this vital communication route reopens will Panjakent stand a chance of recovery.

HISTORY The banks of the Zarafshan River, at a significant Silk Road crossroad, were the ideal location for an ancient city to grow and flourish. The Sogdians constructed an impregnable-looking fortress with walls 12m thick on a hill 4km east of the modern town, and it supported a thriving population of 5,000 people during the height of the silk trade. It was a melting pot of Silk Road cultures, with Zoroastrians, Buddhists, Manicheans and Nestorian Christians all making their unique contributions.

Arab invaders sacked the city in 772 and burned many of the buildings to the ground. Rather than attempt to rebuild their magnificent palaces and temples, Panjakent's inhabitants abandoned their city, inadvertently preserving it in time for archaeologists to uncover more than a millennium later. The last Sogdian ruler, Dewashtich, retreated into the mountains but was captured and, by one account, crucified. His followers, including women and children, were massacred as they fled Panjakent for Khujand. The few survivors of this bloodshed are the ancestors of the modern Yagnobis (see box, page 99).

GETTING THERE AND AROUND

By road At the time of going to print, the border crossing to Uzbekistan to the west of Panjakent was closed and showed no sign of reopening in the immediate future. If it does reopen during the lifespan of this edition, it will once again be possible to drive to or from Samarkand in under 2 hours, and border formalities here were always somewhat faster than at other crossing points.

The 97km of road between Panjakent and Ayni have been improved and the drive takes around 2 hours. If you are coming from the direction of Dushanbe, the turning to Panjakent is not signposted. Come through Ayni, out the other side, then turn left at the crossroads-cum-roundabout. If you overshoot you will end up heading through the mountains to Khujand. The minibus takes around 3 hours (more if it is wet) and costs TJS70. Shared taxis to Panjakent depart from the Stoyanka Khujanda at the north end of Rudaki, near Vodonasos, and cost TJS80–120, though a cheaper fare can possibly be negotiated with a driver willing to leave you somewhere along the 97km stretch from Ayni to Panjakent. From Khujand, shared taxis cost TJS80–100 and take 5 hours to make the trip.

There are two bus stands in Panjakent. The eastbound intercity buses leave from the **East Gate bus stand**, and local buses also use the **Bazaar bus stand**. Minibus #1 goes from the bazaar to the airport, and #4 travels most of the length of Rudaki. Both cost TJS1.

4

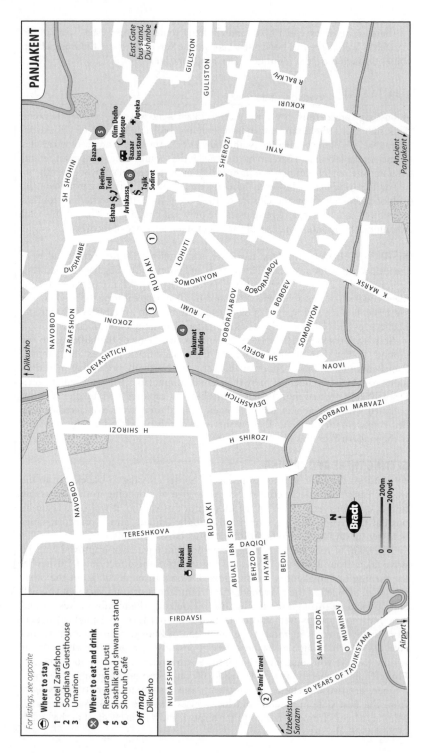

PANJAKENT

For listings, see opposite

Where to stay

1 Hotel Zarafshon
2 Sogdiana Guesthouse
3 Umarion

Where to eat and drink

4 Restaurant Dusti
5 Shashlik and shwarma stand
6 Shohruh Café

Off map
Dilkusho

By air Panjakent does have its own **airport** on Let Nezavisimosti in the south of the town, but flights take place in winter only and do not conform to a regular itinerary. Departure details and tickets are all available from the airport's information office.

TOURIST INFORMATION AND TOUR OPERATORS Panjakent unexpectedly has the best tourist information provision of any city in Tajikistan, including Dushanbe. This is thanks to the German Welthungerhilfe- and EU-backed **Zarafshan Tourism Board** (*125 Rudaki;* 53 680; e *info@zerafshan.info*) and its larger sister organisation, the **Zarafshan Tourism Development Association** (m *092 770 3995;* e *ztda_zarafshon@ yahoo.com;* w *ztda-tourism.tj*), in Khujand. The ZTB was established in 2009 to develop and support sustainable tourism in the Zarafshan region. It provides information (including maps), equipment and vehicle hire, trekking guides and pack animals, and can also arrange homestays in the Zarafshan and Yagnob valleys, Iskanderkul and the Seven Lakes, and near to the Marguzor and Alaudin lakes. All the homestays have a set price of US$10 per person, with an additional US$5 if you want meals.

Pamir Travel (*Geolog village;* 55 088; e *pamir-travel@list.ru;* w *pamir-travel.com*) was founded in Panjakent in 1992 and has since opened branches across Tajikistan. From this original office director Sadoullo Khasanov arranges historical tours to ancient Panjakent and Sarazm, treks in the Seven Lakes and Fann Mountains and, intriguingly, ethnographic tours as well.

WHERE TO STAY Our favourite place to stay in Panjakent is the **Sogdiana Guesthouse** (*24 Rudaki;* 53 134; e *sadoullo@mail.ru;* **$$**), formerly the Elina Guesthouse, which is down the last road on the left before you reach the roundabout at the western end of Rudaki. Comfortable rooms are arranged around a simple courtyard, and the bathrooms are immaculate. The staff frequently appear from nowhere with pots of tea and plates of fruit, showing off the finest Tajik hospitality.

Unfortunately, the guesthouse is closed from the end of October until late April due to lack of heating, during which time **Pamir Travel** (see above) will happily arrange you a homestay in the city instead.

The **Hotel Zarafshon** (*24 Loiq Sherali;* m *092 902 5999;* e *hotelzarafshon@mail.ru;* **$$**) is a clean, welcoming alternative with an English-speaking proprietor and free Wi-Fi. The **Umarion** (*157 Rudaki;* **$$**), right on the city's main commercial strip, also has 14 air-conditioned rooms with Wi-Fi.

WHERE TO EAT AND DRINK There are numerous small cafés around Panjakent's bazaar, the pick of which are **Shohruh Café** (*150 Rudaki*) and the *shashlik* and *shwarma* stand just along the road at 197 Rudaki. Somewhat larger is **Restaurant Dusti** (also on Rudaki), next to the Hukumat building. Down by the river, don't miss the quaint **Chaykhona Dilkusho** (*$$*), which has delicious Tajik favourites (ask if the *osh* (hearty rice and beef dish) is on offer) and, conveniently, menus in English.

OTHER PRACTICALITIES Almost all of Panjakent's facilities are on Rudaki in the blocks either side of the bazaar. **Tajik Sodirot Bank** is at 146 Rudaki, and **Eskhata Bank** is almost immediately opposite, along with agents for **Beeline** and **Tcell** phone credit. Internet access is available from the **ZTDA Information Centre** (*47 Sherozi*). There are two *apteka* at 164 and 168 Rudaki.

WHAT TO SEE AND DO Ancient **Panjakent** is remarkable due to the state of its preservation. Having been abandoned suddenly and never built over, it is still possible to walk the streets laid out much the same way as they were the day the Arabs came. At its height in the 8th century, the city covered around 20ha, and about half of this area has been carefully excavated, with finds being removed to the National Museum in Dushanbe (page 89) and the local Rudaki Museum (see below). Most impressive among the buildings are the citadel on top of the hill overlooking the city, the necropolis, and the fine, once multistoried buildings where the famous frescoes were discovered. There is a small **museum** (08.00– 17.00 Mon–Fri; admission to museum & ruins TJS10) near the entrance to the ruins, featuring a handful of artefacts and detailed information about the life of Russian archaeologist Boris Marshak, who spent half a century excavating the site and lobbying for its preservation. As per his will, Marshak is buried on the grounds. Taxis can be hired to visit the ruins, which overlook the modern city a mere 2km south of Rudaki, adjacent the airport. The labyrinthine ruins are open around the clock, but it is advisable to visit only within the operating hours of the museum.

The easiest place to see Panjakent's remarkable frescoes, however, is in the much larger **Rudaki Museum** (67 Rudaki; 08.00–17.00 Mon–Sat; local/foreigner TJS2/10) in the centre of the modern town. It's an attractive, white building with well-laid-out displays, plenty of information and an enthusiastic curator. The Sogdian frescoes are undoubtedly the biggest draw, and although the best and largest examples (one of which was 15m in length) have been spirited away to Dushanbe and the Hermitage Museum in St Petersburg, you can still admire murals depicting many-headed gods, ancient heroes and the Sogdian aristocracy. Other notable artefacts include ornaments carved from wood and clay, domestic and ritual pottery, ossuaries (vessels for the bones of the dead) and altarpieces, many of which show marks of the apocalyptic fire.

Panjakent's lively **bazaar** has a substantial, decorative gateway, and immediately opposite is the **Olim Dodho Mosque**, the multi-domed roof of which is reminiscent (albeit in miniature) of the Grand Bazaar in Istanbul.

AROUND PANJAKENT Some 15km west of Panjakent, just before the closed Uzbek border, are the impressive ruins of one of Tajikistan's other great archaeological sites: **Sarazm**. Discovered in 1976 by the Soviet archaeologist Abdullojon Isakov, it is remarkable for both its size and its antiquity. Sarazm is an open-air site so there are no fixed opening times, and no entrance fee. Local people may appear to 'guide' you around the site, in which case give them a small donation for their time.

THE PRINCESS OF SARAZM

Of all the discoveries at Sarazm, the most significant is the body of a noblewoman buried in richly embroidered clothes and decorated with semi-precious stones. She is known as the Princess of Sarazm.

Archaeologists have estimated that the woman died around 3000BC; the dry, sandy ground of Sarazm has left her grave goods unusually well preserved. Her beads are made from lapis lazuli, jet and turquoise, confirming that, even 5,000 years ago, Sarazm was already trading with Afghanistan and the Indian subcontinent. The beads are on display in the National Museum in Dushanbe (page 89) along with her bronze mirror: then as now, a girl had to make sure she looked her best.

Known by archaeologists as a 'proto-urban site' because of its status as one of the world's oldest cities, the Sarazm settlement originally spread across 130ha. Carbon dating confirms it was already inhabited by 3500BC, peaking at the start of the Bronze Age when it was likely the largest metallurgical centre in central Asia. It thrived until the 3rd millennium BC and was added to UNESCO's list of World Heritage Sites in 2010 in recognition of its historical significance, the first UNESCO site in Tajikistan. The name 'Sarazm' means 'where the land begins', and for several millennia the settlement served as a great centre of trade and industry, producing handicrafts, tools and other artefacts that were sold and utilised throughout the ancient world.

The archaeological excavation at Sarazm is divided into three main areas, each covered by a corrugated roof to protect it from the elements. The walls of the different buildings are superbly preserved: you can easily still walk through their doorways and follow the grids of streets, imagining that you are bringing agricultural goods to market from your family's farm, or that you're an urbane city dweller taking to the pavements for a bit of socialising.

As with ancient Panjakent, Sarazm's most important archaeological finds have been removed to major museums in Dushanbe and abroad, but a small collection is still housed in the adjoining, almost hidden **Sarazm Museum**. The artefacts demonstrate this was a well-developed city with sophisticated agriculture, metallurgy (bronze, copper and precious metals) and craftsmanship, and that it had trading partners as far afield as Iran and India.

From Panjakent, minibus #3 can take visitors from any point along Rudaki west towards Sarazm and the now-closed border just beyond. The half-hour trip should cost no more than TJS5. You can see the protective roofs over the site to the north of the road as you approach. It is advisable to plan your trip for earlier in the day, as minibuses returning to Panjakent become scarce in the afternoon.

UPDATES WEBSITE

You can post your comments and recommendations, and read feedback and updates from other readers online at w bradtupdates.com/tajikistan.

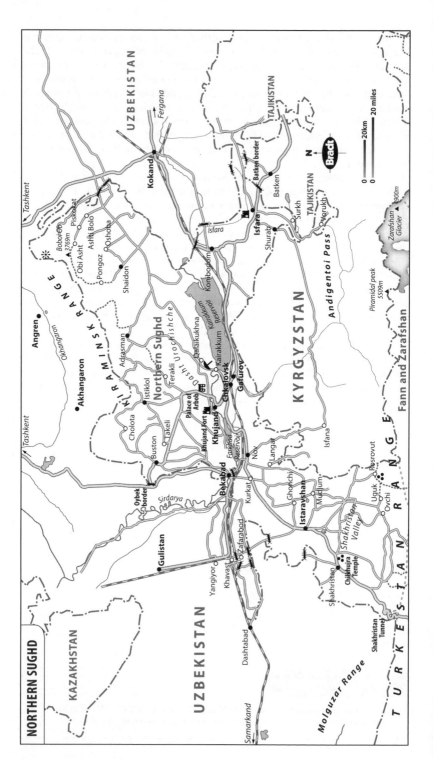

NORTHERN SUGHD

5

Khujand and Northern Sughd

The northernmost region of Tajikistan, Sughd, takes its name from the ancient Sogdians, whose empire flourished from the 2nd century BC until the late 10th century. The Sogdians' capital was Samarkand, but they retreated to the mountains in times of war, and were responsible for spreading goods and ideas in both directions along the Silk Road.

The Sughd region remains ethnically and culturally diverse and, thanks to its rich agricultural land, profitable mines and border crossings with both Kyrgyzstan and Uzbekistan, it is Tajikistan's wealthiest province. There are numerous sites of interest for tourists, from mosques and mausoleums in Istaravshan to forts and a copy of St Petersburg's Winter Palace in Khujand. The region is easily accessible both from neighbouring countries and, as road infrastructure slowly improves, also from Dushanbe. In fact, entering the region from the south is quite dramatic, requiring high-altitude drives through the Turkestan Range before descending through the Shakhristan Pass and into the broad Fergana Valley. *En route* to bustling Khujand, there are plenty of quiet country escapes, camping and trekking opportunities, and cultural sites to divert you from the main road.

ISTARAVSHAN   *Telephone code: 03454*

The general atmosphere of 'modern' Istaravshan might be grim, but the bustling bazaar and architecturally priceless old town make a day trip to the city from Khujand, or a stop *en route* from the south, worth the effort.

Istaravshan has archaeological and architectural gems to rival those anywhere in Tajikistan. The mosques and *madrasas* of the old town would not be out of place in Bukhara or Samarkand, and the imposing position of the Sogdian citadel is the perfect place from which to watch the sun go down.

HISTORY Istaravshan was founded as a Silk Road trading post sometime in the 6th century BC. It grew quickly, and merchants and travellers passed through on the east–west axis of the Silk Road and also when journeying south to Afghanistan and the Pamirs.

The city's wealth and strategic location made it an attractive target for its invaders, and three times Istaravshan was destroyed almost to the point of no return. Alexander the Great took the city by force in 329BC; he ordered every man in the city be executed, and the women and children sold as slaves. Mongol forces wreaked havoc and an equivalent level of bloodshed in the early 13th century, and tsarist artillery shelled the city into submission most recently in 1866.

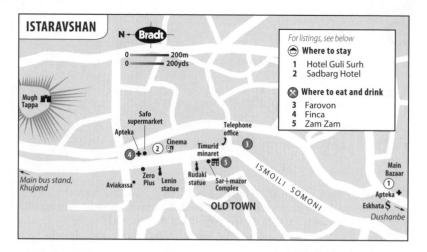

For listings, see below

Where to stay
1 Hotel Guli Surh
2 Sadbarg Hotel

Where to eat and drink
3 Farovon
4 Finca
5 Zam Zam

GETTING THERE AND AROUND

The drive from Dushanbe to Istaravshan, a total of 268km, has been immeasurably improved with the opening of the Shakhristan Tunnel in the autumn of 2012. It cuts off a back-breaking stretch through the mountains where lorries all too often jackknifed or skidded on the gravel, usually with dire consequences. There are two road tolls between Ayni and Istaravshan, one by the tunnel (*TJS23*) and the other just before Istaravshan (*TJS6*). Minibuses and shared taxis, departing throughout the day, take just over 4 hours, and cost TJS120.

There is an excellent road between Istaravshan and Khujand, and consequently the 70km journey takes just an hour by car. There are two road tolls, one at Dehmoy (*TJS2*) and the other at Chorukh (*TJS4*). The journey by shared taxi costs just TJS10.

Istaravshan's **main bus stand** is on Ismoili Somoni at the outskirts of the town as you head towards Khujand or Dushanbe. The intercity minibuses stop here, as do the numerous local minibuses that whizz up and down to the bazaar.

TRAVEL AGENTS

There is an *aviakassa* at 102 Ismoili Somoni, in the same building as Hotel Istaravshan.

WHERE TO STAY

Istaravshan's accommodation options are underwhelming in the extreme, so it's best to visit the city as a day trip from Khujand, or *en route* from Khujand to Dushanbe. If you do get stuck here, however, these are the pick of the miserable bunch.

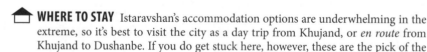

Sadbarg Hotel 105 Ismoili Somoni; m 091 873 7788; w sadbarg.tj. This large modern hotel is well situated opposite the Rudaki statue on Ismoili Somoni. The shiny façade disguises a fairly rundown interior, however, & rooms are not always clean. There is a small convenience store on the ground floor. **$–$$**

Hotel Guli Surh Main bazaar; m 092 749 4884. The hotel has been recently renovated & rooms upgraded to have hot water in the bathrooms. New windows cut down the noise. It's basic but that's reflected in the price. **$**

WHERE TO EAT AND DRINK

For a sit-down meal, Farovon (*91 Ismoili Somoni*; **$**) is the new spot in town for a nice dinner, while **Zam Zam** (*114 Ismoili Somoni*; **$**) is a small, no-frills fast-food joint in the basement of the building that attracts a motley crew of teenagers. Alternatively, at the corner of Ismoili Somoni and the bridge that leads up to Mugh Tappa is **Finca**, a large *chaykhona* with indoor and outdoor tables and the usual menu of *shashlik*, salads and flatbread. There are two more *chaykhonas* near the bazaar, but they're rather less clean than Finca.

ENTERTAINMENT There is a small **cinema** (*105 Ismoili Somoni*) to the right of the Sadbargi Hotel that claims to have 5D showings during the summer. We were really intrigued as to what this fifth dimension might be, but sadly in too much of a rush to take in a film.

SHOPPING For fresh produce and household goods, the **main bazaar** (page 118) is well stocked; it's also possible to buy craft items (such as decorative knives and small wood carvings) direct from the workshops on the edge of the market. There is a small **convenience store** beneath the Sadbarg Hotel and the larger, better-stocked **Avis** and **Safo** supermarkets are also on Ismoili Somoni a few doors down.

OTHER PRACTICALITIES
Communications Harking back to the days before mobile phones (for there was indeed such a time), Istaravshan still has its own **telephone office** (*Ismoili Somoni;* ⊕ *08.00–17.00*) where it's possible to make inexpensive international calls. Calling the UK, for example, will set you back TJS1.41 a minute.

Immediately opposite, **Zam Zam** (opposite) has Wi-Fi and a few rather dusty computer terminals.

Medical There is a **hospital** at 102 Ismoili Somoni and an apteka to the right-hand side of the main bazaar.

Money Khujand has a number of ATMs should you be stuck for cash, and there is a branch of **Eskhata Bank** immediately opposite the bazaar.

WHAT TO SEE AND DO
Mugh Tappa Wherever you are in Istaravshan, it's impossible to miss the imposing mud-brick **gateway** atop the hill overlooking the city. A modern reconstruction of one of the citadel's Medieval gateways dominates the site and, though it's unlikely to be historically accurate in its design, it nonetheless gives an indication of the fort's original scale.

Less dramatic, but historically more significant, are the mounds of earth in the corner of the site. Though they bear more than a passing resemblance to builders' rubble, they are in fact all that remains of the **Sogdian fortress** attacked by Alexander. There is, unfortunately, neither information boards nor anyone to ask, but you can nonetheless appreciate the defensive advantage that this position would have given the fort's earliest residents.

Shahr-i Kohna Istaravshan's **old town** is tucked away in the labyrinth of alleys back from Ismoili Somoni. To find it, locate the **Timurid minaret** (the tallest structure in the area), then simply dive into the streets behind and start exploring.

The minaret is situated within the **Sarimazor complex**, which includes two mausoleums and a beautiful wooden mosque. The older mausoleum is known as the **Ajina Khona** (House of Demons), but this seems to be a relatively recent name and no-one is entirely sure of its origin. The **mausoleum of Hazrati Mekhdoni Azam** is rather more intricate. The exterior displays some fine 16th-century tile work and the interior, though simple, was once decorated with calligraphy, of which a few traces remain. The **wooden mosque**, begun in the 1500s but with later additions and significant 20th-century renovations, is fabulously carved and with a ceiling painted in riotous colours. The pillars are reminiscent of the hall of Solomon and taper elegantly as fresh air breezes between them. Though the complex is free to enter, it is respectful to make a small donation to the elderly watchman to assist in its upkeep.

The old town's most photogenic sight is the **Kok Gumbaz** (Blue Dome), an intricately tiled mosque and *madrasa*. Underneath the turquoise dome is the final resting place of one Shah Fuzail ibn Abbas, about whom little is written in English. The mosque dates from the 1600s and was built by Abdul Latif Sultan, son of Ulugh Bek, the architect of Samarkand's exceptional Medieval observatory. Despite a hiatus during the Soviet period, the *madrasa* is still teaching students today, and visitors are welcome to come inside. English is on the curriculum and the students are keen to practise.

Ismoili Somoni Avenue Where the old town meets the Soviet-era thoroughfare formerly known as Lenin Street, there is a pleasant square planted with roses and, at its centre, the seemingly necessary **statue of Rudaki** (*98 Ismoili Somoni*). The back wall of the square also displays a number of **plaques**, each commemorating the life of a different writer or artist with links to Istaravshan.

Across the river, the four-storey yellow building marks the centre of the **bazaar**. Among the *shashlik* stands and fruit stalls are a few interesting buildings, including the crumbling remains of what was once a domed, tiled *chaykhona* and, on the opposite side of the street, a newer building designed in a traditional style and complete with ornately carved pillars and fascia boards. It houses the Eskhata Bank. The most interesting sight, however, is the row of tiny **workshops** where metalworkers, carpenters and other artisans are still producing traditional goods, predominantly for the local market rather than for tourists. Many of the craftsmen are happy for you to enter their premises to watch them work and, of course, even happier if you see something you'd like to buy.

AROUND ISTARAVSHAN A half-hour south of town is the gorgeous **Shakhristan region**, a swathe of cool, verdant mountains dotted with farms, villages and summer holiday cabins. Starting from the M34 highway at the oddly placed **statue of Romulus and Remus** and heading east for 15km, the road leading to the lush **Okhtagi Canyon** runs past several lodges, including the quaint but basic **Edelweiss** (**$**), with its triangular cabins and communal privy, the **Obshoron guesthouse** (m *093 837 5702*; **$–$$**), with a swimming pool and other sports-centred amenities, and the **National Bank of Tajikistan Training Centre**, a seasonal retreat open to the general public, with cosy, modern luxury cabins and en-suite bathrooms (m *092 270 3881*; **$$**). Taxis can be hired from Istaravshan and Khujand (*TJS150*), but the return trip would need to be negotiated in advance. Another option is to secure transport through a local tour operator such as **Paramount Journey** (m *092 717 3422*).

On the road to Khujand is a Soviet-era reservoir (still in use), which is decorated with a vast concrete **bust of Lenin**. The site has definitely seen better days, but you can still scramble up the hill and have your picture taken with the glorious dictator himself.

KHUJAND   *Telephone code: 03422*

One of Tajikistan's largest and wealthiest cities, Khujand has an almost cosmopolitan air and it bears the weight of its turbulent history well. Parks and monuments have all been sensitively restored, the bazaar is one of the liveliest in central Asia, and the mighty river, Syr Darya (Jaxartes), is a striking urban centrepiece. The well-paved streets, commercial centres and modern airport all reflect the city's relative prosperity and solid position as an economic engine in the Fergana Valley.

We've found Khujand to be a friendly place, particularly for a city. On our first night, we arrived late from Dushanbe and ripped open a tyre on a broken asbestos pipe outside the Khujandi Theatre as we drove in circles looking for our hotel. A gang of young men, somewhat intimidating under other circumstances, sprang into action, keen to test their strength against the too-tight nuts on the Land Rover's wheel. The Chinese-made jack was broken, the nut key was missing and it was close to midnight, but a party with beer and charades ensued and by the early hours we were tucked up in bed with a vehicle that was fit for the road.

HISTORY Khujand was founded twice, each time by one of history's mightiest kings. First the city was **Cyropolis**, the City of Cyrus, as the Persian Cyrus the Great came here on his final expedition against the Saka tribe shortly before his death in 530BC. Two centuries later, Alexander the Great also determined it a fitting place for a city, and he named it **Alexandria Eschate**: the furthest Alexandria. For the Greeks, the Syr Darya was an ideal natural defence against the Scythian tribes to the south.

Khujand became part of the Abbasid Caliphate in the 9th century AD as a result of the Arab invasion of central Asia. Maintaining control of such a distant territory was nigh on impossible, however, and so the city fell in quick succession first to the Samanids and then to the Karakhanid Khanate. It flourished as a centre of Silk Road trade and culture, and gave birth to a number of notable writers and intellectuals, including the 10th-century astronomer and mathematician Abu **Mahmud Khujandi**, and the 14th-century Sufi poet **Kamoli Khujandi**.

Unsurprisingly, Khujand attracted the attentions of Genghis Khan and was laid to waste in 1220 having initially resisted his forces. The city was occupied in turn by the Timurids, Shaybanids, the Kokand Khanate and then the Russian Empire, who held it as part of the Governorate of Turkestan.

With the arrival of the Soviets, Khujand was initially incorporated into the Uzbek SSR, but then reassigned to the Tajik SSR in 1929. It was rechristened **Leninabad** in 1939 in light of its new-found importance as Tajikistan's second city, a name which it held until 1992.

GETTING THERE AND AWAY

By air Khujand's airport [122 D4] is 15km south of the city and can be reached by taking the #80 minibus from Panjshanbe bazaar (*TJS3*). It offers a surprisingly good range of routes with a daily flight to Dushanbe (*around US$75*) as well as regular services to Moscow, St Petersburg, Sochi, Orenburg and Yekaterinburg.

The two most useful airlines using the airport are Tajik Air and Somon Air. Tajik Air has an office at 56 Ismoili Somoni, but it's frequently easier to book an e-ticket online.

By rail Khujand is one of the few cities in Tajikistan to still have a functioning rail service. There are thrice-weekly trains in each direction between Khujand and Saratov via Samarkand (*TJS1,000*), and also a weekly service to and from Moscow (*TJS1,260*).

The train station is in the south of the city on Rahbar Kosimov, just west of the junction of Ismoili Somoni and Gagarin.

By road The main road border crossing with Uzbekistan (Oybek) is situated 60km north of Khujand near Buston, and this is the easiest way to reach Tashkent, 100km

TEMUR MALIK

No-one wants to have to stand up to Genghis Khan, but to be the governor of a city in his path must be one of the most thankless tasks. Temur Malik was one such unfortunate individual.

Hearing the Mongols were on their way, Temur Malik called his followers to an island in the middle of the river and gave them the choice to flee and hopefully save their skins or to stay, fight and almost certainly die. To a man they stayed and fought, and to a man they died: they were besieged in the river, ran out of supplies and consequently fell to the Mongols' swords. Temur Malik himself was the only man to survive.

The legend of Temur Malik gained popularity among Tajik nationalists in the 20th century as he was easily promoted as a patriot who risked everything to resist foreign invaders. It is for this reason that he is commemorated with such a substantial modern statue in the city's historical museum.

on the other side of the border. The Oybek border post is open 24 hours for foreigners and, providing your papers are in order, it's a relatively easy crossing. The minibus to Buston from Khujand costs TJS5, as does a taxi from Buston to the border. Minibuses to Buston, as well as buses to Istiklol (formerly known as Taboshar) leave from the **Abreshim bus stand** in the northeast of the city several times daily.

The new tunnel at Shakhristan and the cleaned-up Anzob Tunnel have reduced the journey time between Khujand and Dushanbe to around 5 hours. For details on the road tolls between Khujand and Istaravshan see page 116, and for the stretch between Ayni and Dushanbe see page 105. There are no minibuses to Dushanbe, but shared taxis depart multiple times daily from the **Avtovokzal bus stand** [122 A4] on Kamoli Khujandi and cost between TJS100 and TJS150, depending on your haggling skills. If you are only going as far as Istaravshan, hourly minibuses ply the route, which takes around an hour and costs TJS10, also departing from Avtovokzal.

Minibuses travelling east to Isfara depart from the **South Avtostansiya bus stand** [122 C3] at the southern end of Ismoili Somoni. A seat either in the minibus or a shared taxi, both of which depart at multiple times throughout the day, should cost no more than TJS10.

LOCAL TOUR OPERATORS The regional office of **Pamir Travel** is in Khujand (*13–36 MOPR;* \ *43 020;* e *pamir-travel@list.ru;* w *pamir-travel.com*) and is a good option for arranging tours, guides and onward travel by land (including to Uzbekistan).

Khujand-based **Paramount Journey** (m *092 717 3422;* e *info@paramountjourney. com;* w *paramountjourney.com*) specialises in trekking, adventure tourism and photography expeditions, especially in the Kiraminsk, Fann and Pamir mountains.

The **Zarafshan Tourism Development Association** [122 A5] (*59 Akademik Rajabov;* m *092 770 3995;* e *ztda_zarafshon@yahoo.com;* w *ztda-tourism.tj*), relocated from its former headquarters in Panjakent, facilitates tours, trekking adventures and homestay excursions in the Zarafshan and Yagnob valleys and surrounding areas.

For airline tickets, there are a number of *aviakassa* on Ismoili Somoni, situated between the junction with Kamoli Khujandi and the bazaar.

WHERE TO STAY Khujand has, all things considered, a good range of accommodation options, from the cheap and exceptionally basic to the pricey and approaching luxurious. In the cheaper hotels, there tends to be a difference in

The peaks and valleys of the Fann
Mountains create one of the best
trekking areas in Tajikistan (m/S)
page 108

above left   Tajik children wearing traditional dress. The colour red is thought to bring good fortune and the elaborate embroidery is a regional speciality (FTJ/WC) page 24

above right   The nomadic residents of Jalang village in the Pamirs still live in yurts made from densely packed felt stretched across a collapsible wooden frame (DBI/A) page 181

below   Traditional suzani embroideries are still hand-sewn in many of Tajikistan's villages (NV/S) page 24

top   Nothing beats the excitement
of watching a horse race on the
Murghab Plateau (SD) page 25

above   A typical wedding feast can
involve as many as 1,000 guests
and takes place over several days
(SS)

right   The Panjshanbe Bazaar in
Khujand has an excellent range
of fresh produce. Pictured here,
women selling pumpkins
(SS) page 123

above left   The most famous and elusive of Tajikistan's fauna, the majestic snow leopard (*Panthera uncia*) is a resident of the high mountains. The country contains about 200 of the cats, approximately 5% of the world's population (AZ/S) pages 7–8

above   Grey wolves (*Canis lupus*) roam the mountains alongside brown bears and wild boar (DMJ/MP/FLPA) page 8

below left   The tugai forests are a key habitat for the endangered Bukhara, or Bactrian, red deer (*Cervus affinis bactrianus*) (MN/FLPA) page 8

below   The Siberian ibex (*Capra sibirica*) is a common sight and has an uncanny ability to climb steep cliffs (I/FLPA) page 8

above left The vulnerable Pallas's fish eagle (*Haliaeetus leucoryphus*) is one of around 350 species of bird that can be found in Tajikistan (JCS/FLPA) page 9

above right Tajikistan is home to eight species of owl, including the European eagle-owl (*Bubo bubo*) (PS/FLPA) page 9

below The Marco Polo sheep (*Ovis ammon polii*) is the world's largest sheep; the horns of the male can measure up to 190cm in length (AP/A) page 168

above The Wakhan Corridor is one of the last great wildernesses and an awe-inspiring destination however you choose to travel there (SS) pages 165–9

left Prior to the Arab invasion, the Wakhan had a thriving Buddhist population as well as Zoroastrians, as evinced by the 4th-century Buddhist stupa in Vrang (MK/S) page 168

below The long-haired yak is an essential part of nomadic life: not only are they a key form of transport but their hair can be woven into clothing and their milk and meat are nutritious (SS) page 8

above The hot springs of Garm Chashma, just south of Khorog, are naturally occurring and are purported to have curative properties (TDC) page 163

right Yurts are the traditional home of nomads across the Pamir mountain range. Thick felt is a good insulator and the interiors are richly decorated (SD)

below The Nurek Reservoir was created in the 1970s. Its dam is the second highest in the world (RV) page 95

KALPAK TRAVEL

The Central Asia Specialists

WWW.KALPAK-TRAVEL.COM

Tajikistan, Kazakhstan, Kyrgyzstan, Uzbekistan, Turkmenistan • Group & Private Tours

+41 78 657 27 01 / info@kalpak-travel.com

PARAMOUNT JOURNEY

BOOK A TRIP IN
FANNS, YAGNOB
& ZERAFSHAN

• TREKKING TOURS
• JEEP TOURS
• EXPEDITIONS
• PHOTO TOURS
• MOUNTAIN BIKING

quality and condition between rooms, so do ask to see several before checking in. The one hotel to avoid at all costs is **Hotel Leninabad** (*51 Nabiev*). Not only is the building dilapidated to the point of squalor, but staff have been known to let people into guests' rooms at night while they are sleeping.

⌂ **Armon Apart-Hotel** [122 C1] (16 rooms) 7 Sir-Darya; m 092 771 6967; w armon-hotels. tj. Spacious, recently renovated rooms with bright, clean bathrooms & attentive staff. Offers movie screenings & a yoga retreat in summer. **$$$**

⌂ **Grand Hotel Khujand** [122 A6] (16 rooms) 20 Maksudjon Tanburi; ☎60 599; e Khujand.grand. hotel@mail.ru; w grand-hotel.tj. Khujand's most expensive hotel is also one of its newest. Superbly situated by the fort & the Khujandi Theatre, bathrooms are immaculate & the rooms clean. There's also a sauna & pool table. B/fast inc. **$$$$**

⌂ **Hotel Khujand** [122 B5] (5 rooms) 1 Mavlonbekov; ☎65 997. A quiet & cosy option close to the opera house. Look out for the bright red roof: it's easy to spot. Staff are attentive & forthcoming with information about the city. **$$$**

⌂ **Hotel Sugd** [122 D4] (129 rooms) 179A Ismoili Somoni; ☎41 188; e hotel_sugd@mail. ru. Fairly new, 3-star property with clean, fresh rooms, neutral décor & helpful staff. Rooms are equipped with TV, stereo & fridge, & the water in the bathrooms is hot. There is a bar in the foyer. Wi-Fi & b/fast inc. Cash only. **$$$**

⌂ **Hotel Vakhdat** [122 B5] 3 Mavlonbekov; ☎65 101, 40 769. Next door to Hotel Khujand, Vakhdat is somewhat dim but generally clean & presentable with large rooms & reasonably comfortable beds. **$$$**

⌂ **Khujand Deluxe** [122 C1] (20 rooms) 63A Mira; m 092 605 5444; w khujand-deluxe. tj. Large, ornate rooms with clean bathrooms & hot water in a mansion-like setting. Wi-Fi & b/fast inc. **$$$**

⌂ **Tavhid** [122 B6] (14 rooms) 117 Firdausi; ☎67 512; e smukin@gmail.com. Conveniently located, well-run hotel just off Ismoili Somoni. Local/foreigner TJS280/310 inc b/fast. **$$$**

⌂ **Hotel Ehson** [122 D4] 171 Ismoili Somoni; ☎66 984. Situated at the junction of Ismoili Somoni & Gagarin, the Ehson is easy to spot as it's the tallest building in the area. The cheapest rooms have shared bathrooms. If you're arriving by car, be aware that this intersection is a popular hang-out for the traffic police. **$–$$**

⌂ **Hostel on Shark 21** [122 D7] (1 room) 21 Sharq; m 090 833 8800. Not to be confused with the aforementioned hotel, this hostel is located inside 3-room apartment owned by a friendly family. Intimate room with 3 beds, clean bathroom, communal area & shared kitchen. Wi-Fi & continental b/fast inc. **$**

⌂ **Hotel Shark** [122 D7] Panjshanbe Bazaar. Khujand's cheapest accommodation option is only for the very hardy. US$3 will get you a dorm bed sleeping cheek by jowl with the market's traders. Bring your own sleeping bag. There's no bathroom &, probably quite predictably, just a single toilet that smells like the mouth of hell. **$**

✖ **WHERE TO EAT AND DRINK** Khujand is a bustling town with, by Tajik standards at least, high levels of disposable income, so plenty of people choose to eat out. Fast-food joints and cafés serving *shashlik* and soups are numerous, and there's little to choose between them. Here are our top choices.

Unless otherwise stated, restaurants are open for lunch and dinner. Telephone numbers are given only when the call is likely to be answered.

✖ **Café Visol** [122 A6] 20 Maksudjon Tanburi; ☎710 1414; ⊕ 10.00–23.00. Right next to the fort, Café Visol is probably Khujand's smartest dining option. The predominantly European menu is varied & tasty, there are cloths on the tables in place of the ubiquitous plastic sheets, & the staff are happy to recommend dishes. **$$$**

✖ **Zaitun** [122 D1] Sir-Darya at 31st Microdistrict fountain; m 092 883 4444; ⊕ 07.00–23.00. Excellent selection of Tajik & central Asian mains, inc a tasty osh, the rice & meat combination that is Tajikistan's national dish. Fun, evocative atmosphere & friendly service. **$$–$$$**

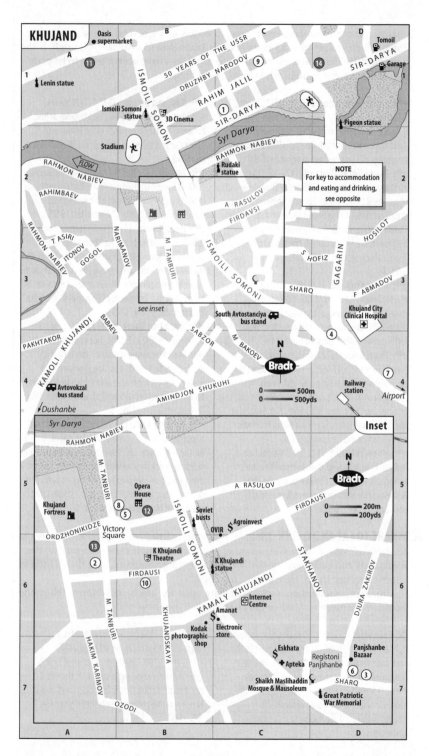

KHUJAND

A
1 Lenin statue

Oasis supermarket

11

B
50 YEARS OF THE USSR
DRUZHBY NARODOV
RAHIM JALIL
SIR-DARYA
Syr Darya

C
9

14

D
Tomoil
SIR-DARYA
Garage

Ismoili Somoni statue
3D Cinema

7

Pigeon statue

Stadium

RAHMON NABIEV

2 RAHMON NABIEV
RAHIMBAEV

FLOW

Rudaki statue

NOTE
For key to accommodation
and eating and drinking,
see opposite

2

RAHMON NABIEV
T ASIRI
ITONOV
GOGOL
NARIMANOV
M TAMBURI

A RASULOV
FIRDAVSI

ISMOILI SOMONI

S HOFIZ
GAGARIN
HOSILOT
F ABMADOV

3

see inset

South Avtostanciya bus stand

SHARQ

Khujand City
Clinical Hospital

4

PAKHTAKOR
KAMOLI KHUJANDI
BABAEV

SABZOR
M BAKOEV

N

Bradt

7

4
Avtovokzal bus stand
Dushanbe
AMINDJON SHUKUHI

0   500m
0   500yds

Railway station

Airport

Inset

Syr Darya
RAHMON NABIEV

M TANBURI

A RASULOV

FIRDAUSI

N

Bradt

5

Khujand Fortress

Opera House
8 5 12

Soviet busts
OVIR Agroinvest

ISMOILI SOMONI

FIRDAUSI

0   200m
0   200yds

5

ORDZHONIKIDZE
Victory Square
13
2

K Khujandi Theatre
FIRDAUSI
10

K Khujandi statue

KAMALY KHUJANDI

STAKHANOV

DJURA ZAKIROV

6

Internet Centre
Amanat
Kodak photographic shop
Electronic store

Eskhata
Apteka

Registoni Panjshanbe

Panjshanbe Bazaar

6 3

SHARQ

7

HAKIM KARIMOV
M TANBURI
KHUJANDSKAYA
OZODI

Shaikh Maslihaddin
Mosque & Mausoleum
Great Patriotic
War Memorial

A   **B**   **C**   **D**

🍴 **Café Kavsar** [122 C6] Ordzhonikidze; ⏰ 08.00–17.00. Start your day with Kavsar's excellent pancakes with honey, an omelette & a pot of tea. Later in the day, the salads (starting from TJS2.50) are reasonable, & the cakes look impressive too. Service is efficient if not particularly enthusiastic. $–$$

🍴 **999** [122 A1] 18th Microdistrict. The wafting smell of *shashlik* reaches you long before you can see the outdoor grills. Catering primarily to truckers & other passers-by, there's no reason to make a detour here, but it's well placed for a quick snack if you're popping up to see Lenin (page 127). $

ENTERTAINMENT There are a handful of theatres and cinemas in Khujand, but no nightlife to speak of: people tend to make their own entertainment.

Definitely worth visiting for its Art Nouveau-meets-Classical façade as much as its performances is the **Kamoli Khujandi Theatre** [122 B6] (*140 Firdausi;* ☎ 63 184). The deputy director, Mirzod, has worked here for the past three decades and, providing you understand Tajik or Russian, he's delighted to talk about past productions and the notable actors and directors who have worked here. Performances of both Tajik and foreign plays still take place relatively frequently and the tickets (*TJS5*) are a bargain.

If you want to watch a film, **3D Cinema** [122 B1] (*cnr Ismoili Somoni & Rahim Jalil*) has a showing of either a Russian or a Hollywood blockbuster most evenings. As the name suggests, they are sometimes in 3D, and always in Russian. Tickets cost TJS5.

SHOPPING Khujand isn't much of a place for retail therapy, particularly if you're after gifts or souvenirs. The gift shop inside the fort (page 125) has a few pieces of embroidery, *ikat* scarves and books on art and archaeology in Russian, but this is really your only option.

For food and household goods, you have rather more choice. The **Panjshanbe Bazaar** [122 D7], close to the junction of Ismoili Somoni and Sharq, has an excellent range of fresh produce, and there are a good number of small convenience stores and supermarkets, of which two of the best stocked are **Oasis** [122 A1] (*18th Microdistrict*) and **Anis** (*cnr Kamoli Khujandi & Kosmonavtov*).

For camera cards, chargers and computer parts, there is a small, fixed-priced **Mir** electronics store at 39 Ismoili Somoni. The prices on the tags are the official prices; you'll get a deduction of around 10% if you're happy to take the item without a receipt. For camera accessories, you can also try the Kodak-branded photo shops on the south side of Panjshanbe bazaar and the southwest corner of Ismoili Somoni and Khujandi [122 B6].

OTHER PRACTICALITIES

Communications Khujand's youth have embraced the web with open arms, and consequently it is very easy to get online in the city. Many of the hotels have Wi-Fi and there are cybercafés on most streets.

📧 **Internet Centre** [122 C6] 162 Khujandi; ⏰ 10.00–20.00. TJS4/hr.

Medical The provision of medical services in Khujand is better than in other parts of Tajikistan, but still below

KHUJAND	
For listings, see pages 121–3	

🛏 Where to stay	
1	Armon Apart-Hotel............C1
2	Grand Hotel Khujand.........A6
3	Hostel on Shark 21............D7
4	Hotel Ehson......................D4
5	Hotel Khujand...................B5
6	Hotel Shark......................D7
7	Hotel Sugd........................D4
8	Hotel Vakhdat..................B5
9	Khujand Deluxe................C1
10	Tahvid..............................B6

✖ Where to eat and drink	
11	999...................................A1
12	Café Kavsar......................B5
13	Café Visol.........................A6
14	Zaitun..............................D1

international standards. In an emergency, the **Khujand City Clinical Hospital** [122 D3] (*Gagarin, close to the junction with Ismoili Somoni*) is the largest medical centre and has a number of efficient doctors, plus some diagnostic equipment. Smaller complaints can usually be solved with a trip to the pharmacy. There are government *apteka* across the city, including at 51 Ismoili Somoni and in Panjshanbe bazaar.

Money Khujand is Tajikistan's wealthiest area, and banks and ATMs have sprung up all across the city to handle all the money. Money changers are numerous, and cash is king, even in the better hotels.

The most convenient bank branches are **Amonat Bank** [122 B6] (*132 Firdausi; ⊕ 07.30–17.00 Mon–Fri, 08.00–14.00 Sat*), where OVIR payments have to be made, its second branch at 37 Ismoili Somoni, and **Agroinvest Bank** [122 C5] (*118 Firdausi*). They all have ATMs and handle Western Union transfers, as well as offer currency exchange.

Registration Khujand's **OVIR** [122 C5] (*120 Firdausi; ℡66 734; ⊕ 08.00–noon & 13.00–17.00 Mon–Fri, 08.00–noon Sat*) is a tiny office tucked behind a somewhat unprepossessing café close to the junction with Kamoli Khujandi. It is considerably more efficient than its counterpart in Dushanbe, so if you do have to register (page 32), then this is a good place to do it. CIS nationals can register within a couple of hours (*TJS85*); foreigners are advised to use an agent (page 120).

Payment for registration and visa extensions (which can take up to ten days) has to be made at Amonat bank.

WHAT TO SEE AND DO The majority of Khujand's tourist sites are concentrated around Registoni Panjshanbe and Victory Square at the junction of Maksudjon Tanburi and Firdausi, with additional statues scattered on squares and intersections across the city.

Starting at the south end of Ismoili Somoni, the **Registoni Panjshanbe** [122 D7] has attractions on three of its four sides. The fairly modern **Sheik Muslihiddin Mosque** [122 D7] is the city's largest place of worship and cuts a striking figure on the skyline: the intricate portico, tiled minaret and turquoise domes would not look out of place in Bukhara or Samarkand. There is an attractive 19th-century **minaret** made of baked-mud bricks. It stands 21m tall and is a particularly popular resting place for the local pigeon population. The interior of the building, however, is much less ornate, save for some geometric wooden carvings on the *sagona* in the centre. The mosque is rarely busy, except for on religious festival days.

Sheik Muslihiddin (1133–1223) is buried in the 14th-century gilded **mausoleum** on the same site. He was a holy poet come miracle worker who was revered by local people. Originally buried in the suburbs, his remains were moved here shortly before the Mongol invasion. The mud-brick tomb and its contents were burned by the Mongols and completely destroyed, so the mausoleum you see today dates from two later periods of construction in the 14th and 16th centuries respectively.

On the opposite side of the square is **Panjshanbe Bazaar** [122 D7], Khujand's central market. The vast pink edifice with its attractive white plasterwork and central semi-dome looks as if it should be the set for a fairy-tale wedding or an 18th-century royal ball, but it in fact dates from 1964 and was always intended to house market traders and their wares. Climbing the stairs to the right of the main entrance enables you to get a closer look at the beautifully painted ceiling, and also offers a good vantage point for photographs across the square. The market itself has a lively atmosphere, particularly in the morning, and you'll scarcely be able to set foot among the fruit stalls before someone will accost you with a slice of melon or handful of pomegranate seeds to try. Every kind of good is for sale here, and the hours fly by as you rummage around, engage in riotous charades and buy all sorts of things you never knew you needed. It's a great place for people-watching, and the market traders are friendly, always keen to chat and pose for photographs.

As you leave the square on to Ismoili Somoni, the three-sided monument in front of you is Khujand's **memorial to the Great Patriotic War** (World War II) [122 D7], also known as the Memorial to Fallen Heroes in the Fight Against Fascism. Two of the three carved panels remember the sacrifice of those who died; the third reminds onlookers of the importance of peace. The monument is very much an artwork of its time, with stylised figures – workers, soldiers and women – striding forth boldly to confront their oppressors.

Not far from the Registoni Panjshanbe is the **Khujand Hippodrome**, the city's main sporting arena. If you are interested to watch a game of *buz kashi* (dead goat polo), this is the place to come. In the winter months (November to April), matches are fairly regular, though there is no set schedule. Paramount Journey (page 120) arranges *buz kashi* tours where you can meet the players, watch a match, and even try it yourself if you're confident on horseback.

Continuing north along Ismoili Somoni brings you to the **Abu Mahmud Hamid ibn Khidr Khujandi statue** [122 B6]. Situated in a small park at the intersection of Ismoili Somoni and Kamoli Khujandi, Khujandi himself sits looking pensive with a large book on his knee. Khujandi is the city's namesake, a Persian romantic poet and Sufi who was born here but lived in Tabriz, Iran, where he died and was buried in 1400. Lines of trees carry the eye further down the road to another war memorial and then a line of bronze busts [122 B5], each belonging to a Soviet-era luminary, that are surrounded by well-kept rose bushes.

Moving now to **Victory Square** (also called Pushkin Square) [122 A5] and the historic centre of the city: **Khujand Fortress** [122 A5]. Archaeological excavations on the site have unearthed Graeco-Bactrian coins, pottery shards and other items which date the earliest parts of the citadel to the 4th century BC. Many of these are displayed in the museum (see below). The fortress was continually rebuilt and expanded for 2,500 years, however, as every time it was attacked, significant reconstruction was required. It reached its greatest extent in the 13th century, with thick clay walls atop an embankment, a water-filled moat, and a city wall encompassing 20ha of land, but even then it was no match for Genghis Khan. The Mongols completely destroyed the fortress.

The buildings visible today follow the lines of the fortress's 13th-century incarnation. The Khujandis quickly rebuilt their city, including the fort, after the Mongols left. The structure has been heavily renovated in recent years and, in the case of the attractive main gateway, completely reconstructed. It does, however, give visitors a good impression of the scale of the original building, and why the besieged Khujandis were able to hold out against the Mongols for so long.

Inside this gate is the **Historical Museum of the Sughd Region** (⏀ 08.00–16.00; *TJS10*) or, to give it its full name, the Historical Local Lore Museum of Archaeology and Fortification. Unusually for a regional museum, this is a modern, well-laid-out space with exhibit labels in Tajik, Russian and English. The basement displays a collection of modern mosaic murals depicting scenes from the life of Alexander the Great, dioramas of Stone Age and Iron Age life, archaeological finds including a three-legged iron pot, and some stones informatively labelled as such. The museum has a small gift shop selling handicrafts and a few books.

The ground floor is dominated by a 4m-tall **statue of Temur Malik** (see box, page 120) and a mock-up of an archaeological dig with 'finds' arranged in chronological order. Highlights include a wooden coffin from the 1st century BC, a 6th-century earthenware teapot, a dervish's dressing gown and some particularly fine gold coins. There are wall displays on Sarazm, the Kushans, the Middle Ages and the arrival of the Chingizids (Mongols), as well are more staid exhibits relating to the October Revolution and Soviet period. Taking advantage of the services of the English-speaking guide really brings the collection to life.

Elsewhere on the square is the attractive **Kamoli Khujandi Theatre** [122 B6] (page 123), a **fountain** and bronze sculpture and, atop the otherwise quite ordinary building to the left of the theatre, a **long mosaic panel** in coral-coloured stone.

A short walk from the square brings you to the **Syr Darya** (see box, page 128) and another **line of bronze busts**, this time of Khujand's historical leaders. There is a **promenade** much of the way along the riverbank, but the best views are to be had from one of the two bridges.

North of the river are three **statues**, two that are important and one that has novelty value. In pride of place on Kahrahmon (the northern part of Ismoili Somoni) is a vast bronze statue of **Ismoili Somoni** [122 B1] crowned in gold and flanked by a pair of lions that would not look out of place on Trafalgar Square.

ISTIKLOL

Known throughout most of its existence as Taboshar, the town 42km due north of Khujand, and called Istiklol ('independence' in Tajik) since 2012, has quite an unconventional history. A trickle of German migrants first settled in small villages throughout the nigh-unpopulated region through the end of the 19th and into the 20th century. After World War I, uranium was discovered near the tiny settlement of Taboshar, and as the Soviet Union raced against the USA to develop the ultimate weapon, the area became indispensable to the USSR's nuclear aspirations. By the 1930s, Taboshar was the largest uranium-mining site in the Soviet Union, and German prisoners of war, as well as German Russians living in other parts of the country, were sent to the town to work in the mines during and after World War II. After the war, the settlers, prisoners and refugees built houses and apartment buildings in lovely German architectural styles along shady, tree-lined streets, resulting in an alpine-looking aesthetic. Taboshar and its main export remained official state secrets through the 1970s, though the residents of Khujand were aware of the off-limits town and provided many goods and services that weren't available in Taboshar proper. After the closure of the mine, the vast majority of the German community left for Germany or other countries, and the overall population fell from a high of some 20,000 in 1989 to 15,600 in 2014, leaving many houses abandoned and the streets eerily quiet. The ruins of the military base that guarded the operation, along with open uranium pits and a radioactive reservoir, are all walking distance from the centre of town, where a small museum outlines Istiklol's history with vivid detail and artefacts donated by residents; ask around for the caretaker, who is knowledgeable but speaks very little English. Buses leave from Khujand's Abreshim bus stop daily, though it may be more prudent to hire a taxi for a surprisingly pleasant half-day trip. Try not to stay too long, though, and pack a lunch, as the few mini-markets in town sell only packaged snack foods.

The numerous choreographed fountains (lit at night in particularly special neon shades of red and green) make it a popular spot for wedding photographs.

Unceremoniously usurped by Ismoili Somoni, central Asia's tallest remaining **Lenin statue** has been moved to a virtual wasteland next to the electricity substation and a car wash. In spite of his 22m height, here Lenin still appears lost and forlorn, a shadow of his former self. Given that Khujand was once Leninabad, it is a pity the city cannot embrace this part of its history and display this important statue somewhere people may actually be able to appreciate it. Other than an occasional tourist, the only visitors here are a few elderly ladies genuinely mourning the passing of the Soviet Union and the economic and political stability it afforded.

Last but certainly not least is the **giant pigeon statue** [122 D1] in Navruzgoh Park. You can see it from the eastern bridge. Quite what this pigeon is doing here no-one is sure, but he's certainly an entertaining addition to the shoreline.

AROUND KHUJAND Of all the things you might expect to find on a collective farm outside Khujand, a 1950s recreation of the Winter Palace in St Petersburg is probably not one of them. The **Palace of Arbob** is there to surprise you.

We drove the 10km east from Khujand late one afternoon, determined to see what must rate as one of the most eccentric Soviet follies. The palace is a real oxymoron: on one hand, it was the centrepiece of the Voroshilov State Collective Farm, and its museum (*entrance TJS3*) is stuffed with Soviet propaganda glorifying the happy peasant and his remarkable achievements in increasing cotton production. At the same time, its very architecture and the water gardens in which it is set imply a very un-Soviet admiration for the indulgences of the bourgeoisie.

Continuing another 10km to the east brings you to **Lake Kairakkum**, an artificial reservoir that was a popular Soviet-era holiday destination and is still the closest thing to a beach resort you'll find so many thousand kilometres from the sea. The **Shifo Sanatorium** (↖ *24 387; www.kurort.tj;* **$$**) in the town of Bukhta Mirnaya has been renovated fairly recently and is a reasonable place to stay.

Trekkers interested in a more uplifting experience than normal can hike up **Boboi Ob**, at 3,769m the highest peak in the Kurama Range, with spectacular views of the Fergana Valley. Muslim pilgrims make the three-day journey to the top at least once a year, though more audacious trekkers can do the 15km trail from Obi Asht, one of

---

ABU MAHMUD KHUJANDI

Khujand's position on the Silk Road made it not only a centre for trade but also a melting pot for new ideas. Indeed, one of the finest scientific minds of the 10th century was born in the city and is colloquially known as al-Khujandi ('the one from Khujand').

Abu Mahmud Hamid ibn Khidr Khujandi was born in Khujand in the mid-900s. He worked in the fields of astronomy and mathematics, and made notable discoveries in both.

In Iran, he constructed a giant mural sextant to determine the tilt of the earth (which he decided to be 23°32'19" for the year 994) and concluded that the axial tilt is in fact decreasing. The slight inaccuracy in his calculations is likely due to the weight of his instruments.

In mathematics Khujandi stated a special case of Fermat's last theorem, for n=3, and he may also have discovered the spherical law of sines, though surviving texts on this point are inconclusive.

Known to the ancient Greeks as the Jaxartes on account of its colour (from the Persian *yakhsha arta*, meaning 'great pearly river'), the Syr Darya became famous in the classical world as the site where Alexander the Great fought the Scythians in 329BC at the Battle of Jaxartes. Subsequent Islamic writings from the Medieval period suggest that the Syr Darya is one of four rivers whose common source lies in paradise. The others are the Amu Darya (the Oxus), the Nile and the Euphrates.

In reality, the Syr Darya rises from head streams in the Tian Shan Mountains of Kyrgyzstan and flows 2,212km west through Uzbekistan and Kazakhstan, and would naturally finally drain out into the Aral Sea. Its water flow is around 37km³ a year.

The diversion of the Syr Darya's water into a network of canals is one of the main reasons for the environmental disaster that is the shrinking of the Aral Sea. So much water is used for cotton irrigation (and lost due to evaporation and leakage from poorly maintained channels) that the river runs dry long before reaching its natural end.

the three approaches to the peak, in only a day. The devout who climb the peak leave shrines of stones and coloured cloth, with the pilgrimage period reaching its zenith in August and September. Trekkers can camp up to 3,500m, though homestays with Tajik or Uzbek families in the starting points of Obi Asht, Oshoba and Pongoz are very common and can be arranged through **Paramount Journey** (**w** *paramountjourney. com*). Single-vehicle transport can also be organised by Paramount, though it is possible to take a minibus from Khujand's Abreshim bus station to Ashti Bolo (*TJS15*), then haggle with village residents for a ride to Obi Asht.

ISFARA Telephone code: 03462

Arriving in Isfara can feel as if you've reached the end of the earth. When the border crossing with Kyrgyzstan is closed there is little reason to come here, but when it is open it can prove a convenient overnight stop before you leave Tajikistan, and there are a few attractive buildings. The city of some 40,000 is situated on the narrow Isfararinka River, spanned by a bridge connecting the bazaar to the small, modern commercial district. Sparsely populated mountains rise in the distance, as Isfara occupies a remote corner of the vast Fergana Valley, but the city has served as a way station and regional trading centre since the 7th century.

GETTING THERE Most people arrive in Isfara on their way to or from Kyrgyzstan, as the road from Isfara continues east to Batken and thence to Osh. For more details on this route, see page 37.

Minibuses and shared taxis from Khujand, leaving frequently throughout the day, cost no more than TJS10 and do the 107km journey in 2 hours. They depart from Khujand's South Avtostansiya bus stand at the southern end of Ismoili Somoni.

 WHERE TO STAY AND EAT Map, page 129.

The Soviet-era **Isfara Hotel** (*36 Ismoili Somoni;* 21 405; **$$**) has large if somewhat uninspiring rooms and basic bathrooms, while the modest **Hotel Vatan** (**$**) is nearby and provides basic lodging and internet. There are a couple of *chaykhonas*

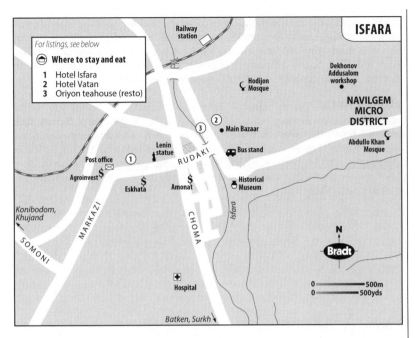

For listings, see below

around the Central Mosque, the newest being the elaborate **Oriyon teahouse** (**$$**), overlooking the river and featuring teas and traditional Tajik meat-based dishes such as *osh*.

SHOPPING Isfara is far from a tourist hub, but hidden in the Navigilem Microdistrict is a workshop producing what may well be the most beautiful souvenirs of your trip. The blue gates of 62 Dukchi open on to the workroom and shop of Dekhonov Addusalom, one of Isfara's last traditional woodcarvers. Watching him work the apricot wood with hand tools (some of which are over 200 years old) is enthralling, and his combs, delicate animal figurines, pots and other curiosities are certainly pieces to treasure.

For fresh produce, bread and household goods, try Navbahor Market on Markazi.

OTHER PRACTICALITIES Isfara's main **post office** is on Markazi, where there is also a **small internet café**.

There are branches of several banks in town, including **Agroinvest Bank** (*38 Markazi;* 22 352) and **Eskhata Bank** (*31 Ismoili Somoni;* 21 451), and there is a branch of **Orienbank** at 158 Kommunarov (24 040). They are all open 08.00–17.00 Monday–Friday and each has an ATM.

WHAT TO SEE AND DO Close to the bridge is Isfara's **historical museum** (*entrance TJS3*) and it's worth starting here to get a picture of the region and the various invaders and settlers who have shaped the city, from its Medieval mosques to the golden statue of Lenin.

The simple **Abdullo Khan Mosque** in the east of the city dates from the 1500s and is adorned with a later minaret. Standing in the central courtyard it is interesting to look up and compare the portions of the mosque that have and have not been renovated, as it's quite rare to see the two side by side.

On Kalima is the **Central Mosque**, also called the Hodijon Mosque, Isfara's largest place of worship. Due to the Soviet Union's restrictions on religion it was closed for almost a third of its 200-year history, but it's experienced an unexpected revival since independence, and thousands of people now regularly come here to pray. In fact, the mosque can hold up to 10,000 worshippers at one time.

AROUND ISFARA Twenty minutes' drive south from Isfara brings you to the otherwise unprepossessing village of Surkh. Ask for the **Mosque of Hazrati Shah** and step inside the quiet courtyard to find the much older and more significant tomb of Kasim. Legend has it that Kasim was descended from Ali, son-in-law of the Prophet, and his burial place has been a pilgrimage site since the 8th century. Look out for the lifelike wooden carvings of birds that decorate the building; the owls are particularly fine.

SEND US YOUR SNAPS!

We'd love to follow your adventures using our *Tajikistan* guide – why not send us your photos and stories via Twitter (🐦 *@BradtGuides*) and Instagram (📷 *@bradtguides*) using the hashtag #Tajikistan. Alternatively, you can upload your photos directly to the gallery on the Tajikistan destination page via our website (w *bradtguides.com/tajikistan*).

6

Khatlon

With dry, undulating terrain interspersed with tufts of irrigated cotton fields and wild brush, no other region of Tajikistan captures such an otherworldly aura as Khatlon. What the district lacks in dramatic mountain ranges, it makes up for in russet Martian canyons, and barren lunar landscapes which change colour with the position of the sun. Baking in summer, with some winter days that see snow, much of Khatlon's semi-arid topography seems to come closest to the stereotypical drylands associated with the 'Stans in Western imagination. But naturally flowing rivers and Soviet-era irrigation channels nourish stands of green trees and vibrant wildflowers in some of the most unexpected spots.

Within easy reach of Dushanbe, and with fast-improving road infrastructure, Khatlon is an obvious choice for visitors keen to explore Tajikistan without the physical challenges of journeying to Khujand or the Pamirs. Three national parks, hot springs and the Amu Darya and Vakhsh rivers reveal the country's natural beauty, while the ancient ruins of the Buddhist monastery at Ajina Tepa, the Khulbuk and Utapur fortresses and the Graeco-Bactrian temple of Takht-i Sangin are indisputable highlights of Tajikistan's cultural heritage.

QURGONTEPPA   *Telephone code: 03222*

Tajikistan's third-largest city has a population of around 100,000 people and is the capital of the Khatlon region. Sprawling over a sun-baked plain, its wide, planned streets, numerous statues and several attractive museums belie the fact that the city was utterly ravaged by the civil war, its infrastructure, industry and population left in tatters. Still, the city has bounced back from the brink with an energetic young populace milling about, and a buzzing economy.

HISTORY The exact origins of Qurgonteppa are unknown; some sources suggest there was human habitation here as early as the 7th century, but if this is indeed the case then the community at Qurgonteppa would have been far smaller than that at nearby Ajina Tepa (page 136). The modern city dates from the Soviet period, with much of the construction occurring in the 1970s and 1980s.

The most tumultuous period of Qurgonteppa's history occurred during Tajikistan's civil war. Qurgonteppa was the home of the Islamic Renaissance Party (IRP), one of the key opposition groups. In 1992–93 some of the most serious fighting took place in and around the city: buildings were burnt out, tens of thousands of people were killed or fled across the border into Afghanistan, and Qurgonteppa's crops and factories were razed to the ground.

GETTING THERE Driving the 100km from Dushanbe and points north to Qurgonteppa is relatively straightforward. The road conditions are generally good, and there is

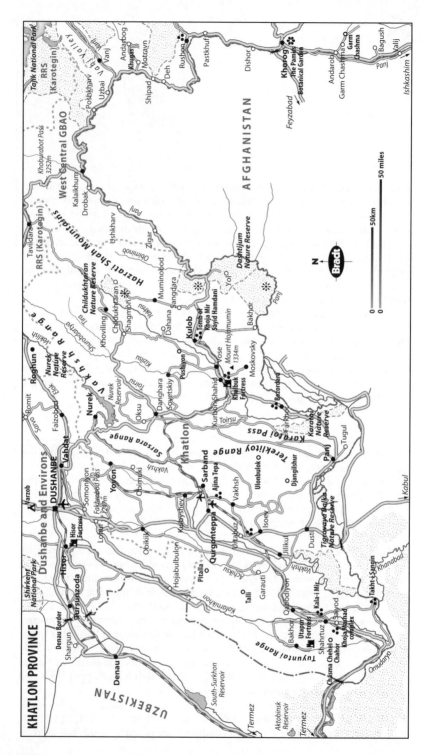

KHATLON PROVINCE

little other traffic. If you are reliant on public transport, shared taxis on the same route cost TJS20 and take 2 hours. They leave from the bus stand in Dushanbe's 46th Microdistrict and drop you at the main bus station in the northwest of Qurgonteppa. The Asian Express bus service offers one daily trip from its terminal in Dushanbe to the bus station (*vokzal*) at the north end of town, as well as the old central bazaar in Qurgonteppa for TJS15 each way. Shared taxis from Dushanbe can be hailed on the southeast corner of the Sakhovat Bazaar and also stop at Qurgonteppa's vokzal and central bazaar; the charge is TJS10–15 for the 90-minute ride each way.

Travelling east, it is 192km to Kulob via Danghara, where an excellent new stretch of dual carriageway has just been laid. Allow 4–5 hours for the drive and be sure to stop at Khulbuk (page 140). Shared taxis also connect Qurgonteppa with Kulob, stopping intermittently along the way.

There is a **railway station** just outside Qurgonteppa, which is on the line to Kulob, but it no longer seems to be operational. The international **airport** is located 9km northeast of the town centre, though the only commercial services at the time of printing were thrice-weekly non-stop flights to Moscow on Tajik Air.

GETTING AROUND Qurgonteppa is small enough to explore on foot easily. **Minibuses** run up and down Vahdat and Ayni (*TJS1*), congregating around the bazaar on B Gafurov.

TOURIST INFORMATION There are several *aviakassa* around the bazaar, with little if anything to choose between them, but they are of use if you need to buy a flight ticket, make changes to your booking, etc. There is no official source of tourist information in the city, but staff at the Khatlon Region Local History Museum (page 135) and the Ramz Hotel (page 133) are happy to make recommendations and offer directions.

 WHERE TO STAY   *Map, page 134.*

Qurgonteppa's accommodation options are a little bit more up to date these days, but there are still a few throwbacks to the not-quite-cosy Soviet era. All the hotels are within walking distance of the city's attractions.

Ramz Hotel Complex 51A Ayni; **m** 090 122 4444; **e** ramzhotel.tj@mail.ru. Modern hotel with helpful, surprisingly cheerful staff & designated off-street parking. Rooms are clean & comfortable & there seems to be plenty of hot water. Front desk staff speak English. Wi-Fi US$2/ day. B/fast inc. **$$$**

Hotel Maftuna 44 Vahdat; **m** 090 111 2153. Rather tired-looking property on the main road into town from Dushanbe. The rooms & public areas are depressing & generally feel neglected. You'll find better value for money up the street at the Ramz. **$$–$$$**

Hotel Bokhtariyon Vahdat; **** (0441) 105 252. Located at the entrance to the city, 2km from the centre, this new hotel is clean, comfortable & modern. **$$**

Hotel Istiqlol Kzivoy; **m** 090 103 0819. Bland but acceptable hotel a little way from the city centre. Shared dorms from TJS50. **$–$$**

Hotel Qurgonteppa 24 B Gafurov; **** 23 694. Soviet hotel close to the bazaar that has seen better days. The basic rooms are really pretty bad; the half-lux & lux rooms are only slightly better. **$–$$**

✗ WHERE TO EAT AND DRINK   *Map, page 134.*

The Istiqlol and Ramz hotels both have restaurants serving basic menus of soups, salads and grilled meats, and the latter is popular for wedding parties too. Other establishments include the following.

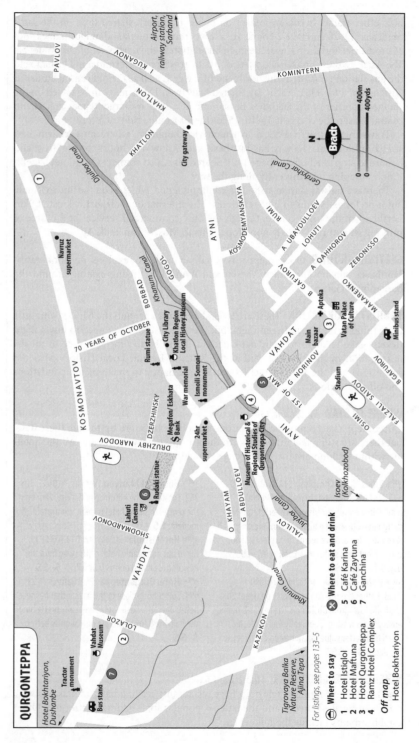

QURGONTEPPA

Where to stay
1 Hotel Istiqlol
2 Hotel Maftuna
3 Hotel Qurgonteppa
4 Ramz Hotel Complex

Off map
Hotel Bokhtariyon

Where to eat and drink
5 Café Karina
6 Café Zaytuna
7 Ganchina

For listings, see pages 133–5

KOMINTERN
PAVLOV
I KURGANOV
KHATLON
KHATLON
City gateway
AYNI
Navruz supermarket
Dulbai Canal
Khanum Canal
BORBAD
GOGOL
70 YEARS OF OCTOBER
Rumi statue
City Library
Khatlon Region Local History Museum
KOSMONAVTOV
DZERZHINSKY
DRUZHBY NARODOV
Megafon/Eskhata Bank
War memorial
Ismoili Somoni monument
24hr supermarket
Museum of Historical & Regional Studies of Qurgonteppa City
VAHDAT
Main bazaar
Apteka
Vatan Palace of Culture
Minibus stand
Stadium
G NORINOV
1ST OF MAY
AYNI
RUMI
KOSMODEMYANSKAYA
A UBAYDULLOEV
LOHUTI
A QAHHOROV
ZEBONISSO
MAKARENKO
B GAFUROV
OSIMI
FALZALI SAIDOV
B GAFUROV
Isoev (Kolkhozobod)
Juybor Canal
JALILOV
O KHAYAM
G ABDULLOEV
KAZOKON
Khanum Canal
SHODMARDONOV
Lahuti Cinema
Rudaki statue
VAHDAT
LOLAZOR
Vahdat Museum
Tractor monument
Bus stand
Tigrovaya Balka Nature Reserve, Ajina Tepa
Hotel Bokhtariyon, Dushanbe
Airport, railway station, Sarband
Geldyshat Canal

0 400m
0 400yds

N

Bradt

☕ **Café Karina** Cnr Vahdat & 1st May; ⏱ 08.00–18.00. Small & pleasant café overlooking the park. Close to the bazaar. **$$**
☕ **Ganchina** Opposite Vahdat Museum; ⏱ 09.00–21.00. Glorified *chaykhona* with helpful staff & good salads. **$$**

☕ **Café Zaytuna** 29 Vahdat; ⏱ 08.00–22.00. In the same building as the Lahuti Cinema, Zaytuna serves up a predictable menu of pizzas & fast food to excitable teens & young families. **$–$$**

ENTERTAINMENT The latest films are shown at **Lahuti Cinema** (*29 Vahdat;* m (*0903*) *458 5050;* ⏱ *10.00–23.00*) and this is your best bet for an evening's entertainment. Film showings (all in Russian) take place five times a day in the 587-person theatre, and tickets are an affordable TJS5.

Occasional films, including less commercial works, are shown at the big blue **Vatan Palace of Culture** opposite the bazaar.

OTHER PRACTICALITIES Qurgonteppa has a branch of **Eskhata Bank** (*cnr Vahdat & Druzhby Narodov*) and **Amonatbonk** (*cnr Ayni & Karl Marx*), both with ATMs and money transfer services. There is also a **Megafon** shop (*also Vahdat & Druzhby Narodov*) and *apteka* (pharmacy) by the bazaar and in the same building as Hotel Istiqlol on Kzivoy. A 24-hour **Navruz** supermarket is located on the corner of Borbad and Kosmonavtov.

WHAT TO SEE AND DO For a relatively small town, and one so badly damaged by the civil war, Qurgonteppa has a surprisingly high number of engaging sites: three museums, a bazaar, a cultural centre and numerous monuments, from the ubiquitous Rudaki to a rather less common monument to tractors.

Probably the most interesting historical collection is held at the **Khatlon Region Local History Museum** (*10 Borbad;* ☏*34 230;* ⏱ *08.00–17.00 Mon–Fri, 09.00–16.00 Sat, closed for lunch noon–13.00; local/foreigner TJS2/15*), a large, new museum opened by President Rahmon himself. The curators are rightly proud of their two-storey exhibition space and its wide variety of exhibits: dioramas featuring stuffed local wildlife; scale models of what Takht-i Sangin and Ajina Tepa might have looked like; cases of dried insects (some disturbingly large); and a good collection of traditional textiles. We were particularly taken with the sculpture of Romulus and Remus being suckled by the she-wolf, though bemused as to what its connection with Khatlon could possibly be.

Next door to the museum is the **City Library** (*12 Borbad;* ⏱ *08.00–17.00 Mon–Fri, 08.00–noon Sat, closed for lunch noon–13.00*) with a reasonable selection of books and journals (including some books on archaeology) and a room of computers with internet access.

The tongue-twisting mouthful that is the **Museum of Historical and Regional Studies of Qurgonteppa City in Honour of Bibi Khanym** (*Vahdat;* m *091 745 7079;* ⏱ *08.00–17.00 Mon–Sat; local/foreigner TJS1/4.50*) is a fabulous-looking building on a small hill behind the Ramz Hotel. The colourful minaret protruding through the roof suggests a religious building, but in fact it is, as the name suggests, dedicated to the city's past. The exhibits themselves have seen better days and the displays are distinctly dated, but the architecture of the exterior is what makes the attraction.

Hidden beneath a modernist structure resembling a crown is the small, underground **Vahdat Museum** (*Vahdat;* ⏱ *08.00–17.00 Mon–Fri; local/foreigner TJS1/3*).

Qurgonteppa is endowed with numerous examples of public art. Keep an eye out for the writers **Sino** (*Loginov*), **Rudaki** (*Vahdat*) and **Rumi** (*Borbad*), for the World **War II memorial** with its **Lenin** sidekick (*Borbad*), and for the **tractor on a plinth** (*cnr Vahdat & Kosmonavtov*).

AROUND QURGONTEPPA

Ajina Tepa Some 12km to the east of Qurgonteppa are the archaeological remains of Ajina Tepa, the 8th-century **Buddhist monastery** from which the remarkable Sleeping Buddha (now in the National Museum in Dushanbe) was uncovered in the 1960s. Though all of the finds were removed to Dushanbe or museums in Russia, it is still possible to see remnants of the 2.5m-thick mud-brick walls that protected the internal courtyard and monastic buildings. Approximately 1,500 artefacts have been excavated from the site since the initial archaeological dig in the 1960s, a testimony to the monastery's importance and opulence. Ironically, despite its holy affiliations, the name Ajina Tepa itself means 'Devil's Hill', and fragments of gargoyles and other demon-like sculptures were found among the ruins; scholars believe these items served to scare away opponents of Buddhism. Entrance is free and the site is unattended. Hiring a taxi from Qurgonteppa is the most feasible way to access the complex.

Tigrovaya Balka Nature Reserve About 2 hours' drive south of Qurgonteppa (around 70km), this reserve is described by the World Wildlife Fund as the most important nature reserve in central Asia, with a rare riparian forest ecosystem and acres of wetland surrounded by a semi-desert landscape. At the convergence of the Vakhsh and Panj rivers as they become the Amu Darya, this 50,000ha site takes its name from the tigers for which the area was once famed. They are, sadly, long gone, but if you visit equipped with a reliable 4x4 (and preferably the services of a guide) it is still possible to see Saiga deer, wild boar, jackals and other wild dogs, as well as various species of migratory and resident birds. The park is most easily accessed by hired car and there are about 60km of decent dirt roads within the park, as well as a small museum outside the entrance of the park, which contains stuffed animal specimens and information about hiring guides. Tigrovaya Balka is on the UNESCO tentative list for World Heritage Site designation.

Entrance to the park requires a permit, and this can only be obtained from the **National Parks Office** in Dushanbe (*64 Druzhby Narodov*). The permit costs US$40 per person and it is best to allow at least three days for it to be processed. There are no fixed working hours for the reserve, as there are not a lot of visitors, so the best course of action may be to arrive at the main entrance to the reserve at 8.00 or 9.00 on weekdays, when you should be able to arrange a visit with someone from the reserve's administration. There are no 'official' phone lines.

Sarband A modest launching point for a pair of interesting treks, Sarband has a lovely, relaxing grass-covered '**beach**' at the edge of the Sarband Reservoir, where local residents go boating or swimming in the cool, turquoise waters. A 10-minute drive from town brings trekkers to a favourite filming location for Soviet-era action films, the rusty red foothills of Mount Khojamaston, or to the mountain itself, which rises to 1,822m and features paths to the summit that can be trekked in 2–3 hours. Sarband is also an acceptable stopping point on the road from Qurgonteppa to Kulob should you need one. The town has a single **hotel** (*Borbat;* m *091 787 8786;* **$$**), where breakfast and Wi-Fi are included in the room rate, a *chaykhona* (*Goloba Park*) and a branch of **Tajik Sodirot Bank** (*Borbat*). There is a small **statue of Lenin** close to the bank. Shared taxis to Sarband leave from both the *vokzal* (taxi/bus station) and the central bazaar in Qurgonteppa.

Deep in the south of Tajikistan, not far from the Afghan border, Shahrtuz is famous for its cotton production. It is a convenient base from which to explore some of the country's most important historical sites, as well as the 44 springs of Chasma Chehel Chahor.

GETTING THERE Shahrtuz is 130km south of Qurgonteppa and the minibus between the two cities takes 3 hours (*TJS50*). Shared taxis leave the central bazaar and the *vokzal* in Qurgonteppa more frequently than the minibuses and are only slightly more expensive. Asian Express runs the 5-hour journey from Dushanbe to Shahrtuz twice daily for TJS25 each way, while shared taxis cost about the same, but take less time to drive the route.

WHERE TO STAY AND EAT There is a single, small **guesthouse** close to the United Nations Development Programme (UNDP) office that also serves good evening meals. The UNDP office is the closest landmark – ask to be dropped there.

OTHER PRACTICALITIES The **Agroinvest**, **Eskhata** and **Tajik Sodirot** banks all have branches on Lenin where you can change money and send/receive Western Union transfers. Shahrtuz does have a local **hospital**, but it more or less collapsed during the 1990s and is only now being rebuilt (both physically and in terms of staffing and equipment), with the assistance of UNDP. Medical services in the region are already exceptionally overstretched and the hospital cannot be relied upon to provide care for foreigners too.

AROUND SHAHRTUZ
Chasma Chehel Chahor Just 8km from Shahrtuz, Chasma Chehel Chahor is a lush oasis fed by 44 **mountain springs**. Legend has it that Ali, son-in-law of the Prophet Muhammad, came here with his army and, as the surrounding area was arid (and remains so to the present day), he prayed to Allah to provide them with water. Morning came and Ali's prayer was answered: every time he took a step, another spring burst forth from the ground.

Today Chasma Chehel Chahor is an important local pilgrimage site. Muslims, in particular women and the elderly, come to pray for healing and to bathe in the numerous warm-water pools, which are believed to have curative properties. Like with holy water from Lourdes or the Ganges, you can bottle water from the spring and take it home with you, if you're so inclined.

There are separate **swimming areas** for men and for women. The small eels might catch you by surprise as they slip and slide around your legs, but we're assured they're perfectly harmless. It is also a popular picnic spot: mulberry and other fruit trees offer shade, while small children splash and shriek in the water. Summer weekends are particularly crowded, so try to time your visit for a day when everyone else is working.

A **minibus** makes the half-hour drive between Shahrtuz and Chasma Chehel Chahor several times a day, and more frequently on holidays and at weekends. It costs TJS2. Shared taxis also depart from the vokzal and central bazaar in Qurgonteppa. There is a basic guesthouse (**$**) close to the site with an animated and friendly owner.

Khoja Mashad complex Khoja Mashad was an Islamic missionary who came to Tajikistan in the late 9th century, most likely from Iran. He was a wealthy man and funded the establishment of a *madrasa*, where he was later buried. Local legend has it that Mashad's mausoleum appeared overnight by the will of Allah, though archaeologists may view this assertion with a little scepticism.

Located just 6km south of Shahrtuz, in the district of Sayed, the Khoja Mashad complex is composed of **two Medieval mausoleums** (the earliest dating from the first half of the 10th century) connected by a vaulted passageway. Both mausoleums are constructed from baked bricks that have been arranged in an attractive fir-tree pattern, but while they appear to be identical, slight differences in the construction and design of the buildings indicate that they were erected at different times.

Outside the mausoleums is a large courtyard filled with graves, and the ruins of **two domed structures** and a **mud-brick portal**. The style of domes is typical of central Asian architecture prior to the Mongol invasion. The rows of *hujras* (narrow cells) along the edges of the courtyard likely housed the madrasa's students. Other rooms would have served as classrooms, a refectory and a mosque. In spring and summer, wildflowers brighten the solemn atmosphere of the premises. Shared taxis leave from Shahrtuz to carry pilgrims to this sacred burial place, so it can often be crowded.

Takht-i Sangin 40km from Shahrtuz, near to the confluence of the Vakhsh and Amu Darya (Oxus) rivers, is the Temple of the Oxus, one of the earliest and most important archaeological sites in Tajikistan. The finest pieces now in the National Museum were excavated here by Soviet archaeologists in the 1970s and 1980s, and it is likely that the remarkable **Oxus Treasure** (see box, below) was also discovered in the vicinity. Whereas elsewhere in the world a site as significant as Takht-i Sangin would be overrun with visitors, here we had only a goat for company.

THE OXUS TREASURE

On rare occasions, all that glisters is indeed gold, as the British captain F C Burton discovered when he rescued a group of merchants from bandits on the road from Kabul to Peshawar in the spring of 1880. Intrigued by the treasure the merchants carried, Burton purchased from them a gold lion- and griffin-headed armlet and alerted colonial colleagues to scour the markets of Rawalpindi where the merchants were thought to be headed.

Major-General Sir Alexander Cunningham, director general of the Archaeological Survey of India, and Sir Augustus Wollaston Franks, a curator of the British Museum, managed to reunite around 170 gold and silver artefacts from the original treasure hoard, including vessels, coins, armlets and rings, and a beautifully intricate figurine of a charioteer.

The Oxus Treasure is the most important surviving collection of Achaemenid Persian metalwork and it dates from the 5th–4th centuries BC when the Achaemenid empire stretched from Egypt in the west to the Indus Valley in the east. Though the exact site of its discovery is unknown, it is thought to have been found on the riverbank at Takht-i Kuwad, and archaeologists have subsequently hypothesised that it would have originally been collected and stored at the Oxus Temple in Takht-i Sangin.

Today the Oxus Treasure takes pride of place in the Ancient Iran gallery at the British Museum, where it was bequeathed by Franks upon his death in 1897. President Rahmon called for its return to Tajikistan in 2010, but this is unlikely to occur, as the British Museum gifted Tajikistan replicas of the treasure for display in the Tajik National Museum back in 2013.

Founded in the 6th century BC at the end of the Achaemenid period, this ancient settlement was centred on a fortified citadel. Inside was a monumental temple – the Temple of Oxus – with a columned hall encircled by two rows of corridors and finished with a Classical portico. The walls of the inner sanctum were an impressive 5m high, and in places they were 3m thick. The pillars would have been topped with Ionian finials, and there were numerous statues atop pedestals.

Central to the temple was a magnificent carved altar at which worshippers made offerings of coins, precious metals, artworks and ritual weapons. Almost 5,000 artefacts have been excavated, and they clearly show Hellenistic influence. Discoveries of gold and ivory goods, fine glassware and alabaster also affirm the importance of Takht-i Sangin as a Silk Road trading post.

Located on the border with Afghanistan, the site is quite challenging to visit without a permit and an escort (contact the National Parks Office in Dushanbe; *64 Druzhby Narodov*). It is reported that border guards often close the area to visitors without warning.

Utapur Fort Some 10km outside Shahrtuz, on the road towards Voroshilov, is the Utapur Fort, known to locals as Beshkent Kala. Dating from the 1600s, Utapur is unusual among forts in Tajikistan by virtue of the fact that it has a moat. As with the Kala-i Mir (see below), it was severely damaged by the Red Army, but it remains a pleasant spot to spend an hour and to picnic. The walls are reasonably well preserved and the fine stone carvings indicate the skilled craftsmanship used in the fort's construction.

Qabodiyon Named in honour of Kaboti Shahnour, a legendary king in Firdausi's *Shahnama* (Book of Kings), the modern town of Qabodiyon hides a Medieval gem: the **Kala-i Mir Fortress**. Covering 4ha, the fortress was occupied by local rulers until its destruction by the Red Army in 1921.

Although many of the archaeological finds are held by museums in Russia, the town **museum** has a few interesting pieces and the curator will also guide you around the fortress site. Unlike elsewhere in Tajikistan, no renovation has followed the excavation, but it is still possible to make out the gatehouses, strong defensive walls and living quarters.

The town is also known as the birthplace of the great Persian poet and religious philosopher Nasir Khusraw. Born in the year 1004, Khusraw's best-known work is also one of the world's oldest travel memoirs, *Safarnama*, which chronicles his journey through 11th-century Jerusalem, Mecca and Cairo. Qabodiyon is 12km north of Shahrtuz, on the main road to Qurgonteppa, and shared taxis from both towns can drop you along the way.

KURBON SHAHID *Telephone code: 03322*

Today Kurbon Shahid is a small and underwhelming town, but its impressive fortress (albeit a reconstruction of its historic self) makes it a must-see destination in Khatlon.

HISTORY Archaeologists and cartographers first began to study southern Tajikistan seriously in the 1870s, and they started to link physical territories and historical sites with ancient Buddhist texts.

The 4th-century AD Bactrian kingdom of Khuttal (also known as Takhristan) was mentioned in the writings of Chinese traveller Sjuan-Tszjan when he visited central Asia in 630. Its boundaries were initially determined by the Amu Darya and

Vakhsh rivers, but by the 10th century rulers were seeking alliances as far south as Balkh in Afghanistan. A number of prominent cities within the kingdom have been identified, but the centre of regional power was Khulbuk.

Khuttal reached the peak of its power between the 9th and 11th centuries. Khulbuk was strategically important and grew wealthy on the back of trade; both of these things necessitated the construction of strong defences to protect the town against invasion from the south.

Khulbuk's fortunes changed in the 11th century with the fall of the Samanids. Khuttal became a buffer state and was pillaged from both sides but particularly by the Karakhanids. Khulbuk was ravaged and never recovered.

The modern town of Kurbon Shahid exists because of the ruins, and the need to house archaeologists and labourers working on the site.

GETTING THERE Kurbon Shahid is situated on the main road midway between Danghara and Kulob, so it makes a good picnic stop when driving between Dushanbe and Kulob or between Kulob and Qurgonteppa. If you are travelling by minibus, take one of the main intercity routes and make sure the driver understands you want to alight partway and that he adjusts the fare accordingly. Shared taxis plying the route from both Dushanbe and Qurgonteppa to Kulob also pass through Kurbon Shahid.

WHAT TO SEE AND DO The **Khulbuk Fortress** is Kurbon Shahid's indisputable highlight. You round a bend in the road, your jaw drops, you slam on the brakes and squeal to a stop on the gravel in front of the gates. The massive structure has been completely rebuilt, a multi-year process, particularly given the scope of the project. Purists may baulk at the somewhat Disneyfied reconstruction, but it really helps you to see how impressive a structure of this size and strength must have been. The curator, who appears from nowhere in great excitement at the sight of a tourist, assured us that full excavations were undertaken before the builders were allowed to start.

The Khulbuk Fortress was built twice: the initial structure was destroyed by fire in the late 10th century but became the foundation for the subsequent building in the following century. The brick walls were originally coated with adobe plaster and, in the room that later became the palace mosque, this plaster was highly decorated with an ornate *mihrab*. In places it is still possible to see the Kufic script and original paving slabs.

The refurbished **Khulbuk museum** is immediately opposite the fortress, and it houses finds from the site and the accompanying information boards. Contact the curator (m *090 666 7766*) for information in English.

AROUND KURBON SHAHID
Vose Somewhat larger than Kurbon Shahid, Vose is the place to stop if you need a café or a basic shop. Rather more interestingly, the town is also the site of the **Khoja Mumin salt mountain**, a deposit more than 500m tall that is thought to contain at least 30 billion tonnes of salt. It's the second-largest salt mountain in the world, and Marco Polo describes it in his *Travels*. The salt is extracted commercially, but it's still possible to climb to the top for views across the valley.

KULOB *Telephone code: 03322*

With a tiny, bustling centre ringed by quiet residential suburbs, Kulob has the faraway feel of a city isolated in the middle of a continent. Literally translated as 'the swampy place', Kulob is nonetheless politically significant, as Rahmon was the city's governor before taking the presidency in 1992. Its population of 150,000 makes it one of Tajikistan's largest urban centres. Kulob is twinned with the Iranian city of Hamadan, as the poet born there, and after whom the city was named, is buried in Kulob (page 143). Residents are friendly and engaging, pleased to see outsiders in their corner of the world, and particularly embody the warm and welcoming attitude towards guests that pervades the country.

HISTORY The Kulob monument (on Ismoili Somoni) is supposed to celebrate 2,700 years of Kulob, but in reality the city you see today is almost entirely a 20th-century creation, its archaeological heritage well buried beneath the Soviet-era concrete. Historically Kulob was a settlement of some note, with a substantial-sized fortress. It is mentioned in the accounts of early travellers Ibn al-Atir and Saudi Ali Rais. The last king of Kulob (then known as Khatlon), Kai-Khatloni, fought for Timur on his campaigns in Afghanistan and achieved some local notoriety; his rule and that of his successors brought Kulob to regional prominence, and the city became the provincial capital in 1555. It was not strong enough to retain its independence, however, and it was incorporated into the khanate of Bukhara in the 16th century. Kulob continued to act as a buffer state between Bukhara and Afghanistan well into the 19th century when it briefly fell into the hands of the khan of Kokand, was destroyed and rebuilt, then returned to Bukharan control. After the Bolshevik Revolution, Kulob became a stronghold for Basmachi resistance fighters (see box, page 15) and remained so for several years after the rest of central Asia had fallen to the Red Army.

The Soviets industrialised Kulob and intensified farming in the province, focusing on cotton and cereal production in large-scale collective farms. After independence, the Kulobis were one of the main civil war factions, and they directed and undertook some of the greatest atrocities of the early 1990s, including ethnic cleansing and a scorched earth policy for rival territories. It was the former communist leader of Kulob, Emomali Rahmon (see box, page 18), who would rise to the top as Tajikistan's president in 1992, and many other members of government then and now hail from Kulob and the surrounding towns.

GETTING THERE AND AROUND There is an excellent new road between Dushanbe and Kulob with smooth tarmac. Local drivers do tend to speed along, but it's wide enough to keep out of their way. The minibus ride takes 3 hours and costs TJS25, while shared taxis cost TJS50. Minibuses and taxis drop off and pick up passengers from the large bus stand at the western end of Ismoili Somoni. Asian Express buses make the 5-hour trip from Dushanbe twice daily for TJS25 each way.

Numerous **minibuses** whizz up and down Ismoili Somoni and between the bus stand and the hospital. Expect to pay TJS0.60 per journey.

TRAVEL AGENTS There is an *aviakassa* at 1 Ismoili Somoni (⊕ ✆ 30 908; ⊕ 07.00–18.00). Though the service may be gruff and slow, the staff are in fact trying to be helpful. A second aviakassa is inside the **Eskhata Bank** building at 2 Ismoili Somoni and has the added bonus of being able to change currency if the bank has insufficient cash.

 WHERE TO STAY *Map, page 142.*

⌂ **Khatlon Hotel** 6 Ismoili Somoni; m (0902) 221 221. Large, Soviet-era hotel with stony-faced staff & the usual erratic plumbing. Rooms are overpriced for what they are, especially as foreigners pay almost 3 times the price as locals. Apts start from US$100. **$$$**

⌂ **Mahsus Guesthouse** 105 Borbat; m 091 843 8743. Away from the city centre, just along

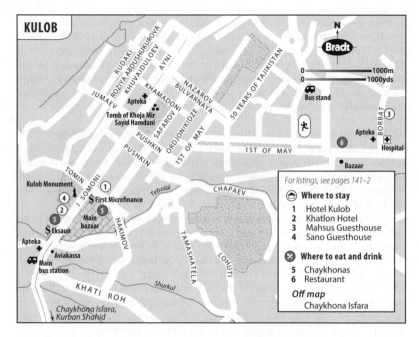

KULOB

For listings, see pages 141–2

Where to stay
1 Hotel Kulob
2 Khatlon Hotel
3 Mahsus Guesthouse
4 Sano Guesthouse

Where to eat and drink
5 Chaykhonas
6 Restaurant

Off map
Chaykhona Isfara

---

from the hospital, Mahsus has large, reasonably pleasant rooms & is generally quiet. Prices are a little high, but they will negotiate if you're staying for a while. **$$$**

Hotel Kulob 7 H Nazapov; m 091 881 3467. Close to the bazaar, this large, pink building has basic, slightly scruffy rooms off somewhat ominous corridors. The babushka standing guard is determined you'll wear the slippers provided

whether you want to or not. The big advantage to the Kulob is the secure parking in the gated compound to the rear. **$$**

Sano Guesthouse 11 Ismoili Somoni; m 091 771 7117. Tucked away from the main road on the lane that runs down the right-hand side of Hotel Khatlon, this small guesthouse is efficiently run by helpful staff. It's popular with NGO workers, so book in advance if you want to secure a room. **$**

✕ WHERE TO EAT AND DRINK *Map, above.*

The **main bazaar**, which is centred on the junction between Ismoili Somoni and H Nazapov, is the best place to buy bread and fresh produce, and there are also a number of *chaykhonas* serving cheap and simple fare. **Chaykhona Isfara ($$)**, near the railway station, has a breezy outdoor seating area with lovely, intricate woodwork on the ceiling and columns. As per usual, the grilled meats are tasty and the traditional Tajik bread is filling.

There is a slightly larger **restaurant** opposite the **small bazaar** by the hospital.

OTHER PRACTICALITIES

Medical Kulob is home to the large and relatively well-equipped **Kulob Regional Hospital** (*Borbat*) where it possible to get basic medical attention in the case of an emergency. There are a number of *apteka* along Ismoili Somoni, the most convenient of which is at number 48, and an additional one opposite the hospital building.

Money Tajikistan's major banks are all represented in Kulob. Most useful are **Tajprom Bank** (*5 Menzhinskogo*), **Agroinvest Bank** (*1 I Somoni*) and the tiny branch of **Eskhata Bank** (*2 I Somoni*), each with an ATM.

WHAT TO SEE AND DO The **tomb of Khoja Mir Sayid Hamdani** is a picturesque tiled structure with a golden dome set among pleasant gardens. Hamdani was an Iranian poet and Islamic missionary who died in Afghanistan but was buried here sometime in the 15th century. Pilgrims still visit the site to seek his blessing. There is a **small museum** alongside the tomb where it is possible to see several historic manuscripts, including Hamdani's own writings. The restoration of the mausoleum and museum was funded by the Iranian government. Admission is TJS15, but women are not allowed inside.

The large and slightly ostentatious **Kulob monument** was erected in 2006 to mark the 2,700th anniversary of Kulob's theoretical foundation. It's set in a pleasant square on Ismoili Somoni, close to the Hotel Khatlon. Expect to do battle with the wedding parties for the best photo-taking spots.

AROUND KULOB
Dashtijum Nature Reserve One of four official nature reserves in Tajikistan, Dashtijum is a relatively small area measuring just 450km² on the lower slopes of the Hazrati Shah Mountains, 77km by road to the northeast of Kulob. Vegetation in the reserve varies from deciduous forest to juniper bushes and its ecosystems support more than 200 species of vertebrates, including 51 types of mammal. Among the rarer species are the Tian Shan brown bear, snake eagles and the world's largest wild goat, the markhor. There are even occasional sightings of snow leopards. The nature reserve is located just outside the town of Dashtijum. Shared taxis depart

---

ENVER PASHA

In the dying days of the Ottoman Empire, a young revolutionary called Enver Pasha cut his military teeth fighting guerrillas in the Balkans, then rose to prominence as Turkey's Minister of War in World War I. His rallying cry to his troops was 'war until final victory'.

When the Russian Revolution took place in 1917, Turkey's Committee of Union and Progress (CUP), of which Enver was a founding member, befriended the Bolsheviks and sent its own troops into the Caucasus, where a power vacuum had been created by the withdrawal of Tsarist forces. Enver named his new army the Army of Islam.

Enver's fortunes changed with the end of the Great War. He was court-martialled *in absentia* for his role in the massacre of ethnic Armenians and condemned to death. Enver fled first to Germany, then offered his services to the Bolsheviks. He thought he could incite the Muslim world to join the revolution.

Lenin dispatched Enver first to Bukhara in 1921, and then to Tajikistan. Caught between his religious brethren and his paymasters, Enver switched sides and joined the *basmachi*. He led a successful attack on Dushanbe in February 1922 but failed to unite his forces and lost the city to the Red Army just five months later.

Enver was killed by the Bolsheviks in the summer of 1922. A truce had been called for Eid, but an informant betrayed Enver's location. He attempted to defend himself with a single machine gun but was shot by a sniper's bullet. The *basmachi* hid his body to prevent its capture, then later buried him alongside fellow fighter Davlat Mandbai in the village of Chagan. His body remained here until the Turkish government carted it back to Istanbul for a state funeral in 1995.

from the bus stand at Ismoili Somoni in Kulob and travel the 80km route to the town. It might be more feasible, however, to hire a private taxi in Kulob to take you directly to the reserve. As with other nature reserves in Tajikistan, entrance to the park requires a permit from the National Parks Office in Dushanbe (*64 Druzhby Narodov*). The permit costs US$40 per person and it is best to allow at least three days for it to be processed. There are no fixed working hours for the reserve, as there are not a lot of visitors, so the best course of action may be to arrive at the main entrance to the reserve at 08.00 or 09.00 on weekdays, when you should be able to arrange a visit with someone from the reserve's administration. There are no 'official' phone lines.

Khoviling About 40km north of Kulob, in a remote district with lush mountain valleys, is Khoviling. Though the town itself has little to offer, it's the stepping-off point for the **Hazrati Shah Mountains** and, in particular, the **Childukhtaran Nature Reserve**. A popular day trek will take you to the **40 Virgins Rocks**; legend has it that 40 young girls prayed for deliverance from the advancing Mongol troops and were turned into stone so that their bodies would forever stay pure. Shared taxis leave from Kulob, making the trip in just over an hour.

The village of **Obigarm** (not to be confused with the spring town of the same name; page 147) was the final battleground of Enver Pasha (see box, page 143) before he was killed by Bolshevik forces in 1922.

TAJIKISTAN ONLINE

For additional online content, articles, photos and more on Tajikistan, why not visit **w** bradtguides.com/tajikistan.

7

Karotegin

With a striking array of rocky, tree-studded cliffs, harrowing mountain passes and marshy river flats, the Karotegin Valley is a beautiful area of Tajikistan rarely seen by foreign eyes. Stretching to the east of Dushanbe and part of the hideously named Region of Republican Subordination (RRS), Karotegin, also known as the Rasht Valley, lies threaded by some of the thinner routes of the tourist trail, from Jirgatal on the Tajik–Kyrgyz border (currently closed to foreigners), or along the challenging northern branch of the Pamir Highway, through Tavildara and thence to Kalaikhum (Darvaz). The snow-capped peaks of the distant Pamirs guard the valley and its warm, engaging citizenry, who dwell in boxy apartment buildings along the main road or on traditional smallholdings which sprawl into the surrounding foothills. The western reaches of the Tajik National Park (see box, page 182) stray into the province, and the area is known for its wildlife, fishing and trekking.

The valley, and in particular Gharm, was the scene of intense fighting during the civil war. Though security has improved, families and buildings are notably scarred by the experience; the derelict factories, resistance hideouts and abandoned personnel carriers are poignant reminders of the violent past.

Minibuses and shared taxis to Faizobod, Obigarm and Gharm can be hired at the intersection of Adkhamov and Mirzo Rizo streets in the southwest part of Dushanbe and the 190km, 3-hour ride to Gharm costs TJS80–100. From Gharm, shared taxis to Tojikobod and the border cost an additional TJS50–80.

FAIZOBOD *Telephone code: 03135*

East of Dushanbe, the small town of Faizobod (alternatively, Faizabad) is a linear settlement that most visitors will only ever pass through. If you have your own transport, however, it's a pleasant diversion to leave the main road and spend an hour at the Sari Mazar shrine. Minibuses travel frequently through Faizobod *en route* from Dushanbe to Gharm, though you would then need to walk or co-opt a local driver to take you on to the shrine.

WHERE TO STAY AND EAT The only accommodation option in town is **Hotel Faizabod** (*47 Ismoili Somoni;* m *093 556 2086;* **$**). It's a small, well-run hotel on the main road with helpful staff. Singles are just TJS20. There is a small **restaurant** on the opposite side of the street.

OTHER PRACTICALITIES There are branches of **Agroinvest** and **Tajprom** banks by the bazaar, and also a **Megafon** office.

WHAT TO SEE AND DO The **Historical Museum** (*Park Pobedy, Ismoili Somoni;* m *093 459 2002;* ⏰ *10.00–17.00 Mon–Fri; TJS1*) is a small, local museum built

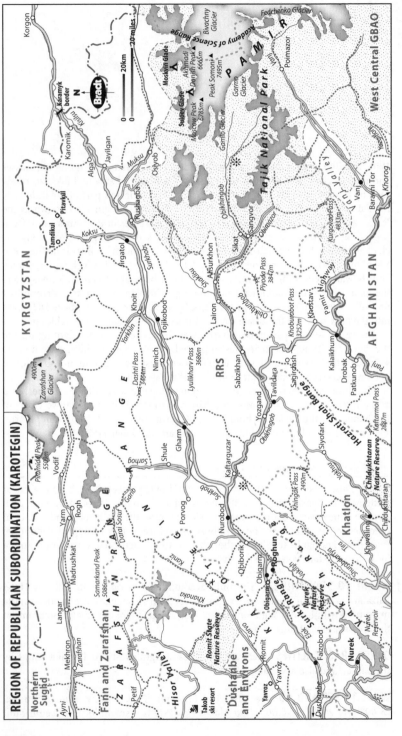

partially in the round, painted salmon pink and with attractively carved doors. Inside is a collection veering more towards the anthropological than historical, which includes items of clothing and jewellery, household goods and a few small items from archaeological sites.

Travelling east out of Faizobod, take the first road on the right as you leave the town, then follow the signs for **Sari Mazar**. Located up a short track behind the garage is the brick-built **mausoleum of Abu Abdurahmon** (AD761–852). A Sufi holy man from Balkh (now in Afghanistan), Abdurahmon was known locally for his piety. The tomb itself seems a more recent construction (though still of significant age) and it is well cared for, with a spotless interior and plenty of places to sit and reflect.

The brick tomb is kept locked, but the keyholder will appear almost straight away. Inside are two graves: the larger, shrouded casket belongs to Abdurahmon and the second is an unknown companion. The elderly and sick still come here to ask Abdurahmon for healing, and locals claim that their prayers are often answered. Whether or not you have an ailment that needs divine intervention, it's a pleasant place to picnic and break your journey, and the place undoubtedly has a feeling of peace.

OBIGARM *Telephone code: 03134*

Obigarm takes its name from the naturally occurring hot springs which are dotted across the area (*ob* meaning 'water'; *garm* meaning 'warm'). The largest business in the town is the Soviet-era **Sanatorium Obi Garm** (m *(0934) 514 4957*), which makes use of the water's supposedly curative properties. Rooms (which include all meals and treatments) start from TJS150 per day, and the doctors expect you to stay for at least a week to gain maximum benefit. Facilities include a variety of saunas and plunge pools, a fitness centre and, for reasons no-one could quite explain, a conference room.

Though one of the larger towns in the area, Obigarm has no visible signs of a café (despite three separate visits) and the shops stock only the most basic foodstuffs. Beware of the Coca-Cola imitation with the blue lid sold in several of the shops: it is flat and unbelievably vile. The **pharmacy**, **Tcell** and **Megafon** shops may come in handy, however.

If you are staying at the sanatorium, reception can arrange transport to and from Dushanbe. Alternatively, you can take the regular **minibus** service. Both the town and the sanatorium itself are clearly marked.

ROGHUN *Telephone code: 03134*

Roghun is the site of the biggest dam that never was. On the opposite side of the river from Obigarm are multicoloured but almost derelict housing blocks built to accommodate workers and their families who were engaged on the construction of the Roghun Dam. Though a few thousand people still live here, it is a community caught in limbo: construction ceased with the fall of the Soviet Union, and after a few subsequent false starts, finally resumed in late 2016.

The dam was first proposed in 1959 and it was intended to harness sufficient hydro-power to create 13.3 TWh of electrical power per year. At 334.98m (1,099ft) it would have been the tallest dam in the world (and more than 30m higher than the nearby Nurek Dam). History had other ideas. The Soviet Union fell, construction stopped at a little over 60m, and an earthquake, mudslide and flood washed even that away in 1993. A Tajik–Russian partnership agreement was signed in 2007 but later blocked by the Russian government, and when the Tajiks launched an initial public offering (IPO) to raise US$1.4 billion in 2010, they received just a fraction

That the Soviets built the Tursunzoda aluminium plant in spite of there being no alumina source of note in Tajikistan is testament to the phenomenal hydro-power potential of the country. Currently just 6% of the country's possible hydro-power is utilised.

The hydro-electric plants of Nurek (3,000MW generating capacity), Baipaza (600MW), Sangtuda 1 (670MW) and Sangtuda 2 (220MW), the latter two built with Russian and Iranian investment respectively, cumulatively go some way to securing energy independence and regulating water supplies. However, industrial development is still hampered by an acute energy shortage. The Roghun Dam (pages 147–8) is much needed by Tajikistan, but despite having been under construction intermittently since the late 1950s, it is only now on the verge of becoming operational. The first units are expected to start producing power in 2018.

In the past, hydro-power projects have frequently failed to live up to expectations and though they can deliver increased energy security, they can also destabilise diplomatic relations with countries downstream and cause significant environmental damage. If these downsides can be mitigated, however, Tajikistan could become an example of how heavy industry (in particular aluminium production) can be supported by clean energy rather than fossil fuels.

of the required sum. A joint French-Italian consortium is providing technical assistance to the dam's developer, which has indicated August 2018 as the time when the first units will go online.

Tajikistan's neighbours have mixed feelings about the project. Pakistan and Afghanistan are expected to purchase electricity generated by the dam, while the late Uzbek president Islam Karimov publicly called the Roghun Dam a 'stupid project' in 2010, accusing the dam of negatively impacting his country's cotton irrigation channels downstream.

Shortly after the village of **Darband** (renamed **Nurobod**, the 'Town Of Light', by excited local officials when it first received an electricity supply) the road crosses the river and then forks. The main road continues south to **Tavildara** (page 150), and the northern road goes to **Gharm**, **Jirgatal** and the Tajik–Kyrgyz border, which is closed to anyone but Tajik and Kyrgyz nationals. Close to the junction are **three interlinking fortresses**, grassy hillocks from the top of which are great views towards the Pamirs.

GHARM   *Telephone code: 03131*

As with most of the towns in the valley, Gharm is a linear development along the road with a relatively small population: many people fled during the civil war; others have left for Dushanbe or Russia in search of work. Still, passers-by can find bustling activity around the town's one and only bazaar, situated on the main street. There is a basic **Mountain Societies Development Support Programme (MSDSP) guesthouse** (*51 Saimuddin Burkhon*), which charges US$20 per person including breakfast.

TOJIKOBOD   *Telephone code: 03154*

With an alpine ambience and a friendly populace, Tojikobod (alternatively spelt Tajikabad) is an altogether more satisfying town, and a better place to overnight,

At 7,495m, Peak Somoni is the highest mountain in Tajikistan, and in the former Soviet Union. On its first ascent in 1933 it was named Peak Stalin, then later Peak Communism, before its current name was settled upon in 1998. Ismoili Somoni was the 9th-century ruler of the Samanid Dynasty, who rejected Zoroastrianism in favour of Islam. He is somewhat of a national hero.

The first ascent of Peak Somoni was completed in September 1933 by Yevgeniu Abalakov from the Tajik–Pamir research expedition via the Bivachnyi Glacier route. Interestingly, Abalakov was a sculptor as well as an alpinist. He died in mysterious circumstances in Moscow in 1948 while preparing for an ascent on Peak Victory, the highest mountain in the Tian Shan range. It would be nearly another 30 years before a foreign team reached the top of Peak Somoni.

Today mountaineers typically take the half-hour helicopter flight from Jirgatal and then make their base camp either at Suloev or Moskvin glades, from which they can climb both Peak Somoni and Peak Korgenevskiy (7,105m). Two permanent buildings were established at Suloev by a team from the Tajik Academy of Sciences in the 1970s, though a seasonal camp is also constructed each year at Moskvin. It operates only between July and September.

The two most popular routes to the summit are Stormy Petrel's ridge, and a shorter route from the Walter Glacier along Borodkin's ridge to the Alp Navruz base camp (4,200m). Both options require a combination of rock, snow and ice climbing, and they are suitable only for experienced climbers. You will require the assistance of a competent guide, most likely brought out from Dushanbe.

---

than Gharm. Situated in the middle of a farming region, the town is on the opposite side of the river from the main road, granting visitors picturesque views of the surrounding mountain peaks. There is a comfortable government **guesthouse** above the town's singular municipal building, with triple and quadruple rooms on offer (**$**).

WHAT TO SEE AND DO There are two shrines located within the town limits of Tojikobod. The **Mazor-i Fathabad**, located inside a cemetery about 1km from the municipal building, remembers an 18th-century Sufi holy man known for his good works. Meanwhile, the **Hazrat-i Bir Pustin**, a mere 200m west of the municipal building, commemorates a Sufi saint who gave away all his worldly possessions, save for a mythical leather coat which would grow wool in the winter months, protecting him from the cold. Neither of the shrines is particularly elaborate, and women are not permitted to enter.

A rather better excursion is to drive up into the **Nushor Valley** to the east of the town. It is exceptionally beautiful, particularly in the late spring, and is home to a substantial amount of wildlife, including bear, wolf, deer, and even occasional snow leopard.

JIRGATAL *Telephone code: 03132*

Jirgatal is the final town on the road before you reach the Tajik–Kyrgyz border, which is 25km to the east. Opened to foreigners in 2012–13, the border is currently closed indefinitely to anyone other than Tajik and Kyrgyz nationals. For details on the border crossing, see *Practical information*, pages 27–62.

Jirgatal has two **guesthouses** side by side (**$**), and they both provide meals on request. There is a small **airstrip** in the town, from which chartered helicopters fly to Peak Somoni.

TAVILDARA   *Telephone code: 03156*

There would be little, if any, reason to come to Tavildara if it weren't for the fact it's on the way to Kalaikhum. We have a certain fondness for it, however, as on our first trip to Tajikistan back in 2010 we departed the **MSDSP guesthouse** (**$**) in torrential rain, only to find that the road had vanished just south of the town. We followed the tracks down into the riverbed (itself no mean feat), only to go 10m or so and sink. We were up to our axles in mud, and there was nothing at all we could do about it.

Soaked to the skin, mud-splattered, in Max's case heavily bearded (we were on our way to Afghanistan), and generally looking like vagrants, we hailed a passing car that happened to be carrying an army officer. We could tell this as there was just a single, uniformed man and his driver inside, while four lower-ranking individuals were left to jog along behind. He was coerced into towing us out of our predicament, but at the critical moment the tow rope snapped (be sure always carry a spare), pinging back violently and denting his paintwork.

The ordinary soldiers, unwilling to leave a job half done, then began to dig out the wheels and lay down rocks while their boss peered out through his increasingly steamy window, less than pleased at the delay. We eventually pushed the car to drier ground and waved goodbye, only to round the next bend and find the same vehicle had blown a tyre. The officer was ready to explode, particularly as our grubby paws were now required to heave his own car up the hill to safety.

AROUND TAVILDARA The village of **Sangor** to the east of Tavildara was a hideout for opposition fighters during the civil war. It is particularly associated with the resistance commander Jumabai Khujayev Namangani, an Uzbek from the Fergana Valley who joined forces with the Islamic Revival Party and fought numerous battles until 1997 when he entered Afghanistan to join the militant Islamic Movement of Uzbekistan. There are some scenic informal **hiking routes** in the surrounding hills, though it is wise to take a local guide as the area was heavily mined during the civil war, and not all the mines have been removed.

FOLLOW BRADT

For the latest news, special offers and competitions, subscribe to the Bradt newsletter via the website **w** bradtguides.com and follow Bradt on:

- BradtTravelGuides
- @BradtGuides
- @bradtguides
- bradtguides

8

West-Central Gorno-Badakhshan

Geographically and culturally it often seems that Tajikistan is a country of two halves: the lowlands in the west, and the Pamirs in the east. Any murmurings about the beauty or scale of the Fann and Zarafshan fade away when compared with the appropriately named 'Roof of the World'.

Tajikistan's hardiest travellers come to Gorno-Badakhshan Autonomous Oblast (GBAO). It's both a desirable destination in its own right, particularly for trekkers and mountaineers, and also the popular route through to Afghanistan and Kyrgyzstan. Ruined fortresses, shrines, and villages seemingly cleft out of the rock line the banks of the River Panj, which is also the imposing physical border with Afghanistan, while inland valleys offer some of the most spectacular and physically demanding treks in the country. The Wakhan Corridor is one of the last great wildernesses, and an awe-inspiring destination however you travel there.

Though GBAO is a place of great natural beauty, it is also the poorest part of Tajikistan. Discontent simmers, particularly between the local population and the state – a relic of the civil war in the 1990s when Pamiris in particular were targeted – and so you are advised to keep abreast of the latest security advice.

KALAIKHUM

Kalaikhum's alternative name, Darvaz, means 'gateway', which is fitting as this is undoubtedly the gateway to the Pamirs. The town is at an altitude of 1,200m, and the Panj River changes direction here, making a gigantic U-turn, with Tajikistan to the north and Afghanistan, now just spitting distance away, to the south.

Few people seem to live in Kalaikhum, but everyone passes through. The *chaykhona* on the bridge, scruffy as it is, has one of the most perfect settings in Tajikistan, poised overlooking the confluence of the Panj and Khumbob rivers. The *shashlik* is really rather good, and the break from the journey welcome. We've spent several happy hours here watching the waters swirl and small, semi-clad boys dive off the rocks for what must be one of the chilliest baths around. If you need to stay the night, there are several **homestays** nearby: ask at the *chaykhona*, or book in advance through **PECTA** (page 157). There is also an **MSDSP guesthouse ($)** just to the south of the town.

AROUND KALAIKHUM The village of **Yoged** lies 30km from Kalaikhum on the road from Kulob. In addition to a **small museum**, there are **four small shrines**, each several hundred years old. The shrines (*oston* in the local dialect) are dedicated to holy men, most likely sufis or Ismaili pirs. There are two **homestays** in the village: it is not possible to pre-book them as they have neither email nor phone lines. You will have to ask locally.

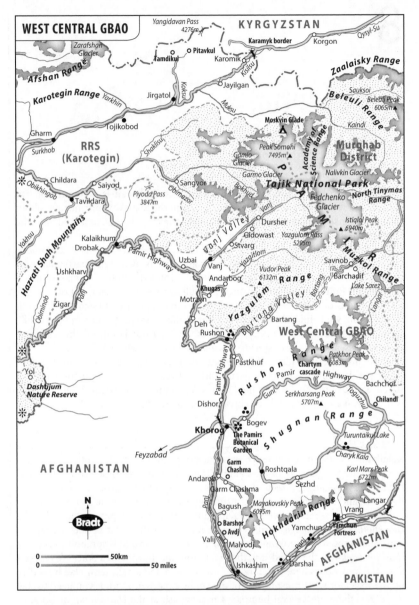

To the south, the wide and fertile **Vanj Valley** makes an attractive detour from the main road and is also the site of several good day-long treks. It is the northernmost of what are known as Tajikistan's great valleys, and runs a distance of 100km fairly straight up to the **Fedchenko Glacier**, the longest non-polar glacier in the world. The upper reaches of the valley are part of the **Tajik National Park** (see box, page 182), and it is the most common access route for ascents of Peak Ismoili Somoni, which at 7,495m is the highest mountain in Tajikistan.

The opportunities here for **mountaineering and glacier trekking** are superb, although, as even parts of the valley floor are at an altitude in excess of 3,000m, you might need to allow yourself time to acclimatise before starting to trek or climb. If you stick to the roads, you will miss out on the chance to see the valley's flora and fauna up close, but there are a few notable cultural sites: look out in particular for the ancient *dashtirogh* (burial ground) shortly before Vanj town and the ruins of a fort at Gidowast. The **shrine at Poi Mazor,** the last village in the valley, may not look like much, but local tradition holds it as the final resting place of Hazrat Ali (c607–61), the son-in-law of the Prophet Muhammad.

From Vanj Valley it is also possible to trek to the neighbouring Bartang Valley (see below).

RUSHON AND THE BARTANG VALLEY

The district capital, Rushon, is also known as Vomar, and you may see this alternative name on some maps. If you have the time it is worthwhile stopping here and also, if you're into impressive views, heading up further into the Bartang Valley. The Bartang River is part of the longest river system in the GBAO region: it starts at the Aksu at Shaymak in the southeast of the Pamirs, crosses the Murghab Plateau and runs into Lake Sarez, which in turn drains into the river running along the Bartang Valley to Rushon, where it empties into the Panj.

The people in this valley would make a fascinating anthropological study. In spite of the fact that Bartang was physically cut off, part of the population shows clear Caucasian genetic characteristics, including blonde and red hair, which is in distinct contrast with the darker, Mongolic features of their neighbours. They have maintained strong, distinctive local traditions of music and dance, and if you are staying in one of the homestays (page 154) on the occasion of a festival or other important celebration such as a wedding, you might well see a performance first-hand.

GETTING THERE The Bartang Valley is exceptionally narrow, and well into the 20th century, the only way to travel along it was in a succession of *ovrings*: baskets on wires attached to the cliffs. Thankfully access has since improved and there is a road of sorts, though you will still require a 4x4 if you want to get to the upper reaches.

If you do not have your own vehicle, you will need to start (and end) your trip to the Bartang Valley from Khorog (pages 156–63). **Minibuses** run once a day to Bashid (*TJS60*) and more frequently to Rushon (*TJS40*). It is also possible to **hire**

BARTANG BOATS

The summer months see a rather unusual mode of transport come into use in the upper reaches of the Bartang Valley: the Bartang boat. Most famously used by Alexander the Great and his forces to cross the Oxus in 329BC, the technology is unchanged in more than 2,000 years.

The boat is prepared by beheading and skinning a goat, then sewing up its various orifices. The skin is then inflated by blowing into a small opening on one of the legs, thus creating an inflatable raft.

You ride the boat lying on your stomach, holding on tightly around the goat's neck. You paddle ferociously with your legs to steer, and allow the buoyant skin to transport you in the current downstream. As you might imagine, it takes a certain amount of skill, and those less accomplished in the art get very, very wet.

8

a car and driver to take you there and back, for which you should budget at least US$400 if you want to travel the full length of the valley. A 4x4 vehicle, though not essential, is highly recommended and will greatly increase your comfort. You can book these from the stores in Kalaikhum (page 151), which are stocked with basic foodstuffs.

🏠 **WHERE TO STAY AND EAT** There are a number of **homestays ($)** in the valley, and the hot tea, warm smiles and beds are incredibly welcome at the end of a long day's trek or drive. There are two homestays in **Bashid**, three in **Savnob** and two at **Bardara**. We have also heard reports of another homestay in the **Devlokh Valley**, though have not visited this ourselves.

If you are staying at a homestay, your breakfast and evening meal will be provided. There are no other places to purchase food: if you are camping or want snacks to eat in between meals, you will need to bring supplies with you.

OTHER PRACTICALITIES You will need a trekking guide to get the most out of the valley. The best source of these is **PECTA** in Khorog (see page 157).

Check with a travel agent prior to trekking to **Lake Sarez**, for this typically requires a *propusk* (permission) in addition to your GBAO permit. This can be

---

TREKKING TO LAKE SAREZ

Treks focused on Lake Sarez (3,263m) start in Barchadif, the last settlement where you'll find a homestay.

The first day of the trek takes you south along the Murghab River and to the vast, natural dam at Usoi, the village now buried beneath the rockfall. It is possible to return from here to Barchadif if you only have time for a short trek, though most people prefer to continue round the lake to Irkht. There are two variations to this part of the route: a boat trip across the water to Zaval, or the strenuous and vertigo-inducing climb over the Marchansoi Pass.

Irkht was once a meteorological station, but little indication of this now remains. It's another day's hard walk up the Langar River to Vykhinch and thence the three headlike lakes at Uchkul. There is another steep climb, this time to the Langar–Kutal Pass (4,630m), from where it is 20km to the summer pastures at Langar (not to be confused with Langar in the Wakhan Corridor). You'll be welcomed with bread and tea, and possibly fresh ewes' milk too.

Langar lies just below the Yashilkul, one of the four largest lakes in the Pamirs. The final leg of the trek winds its way down the river valley to Bachchor at the northeastern end of the Gunt Valley. The path rejoins the road at Bachchor, whence it is 22km back to the Pamir Highway or 116km to Khorog. We would advise driving.

To complete this trek you will need detailed topographical maps of the area. The best currently available ones are those produced by the Soviet military, and thankfully the topography of the area has changed little since they were drawn up. You can download the complete set from Mapstor (**w** *mapstor.com*) for €48. They go down to 1:50,000 scale.

Maps are no substitute for a competent guide who knows the local area and can read the conditions on the mountains. You should contact PECTA (page 157) or Pamir Silk Travel (page 158), both of which are in Khorog, to get a reliable recommendation.

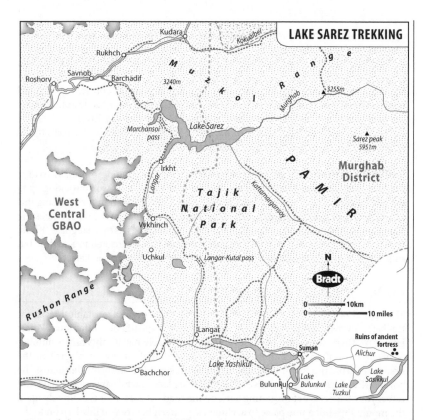

arranged through travel agents in Khorog (pages 157–8) or obtained directly from the **Committee for Emergency Situations and Civil Defence** (*26 Lahuti, Dushanbe;* *(0372) 211 331*). You will need to apply at least ten days in advance of your intended date of travel to Lake Sarez to ensure that the permit is processed in time. As we go to press, we've had news that it may be difficult for foreigners to get a permit to visit Sarez. Contact the tourist office in Khorog (page 157) regarding the latest availability of permits.

WHAT TO SEE AND DO In Rushon town there are **two shrines** which are associated with Shoh Tolib and Sayyid Jalol Bukhari, the missionaries credited with spreading Ismaili Islam in this part of the Pamirs. Jalol Bukhari (also known as Jalaluddin Surkh-Posh Bukhari) was an exceptionally well-travelled figure for his time: he was born in Bukhara in 1199 and lived well into his 90s, preaching not only in central Asia but deep into the Indian subcontinent. It is said that he met Nasiruddin Mahmud, Sultan of Delhi, and also that he heavily influenced the Kashmiri mystic and poet Lalleshwari, or Lal Ded.

The best way to explore the Bartang Valley is on foot, and you will need a local guide to get the most out of the trek. Almost every village has its own shrine or fortress, each with accompanying legends. The most important of these is the Bobo Alisho shrine at Bartang, another supposed tomb of Ali, which has an attractive carved wooden alcove. There is a 19th-century fortress at Roshorv, though it is not of any particular historical or architectural note, and there is a shrine in the village of Savnob. The shrine's name, Hozirbosht, means 'be prepared', and as it lies opposite a cave complex which was used as a place of refuge in times of attack by marauding Kyrgyz, the name is probably quite appropriate.

Up above the shrine are the ruins of a **fortress**, said to have been built by Hasan. Legend has it that Hasan was the preferred builder of the King of Khorasan, and when he finished the king's fortress there, his right hand was cut off so that he could not repeat the work for anyone else. Luckily for Hasan, he was equally able with his left hand, and built his own castle here, overlooking the Bartang River.

Not far past Savnob, the village of Barchadif is the starting point for treks to the spectacular but ultimately doomed **Lake Sarez** (see box, page 154).

AROUND RUSHON Half an hour's drive south of Rushon along the main road is Pastkhuf, with its **ruined fortress** in the hills above the village. It's worth walking up to the fort (there are clear views along the valley, no doubt the reason for choosing this as a defensive position) and also to the Mustansiri shrine. One of the most interesting things about Pastkhuf (and its sister village, Khuf) is that it has its own language, Khufi, spoken nowhere else. It's a Pamiri language, and quite closely related to Shughni, but sufficiently distinct to be classed as a separate language rather than a dialect.

KHOROG *Telephone code: 03522*

The capital of GBAO is the liveliest city in the Pamirs and a veritable Mecca for trekkers, cyclists and overlanders traversing the justifiably infamous Pamir Highway. There are plenty of places to stay, reasonable restaurants and a number of excursion options including the world's second-highest botanical garden, the first car to cross the Pamirs, and the Afghan–Tajik market on the bridge across the border. Khorog is an easy, relatively comfortable place to while away a few days and refuel your batteries before getting back on the road. At 2,042m it is definitely up in the mountains, but a fine place to acclimatise yourself before you head up on to the Murghab Plateau and the Great Pamirs.

HISTORY Prior to the 19th century, Khorog was a minor settlement on the Gunt riverbank, the possession of a succession of local rulers. The population expanded substantially with the construction of a Russian garrison following the signing of the 1896 Anglo–Russian–Afghan Border Treaty, and again when it became the provincial capital in 1925.

Since independence Khorog has had mixed fortunes. Economic collapse and the blockade of the Pamirs during the civil war led to a wide-scale exodus among Khorog's younger population, but the city has been experiencing a revival since the establishment of a University of Central Asia campus in 2003 (page 22) and the influx of money brought by foreign tourists. Of all the towns and cities in Tajikistan, Khorog feels most like it's part of the overland backpacker trail, and you might well want to spend a few days chilling out here, especially before or after tackling the challenges of the Murghab Plateau.

GETTING THERE AND AWAY

By road There are two routes between Dushanbe and Khorog: the slightly shorter northern road goes via Tavildara, but is poorly maintained and closed in winter; and the smoother southern road through Kulob which is open (avalanches permitting) all year round.

On a good run, the 525km drive takes between 16 and 18 hours. If you are driving yourself, you should break frequently, ideally stopping overnight *en route*, as the slightest catnap or error of judgement will see you and your passengers plunge unceremoniously to your deaths. This is not an exaggeration. You will be physically and mentally exhausted when you reach your destination, whichever route you choose.

Travelling by public transport, minibuses and taxis leave at first light to maximise the daylight hours available for driving. Providing your minibus doesn't suffer a puncture or other form of breakdown (seemingly a rite of passage on this road), you arrive not long before midnight. The fare is TJS250 and buses depart most days from Dushanbe's Badakhshan bus stand at the corner of Ayni and Ahmad Donish. Add an extra TJS100 if you're travelling in a shared taxi. The ride is uncomfortable and you should satisfy yourself before leaving as to the safety of both the vehicle and its driver. Insist that he – and you – take regular breaks along the way.

To travel from Khorog to Ishkashim, minibuses take 3 hours and cost TJS50. They leave from the bus stand by the bazaar at the western end of Somoni. It's a relatively easy drive, with interesting diversions to the hot springs at Garm Chashma (page 163) and the ruby mines (page 163).

The drive along the Pamir Highway to Murghab follows the Gunt Valley, then climbs towards the Murghab Plateau. The journey takes 9 hours and, if you're travelling by minibus, it costs TJS80. The minibuses leave from the stand to the east of the bazaar and only leave when full. If you want to speed up the departure, you may be able to pay for the empty seats, and this will also give you a bit more room. You could instead hire a car.

By air Tajik Air operates a daily flight between Dushanbe and Khorog for approximately US$100 per person. It is one of the most spectacular flights on earth, soaring just above the mountain peaks before virtually nosediving on to the narrow airstrip between the river and Somoni. The downside is that with the slightest flurry of snow, rain or fog the flights are cancelled, often causing days of delay as passengers are shunted from one scheduled flight to the next. There is also only a maximum of 16 passengers on any one flight, so getting on board can be hard, especially if the previous day's flight was cancelled. Tickets can theoretically be booked online via the Tajik Air website (w *tajikair.tj*), but you are more likely to get one if you ask a local ticketing agent to book you a seat in advance, or buy at ticket at the ticketing office at the airport the day before you wish to fly.

GETTING AROUND Khorog is a relatively compact town, and most places you'd want to go to are within easy walking distance. The extremities are the **Serena Inn** (5km west of the main town) and the **botanical gardens** (5km to the east), though in reality you'll spend the bulk of your time in the few blocks either side of Central Park.

Khorog is well served by both **minibuses** and **shared taxis**. The most useful of these is minibus #3, which runs from the bazaar, across the river to the south side of the town, then east to the botanical gardens. The journey costs TJS1–2 (TJS10 if you prefer a taxi).

TOURIST INFORMATION AND TOUR OPERATORS The **Pamir Eco-Cultural Tourism Association** (PECTA) (*10 Elchibek;* m *093 442 5555;* e *info@pecta.tj;* w *pecta.tj*) has its main office and information centre in Khorog. It's a non-commercial organisation set up with the support of the Aga Khan Foundation to support tourism and economic development in the Pamirs. It provides comprehensive tourist information, rents out equipment such as tents, sleeping bags and climbing gear, and can arrange homestay accommodation, guides and onward transport into the mountains.

HIRING A CAR

Hiring a car in GBAO actually means hiring a car and driver. The advantages are that the drivers tend to know the roads and the foibles of their particular vehicle and will be responsible for fixing it when it inevitably breaks down or blows a tyre; the downsides are that you'll be paying for the driver's food and accommodation not only while you travel but also any days you spend away from the vehicle (for example time spent sightseeing or trekking), and on the driver's return journey. This is the case regardless of whether or not you are still in the car as he drives back.

You need to hire a 4x4 vehicle. Though you might want a Land Rover or a Toyota Land Cruiser, the reality is that your choice is likely to be limited to a Lada Niva (small but with surprisingly good suspension and greater fuel efficiency) or a larger, clunkier Russian-made jeep. Check the vehicle over yourself before agreeing to any journey (page 44) and make sure there is both a spare tyre and at least one jerrycan of additional fuel as it can be hard to come by once you leave Khorog.

You will need to agree a price before leaving, and be explicit about what that price includes. Hiring a car is slightly more expensive in Khorog than in Murghab, but making arrangements here does at least guarantee you an onward ride, as vehicles in Murghab can be in short supply. The price will be determined by the type of vehicle and the current fuel price. Make sure it also includes any repairs, extra time due to breakdowns, and the driver's expenses. At the time of going to print, you are looking at a minimum of US$0.75 per kilometre, so it's advisable to find travelling companions heading the same way (the Pamir Lodge is a good bet for this) so that you can split the bill between you.

There are also a number of private travel agencies providing a reliable service:

Pamir Alpine Club 10 Lenin; m 093 542 7339; e pamirguides@gmail.com. Also known as the Pamir Guides Association, this is best organisation to contact if you are intending to climb in the Pamirs. It provides specialist mountain guiding services, including to professional climbers, & is well placed to advise on ascent attempts on any of Tajikistan's peaks.

Pamir Silk Travel 1 Azizbek; ☏ 22 299; e info@ pamirsilk.travel; w pamirsilk.travel. A well-run, professional outfit specialising in adventure tourism & expeditions, including supporting summit attempts. Owner Shagarf is especially helpful.

Safar Drivers' Association 68 Jomi; ☏ 22 035; e assafar@yandex.ru; w visitpamirs.com/ drivers-association. This drivers' co-operative is a good option for cars & drivers if you're heading up to Murghab or the Kyrgyz border. Their prices are fixed & are listed on the website, so you won't have any nasty surprises, & they also make suggestions for tours.

Tour de Pamir Lenin; m 093 500 7557; e tourdepamir@yahoo.com; w tourdepamir.com. This company arranges 5-, 8- & 9-day tours of the Pamirs.

 WHERE TO STAY *Map, page 160.*

Khorog is the only place in the Pamirs with a wide range of accommodation options. From the tranquil Serena Inn with its gardens running down to the river, to the family-run homestays south of the river, there's something for every budget. Khorog has a good range of homestays, most of which are situated within easy walking distance of the bazaar. All of them charge around US$10 per person (*US$15 with meals*) and can be booked through PECTA (page 157). Expect basic toilets and bathrooms,

In July 2012, the murder of a high-ranking local official led to serious fighting. The Tajik government launched a military operation in GBAO, centred on Khorog, on 24 July in which a number of civilians were killed and others injured. A ceasefire was called from 26 to 28 July, during which time foreigners were evacuated from the area. Twenty-two British and Commonwealth nationals were evacuated by helicopter and by diplomatic car, a major undertaking by the embassies and the Aga Khan Development Network (AKDN). All GBAO permits were cancelled during this period, and no more were issued until October 2012, effectively prohibiting all foreigners from travelling in the Pamirs. The Foreign and Commonwealth Office advised against all travel to the area.

Subsequent to this there have been occasional incidences of violence along the border – most recently in 2014 when there was a clash between drug smugglers and border forces.

Though the situation has now stabilised and both the Tajik government and foreign embassies are happy for tourists to again visit the area, you should seek advice from your embassy prior to travel and keep abreast of news reports before and during your stay.

but warm hospitality and lively charades. We stayed with the wonderful **Lalmo Muborakkadamova** (*61/10 Bandaliev;* ☎*26 999*) and would certainly do so again.

☗ **Serena Inn** (6 rooms) Tem; ☎ 23 228; e reservations.kci@serena.com.tj; w serenahotels. com. Built to accommodate the Aga Khan on his visit to Khorog, the Serena is a boutique hotel that infuses traditional Pamiri architecture, artworks & textiles with proper bathrooms, crisp linens & quiet, understated service. It feels like you're staying in someone's home. There is a restaurant but it's not always open; room service is the alternative option. B/fast inc. Highly recommended. **$$$$**

☗ **Hotel Delhi Darbar** (10 rooms) 2 Azizbek; ☎ 21 299; e khorog@delhidarbar.in; w delhidarbar.in. Situated above the excellent restaurant of the same name (page 160), the hotel has large, clean rooms & good private bathrooms & is right in the town centre. **$$$**

☗ **Hotel Parinen** (9 rooms) 193 Lenin; ☎ 25 417; e parinen_hotel@mail.ru. Parinen is the next best thing if your budget won't stretch to the Serena, but call ahead, as it frequently gets booked up. In this family-run guesthouse the rooms are clean, as

are the shared bathrooms, & the riverside garden is the perfect setting to enjoy a quiet beer. **$$$**

☗ **Lal Hotel** (9 rooms) 5/1 Azizbekov; ☎ 29 192; e lalhotel@inbox.ru; w lalhotel.tj. Warm & welcoming guesthouse with colourful embroideries & carpets lining the walls. Rooms are clean, as are the shared bathrooms. Laundry service available. B/fast inc. **$$**

☗ **Pamir Lodge** (6 rooms) 46 Gagarin; m 091 948 8958; e pamirlodge@hotmail.com; w pamirlodge.com. The most popular spot for backpackers, Pamir Lodge is south of the river & a short walk from the bazaar. It's our first choice when we stay in Khorog. It shares its premises with the local Ismaili prayer hall, so if you're lucky you might catch a late-night concert with traditional (if somewhat mournful-sounding) songs. It charges US$9 pp if you are in a dbl or tpl room, & the rooms are clean & comfortable. Alternatively, you can choose to sleep out on the veranda or pitch your tent in the garden (*US$5*). Bathrooms are basic & shared. **$**

✗ **WHERE TO EAT AND DRINK** *Map, page 160.*

Khorog has struck down two of our travelling companions with unbelievably bad food poisoning on two different trips, so this section should probably come with

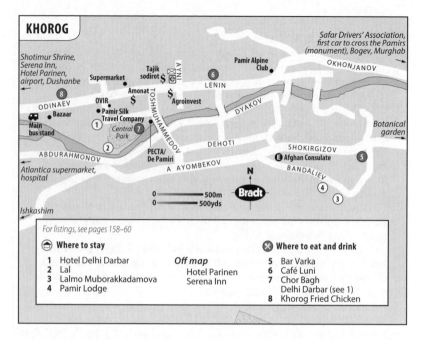

KHOROG

Shotimur Shrine,
Serena Inn,
Hotel Parinen,
airport, Dushanbe

Supermarket

Tajik
sodirot

AYNI

Pamir Alpine
Club

Safar Drivers' Association,
first car to cross the Pamirs
(monument), Bogev, Murghab

OKHONJANOV

6

LENIN

ODINAEV

Amonat

OVIR

Pamir Silk
Travel Company

Bazaar

Main
bus stand

1

Central
Park

2

TOSHMUHAMMEDOV

Agroinvest

DYAKOV

7

PECTA/
De Pamiri

DEHOTI

A AYOMBEKOV

N

SHOKIRGIZOV

Afghan Consulate

BANDALIEV

5

Botanical
garden

ABDURAHMONOV

Atlantica supermarket,
hospital

Ishkashim

0 ——— 500m
0 ——— 500yds

Bradt

4

3

For listings, see pages 158–60

Where to stay

1 Hotel Delhi Darbar
2 Lal
3 Lalmo Muborakkadamova
4 Pamir Lodge

Off map

Hotel Parinen
Serena Inn

Where to eat and drink

5 Bar Varka
6 Café Luni
7 Chor Bagh
    Delhi Darbar (see 1)
8 Khorog Fried Chicken

a word of caution. If you have any suspicions about what you're eating, leave it.
The cafés responsible were Bar Varka (*cnr Bandalieva & Gagarin*) and the in-house
restaurant at the Serena Inn, though on other occasions we've happily dined and
had no adverse effects. It's basically luck of the draw.

We have eaten safely, and with relish, at **Delhi Darbar** (*2 Azizbek;* ⊕ *11.00–22.00;*
$$$) and would probably say they do the best naans and paratha outside the Indian
subcontinent, though virtual starvation for the three weeks prior to our visit may
have contributed somewhat to this superlative assessment. The butter chicken was
also good, as was the daal, and it washed down particularly well with Baltica beer.

Chor Bagh, the Serena's other restaurant, has a superb location in Central Park,
and you can choose to sit inside or in the garden overlooking the river. The latter is
infinitely preferable if the weather is warm enough. The continental menu is a little
on the bland side, service is agonisingly slow and it's also quite expensive (**$$$–
$$$$**), but you're paying for the location. If you need to impress a date, this is the
place to take them.

KFC (Khorog Fried Chicken) (⊕ 10.00–late Mon–Sat), opposite New Bazaar
gate serves good, safe fast food (**$**). **Café Luni**, opposite University of Central Asia
central campus, has passable filter coffee and hot snacks; opening times vary.

There are a number of **small cafés** serving snacks on Lenin, and you can also pick
up food either from the **supermarket** next to the university, or from the **bazaar** in
the west of the town.

SHOPPING Khorog has several options for shopping, both for souvenirs and for
items of a more urbane nature. The **bazaar** at the west end of Lenin has a mixture
of Tajik and Afghan goods (including flat Afghan hats), and there are several small
shops around Central Park selling postcards and other trinkets. The best selection
of souvenirs is at **De Pamiri** (*Central Park;* w *pamirs.org/handicrafts/index.htm;*
⊕ *loosely 10.00–17.30 Mon–Sat, but be prepared to pop back several times*), a

HOW TO ESCAPE A MINEFIELD

Some parts of Tajikistan are heavily mined, a sad legacy of the Soviet invasion of Afghanistan in 1979 and the ensuing war against the Mujahideen. Although some landmine clearance has taken place and organisations such as the Swiss Foundation for Mine Action (w *fsd.ch*) are continuing to identify and make safe sites where mines are known to have been laid, border areas (specifically the banks of the Panj River) remain high risk and you should exercise utmost caution when walking in these areas.

Minefields in Tajikistan are often unmarked: records were not always kept of where mines were laid, and with rockfalls and meltwater constantly moving the earth downstream, landmines can in any case move substantial distances from their original locations. If a site is marked, it may only be with crosses, occasional signposts (not necessarily within view) or piles of rocks painted red on one side. You should avoid walking or camping at all on the riverbanks unless you are sure that they are free of mines. You should also keep your distance from abandoned military hardware and avoid undergrowth where you cannot see where you are treading. Bathing in the shallows of the river is also not recommended. If in doubt, ask local people: they will be the most reliable source of information about where it is and is not safe to tread.

If you fear you have stepped into a minefield try to keep calm and think. Stay where you are and look around you. Do not pick anything up. Survey your surroundings for any suspicious objects: although the mines would originally have been buried, wires or pieces of metal may now be visible above the surface. Also, look for anomalies in the terrain: are there any lumps and bumps of earth that may signify something is buried just below the surface?

Having surveyed the area, you need to backtrack along the route you used, stepping exactly on to your original footprints. Look behind you as you walk but try not to turn round. Walk slowly and carefully backwards until you reach a road, established path or other area you believe to be safe.

While you are in the minefield, pay attention for any signs that detonation may occur: this could be an unusual noise such as a click or a pop, or feeling your foot snag upon a trip wire or pressure plate. Drop to the ground immediately if you think detonation may have been initiated, or indeed if someone you are with cries out a warning that they may have activated a device. Dropping to the ground and shielding your upper body will minimise your likelihood of being hit by shrapnel if a mine explodes. You cannot outrun an explosion and should not attempt to do so.

showcase for Pamiri artisans, the majority of whom are women. Products include colourfully striped knitted Pamiri socks, felt animals (some more easily identifiable than others), jewellery and embroidered textiles. Prices are fixed.

For food shopping, the **bazaar** is a reliable source of fresh produce and bread, and the **convenience stores** on Somoni stock dried and canned goods, chocolate and fizzy drinks. There are also two well-stocked mini-supermarkets: **Atlantica** in Balnitzen, near the hospital, and one near the new bazaar, **Caxodat**.

OTHER PRACTICALITIES

Communications The main **post office** (*50 Lenin; ⌚ 08.00–17.00 Mon–Sat*) could theoretically be used to send a letter, but comes in more useful for international phone calls and the **internet café** in the same building ($\oplus$ *08.00–20.00 Mon–Sat; TJS5/hr*). You can also pay to get online at the **Serena Inn**, though the connection (which is probably via a satellite) is irritatingly slow.

Medical Khorog does have a **regional hospital** that has been renovated by the Aga Khan. However, services are still basic and overstretched. It is on the south side of the river in the compound by the bridge. There are several *apteka* on Lenin and around Central Park. The Aga Khan Health Service is investing US$24 million in a state-of-the-art new medical centre for Khorog, and it is hoped that this will open in 2018.

Money There are three major Tajik banks interspersed along Lenin, all of which do currency exchange. These are **Amonat Bank** (*115 Lenin*), **Tajik Sodirot Bank** (*60 Lenin*) and the **Agroinvest Bank** (*101 Lenin;* $\oplus$ *08.00–17.00 Mon–Fri, 08.00–noon Sat*), which also has an ATM that accepts Visa cards.

Registration Khorog's OVIR is at 115 Lenin should you need to register. It is open 08.00–17.00 Monday–Friday and 08.00–noon Saturday, but closes 13.00–14.00.

Visas The **Afghan Embassy** has a consulate in Khorog (*Sukuz Teknica,* ✆*02 492, 22 492;* $\oplus$ *09.00–14.00 Mon–Fri*). The consulate is able to issue visas and also vehicle permits, which are essential if you are planning to cross the border at Ishkashim.

WHAT TO SEE AND DO Khorog is home to the world's second-highest **botanical garden** (the highest being in Yunnan, China). The high altitude enables an interesting selection of plants to grow, many of which are endemic to the Pamirs. It's a beautifully calm spot to picnic, and there are also good views across the town.

The centre of Khorog is built around the appropriately named **Central Park**. Its riverside location, lawns and manicured flower beds all fit perfectly with the concept of a Victorian pleasure garden; it's scarcely possible to believe that it has been entirely rebuilt since the early 1990s when it was used for growing crops. The Chor Bagh restaurant, an ice cream stall and De Pamiri handicrafts shop are all within the confines of the park.

For serious overlanders, the **first car to cross the Pamirs** is almost a pilgrimage site. The Russian-made truck, which has some visual similarities with the Land Rover Series 2, is displayed upon a plinth in the east of the town, just next to the hydro-electric station. We've often gone to pay our respects.

AROUND KHOROG On the western side of Khorog, not far from the Serena Inn, is the **Shotemur shrine** and a rock that purportedly shows the sacred footprints of Ali's horse.

East of Khorog on the Pamir Highway, about 10km away, the village of Bogev has a **Medieval fortress**, the Kofir Kala, comprised of a stone citadel and two round temples, each with a diameter of around 10m. The temples would have had wooden ceilings, with holes in them to see the sun, as they were used for sun-worship. On the overhanging cliff are the remains of a **Zoroastrian fire temple**.

At **Roshtqala** (The Red Fort) 30km southeast of Khorog are the remains of the **9th-century fortress** that gives the town its name. In fact, it is one of four fortresses in the area, the others being Azizkhon, Sezhd and Charyk Kala. Together the fortresses create a defensive chain along the valley. The site was ideal for a settlement as it is a lush, green oasis with plenty of water. It must once have been a site of some importance, as it is mentioned in the writings of the Persian al-Biruni. If you are interested in development and sustainability, Roshtqala is also a fascinating case study: the UNDP Green Villages Initiative (**w** *greenvillagescentralasia.org*) has introduced small-scale photovoltaic systems and efficient cooking stoves, and has trained households how to use them in order to reduce wood consumption. As you might imagine in this dry, mountain desert environment, wood is in exceptionally short supply.

There are also two shrines in the vicinity: the **Pir Yakhsuz shrine** and the **Bobomafil shrine**. Both men were reputed to be able to control the snow and ice: Pir Yakhsuz drove back the glacier, and Bobomafil could melt snow with the power of his prayers.

Some 30km south of Khorog on the road to Ishkashim is the village of Andarob and the turn-off for **Garm Chashma**, the best hot springs in Tajikistan. Legend has it that Ali struck the ground with his sword while fighting a dragon, and hot water spewed forth. The springs, which are surrounded with a vast, cave-like mineral deposit, are used in turn by men and women; if you arrive during the other sex's session you can either wait or use the covered (and far less dramatic) side pools. It is expected that you will bathe naked, and the salts and sulphur leave your skin feeling remarkably soft.

Close to Andarob, a little off the main road, is the **Kuh-i Lal** (Ruby Mountain) described by Marco Polo. The mine here still produces small quantities of spinels (also known as balas ruby) and you will occasionally be offered uncut stones to buy.

ISHKASHIM *Telephone code: 03553*

The town of Ishkashim (altitude 2,652m) is in two parts, one each side of the Tajik–Afghan border. Though there is a bridge across the river, there is little traffic in either direction. The Tajik town is by far the wealthier, as is testified to by the almost complete absence of lights after dark across the border.

Ishkashim is superbly positioned, both for its proximity to cultural and archaeological sites, and for the views across Wakhan and the Hindu Kush. It's a long drive to get here from almost anywhere, but well worth the effort.

HISTORY There has probably been a settlement in Ishkashim, at this bend in the Panj River, for 1,500 years or more. It is likely that the early Chinese traveller Xuanzang passed through in the 7th century, as may have Marco Polo some centuries later.

When the Russian and British empires finally designated their borders in the 1890s (see box, pages 12–13), Ishkashim would have been the southernmost territory under Russian influence, the Wakhan Corridor being the narrow buffer between the two imperial heavyweights.

GETTING THERE AND AROUND From Khorog to Ishkashim, minibuses take 3 hours and cost TJS50. They leave from the bus stand by the bazaar. It's a relatively easy drive, and by car will be slightly faster than by minibus. There is also an early morning minibus twice a week (currently Monday and Thursday) to Langar (*TJS25*).

If you are taking the Wakhan Corridor route from Khorog to Murghab, you will pass through Ishkashim. Hiring a car and driver for this route will cost in the region of US$400–450, as you'll need to pay for the return journey too. Ask the Safar Drivers' Association (page 158) for the best price.

For details on crossing to and from Afghanistan, see page 36. The staff at Hani's Guesthouse (page 164) are able to advise on onward travel both sides of the border and to arrange cars and drivers from US$0.75 per kilometre. Adab Shah (**m** +93 79

841 4748; **e** *agarkan@gmail.com*) has previously helped us to organise transport and trekking guides on the Afghan side of the border, though he is often in Kabul rather than at home. He is reasonably reliable, speaks good English, and is experienced in dealing with the needs of foreign tourists. An alternative fixer, who we haven't used but who does come highly recommended, is Farhad Badakhsh (**e** *farhad. badakhsh@yahoo.com;* **m** +93 79 762 2978). If you are prepared to cross the border to the Afghan side of Ishkashim and make arrangements once you arrived, head to the Pamir Marco Polo Guesthouse (*$25pp*) and ask for Sultan Ishkashim.

WHERE TO STAY AND EAT The main place to stay in Ishkashim is **Hani's Guesthouse** (**e** *vali4hope@gmail.com;* **$**). It's a fairly basic, two-storey building next door to the police station, but there is usually hot water and there is also a proper toilet, a real luxury in the area. There are also two **homestays**, with Basbibi Rahmatulloeva in the town centre, and with Nekusho Sodatsairov just outside the town at Dasht. Book them both through **PECTA** (page 157).

For food, your best option is to eat where you sleep: you'll pay US$5 for breakfast and an evening meal. Other options include **Bahodur Café** and **Sarez Café**, both of which serve cheap soups and *shashlik* and are right in the centre of the village.

OTHER PRACTICALITIES
Medical There is a very basic **community hospital** in Ishkashim. It should not be relied upon to provide care. There is also an *apteka* by the hospital and another in the town centre.

Money Ishkashim is well served by banks. For money exchange, cash withdrawal and Western Union your options are **Agroinvest Bank** (*2 N Rakhmoni*), **Amonat Bank** (*9 Salomatshoeva*), **First Microfinance Bank** (*Lenin*) and **Tajiksodirot Bank** (*1 N Rakhmoni*).

WHAT TO SEE AND DO The highlight of Ishkashim is its **Sunday market**, one of the few opportunities the Afghan and Tajik towns have to meet. The market takes place on an island in the middle of the river; you do not need an Afghan visa to attend but will have to leave your passport with the soldier at the gate.

Ishkashim also has a **small museum** with archaeological finds from the local area, and information about Ibrohim Ismoilov, an early Bolshevik who was born locally. The curator is happy to tell you about his life.

AROUND ISHKASHIM Just outside Ishkashim at Nut are the ruins of an early **Medieval caravanserai**, the walls of which are still clearly visible. They're a poignant reminder that this was not always the back of beyond, but a well-used trade route from Afghanistan through the Pamirs to the north.

At Namadgut, 15km southeast of Ishkashim, is the **Khakha Fortress**, built by the Kushans, probably in the 4th century AD but possibly a little earlier. Its builder, the khakha, was ruler of the Wakhan and is thought to have belonged to the Siah-Posh, a fire-worshipping tribe whose modern descendants survive in Nuristan, Afghanistan. The fortress was the second major installation in a chain of defences (the first being the fort at Yamchun, page 166) and it must have been a vast and impressive structure, built of clay and stone and with no fewer than 56 towers. The ramparts ran for 750m, with a maximum width of 250m.

Time, water and wind have eroded much of the structure, though you can still get a good impression of its original scale. It is possible to go inside the fortress but you should first ask the Tajik troops stationed there, as due to its proximity to the Afghan border, they can understandably be a little sensitive about people wandering around and taking pictures. A packet of cigarettes and a warm smile should do the trick.

In Namadgut there is also a **shrine to Ali**, which has a beautifully carved doorway and decorative gate covered in fine calligraphy. The doors are some of the best examples of early Pamiri woodwork. Ask for the Ostoni Shohi Mardon.

WAKHAN CORRIDOR

Visiting the Wakhan Corridor should come with a warning: having trekked or driven down the Tajik side of the corridor, you will return home and start planning your trip to Afghanistan. It's unavoidable. The Tajik side is majestic, but Afghanistan is so tantalisingly close that it drives you almost to distraction.

The Wakhan Corridor is a spit of land reaching out eastward to China. At its eastern end, known as the Pamir Knot, the Pamir, Hindu Kush and Karakoram mountain ranges meet; the Pamir River is its northern border. In the corridor, Afghanistan, China, Pakistan and Tajikistan meet.

HISTORY The territory now known as the Wakhan Corridor served as an ancient trade route between Yarkand (now in Xinjiang, China) and Badakhshan. Marco Polo writes about the corridor in *The Travels*; he describes the scale of the mountains and lakes and comments upon sheep with horns six palms in length, a reference to the *Ovis ammon polii* or, more popularly, the Marco Polo sheep (see box, page 168).

The Wakhan came to historical prominence during the Great Game (see box, pages 12–13). Agreements between the Russians, British and Afghans in 1873 and 1893 split the corridor in two: the Panj and Pamir rivers became the border between Afghanistan and the Russian Empire (now the border inherited by Tajikistan) and, on the south side, the Durand Line marked the boundary between British India and Afghanistan. The narrow strip between the two lines is what we know as the Wakhan Corridor.

The corridor's status as a buffer zone more or less brought an end to the centuries of through-trade. Requests to China to open its border here have so far fallen on deaf ears and at the time of going to print it is also prohibited for foreigners to cross from the Wakhan into Pakistan, though this is more likely to change.

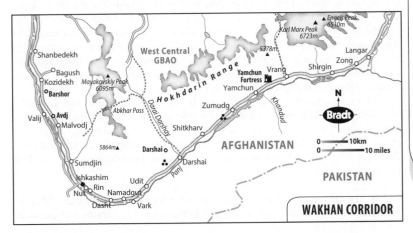

8

GETTING THERE AND AROUND To explore the Wakhan Corridor properly you will require your own transport. There is a twice-weekly **minibus** between Ishkashim and Langar (*currently Mon & Thu; TJS25*) but no other form of public transport. Hitching is possible, but road traffic is fairly thin, and the locals will likely already have snared any spare seats going their way.

For details on car and driver hire, see page 163. Arrangements can also be made via **Hani's Guesthouse** in Ishkashim (page 164), who has helped us secure a lift on more than one occasion.

 WHERE TO STAY AND EAT

Accommodation is in short supply in the corridor, as are places to eat. Bring plenty of food with you for those times that meals are an otherwise remote possibility, and preferably double up on supplies so your driver and/or guide can eat properly too.

The easiest place to break the journey is at Yamchun, where there is a **sanatorium** (**$**) half a kilometre from the spring. It was established to provide care for Soviet war veterans and is fairly run-down, but at least the beds are flat.

PECTA (page 157) has set up a number of **homestays** in the villages, including at Langar, Vrang and Yamg. If you want to stay the night in Langar, there are three different homestays to choose from. Ask for Mulloev Yodgor (**m** *093 428 8869*), Gulshodbegim Tavaloeva (**m** *093 555 0435*), or Nigina Avazkhonova (**m** *093 848 3720*). In Vrang, there are two options, with Rano Tolibshoeva and Jahonbegim Zevarova (**m** *093 771 1201, 093 890 5176*). Last but not least, in Yamg you can stay with Mirzoeva Navruzbeka (**m** *093 807 3309*) or Aidar Malikmadov (**m** *093 456 5519*).

Your driver or guide will probably have several informal homestay options up his sleeve as well. In all cases expect to pay US$10–12 per person, with an extra US$5 for meals.

WHAT TO SEE AND DO

Yamchun Among its numerous smaller sites, the Wakhan Corridor has two absolute gems, the first of which is the **Yamchun Fortress** at Yamchun, just beyond the village of Ptup and 500m above the main road. Its location and the views from the battlements are utterly breathtaking: Hollywood could do no better.

Deciphering the history of the fortress is challenging, as local legends and archaeological theories entwine but often contradict each other in key areas. Locals will tell you that the fortress was built by Zulkhasham, younger brother of the khakha at Namadgut, and that his garrison bravely resisted Arab invaders led by Ali himself. There is, however, no historical evidence that the Prophet's crusading son-in-law ever made it to the Wakhan, and archaeologists have suggested a far earlier foundation. The oldest parts of the fort likely date to the 3rd century BC, with major additions and alterations in the 12th century.

A short scramble uphill from the fort brings you to the **Bibi Fatima springs** (⊕ *06.00–21.00; TJS10*) named after Ali's wife, the daughter of Muhammad. The water is warm, and bathing here is thought to boost fertility. The springs are covered by a small concrete building, so they're not exactly photogenic, but after days of driving and hiking, and staying in homestays with no running water, bathing here is a godsend.

Yamg The village of Yamg is worth a stop for its **house-museum of Mubarak-i Wakhani**, a 19th-century Sufi mystic and astronomer. The curator and guardian,

PEAK ENGELS MEADOWS TREK

A stone's throw north of the Wakhan Corridor, Peak Engels soars to a height of 6,510m. It's a rugged, difficult peak with a sprinkling of snow on top even in the summer months. Though reaching the summit may be beyond most of our capabilities (it's been climbed only a handful of times, first in the mid-1950s), base camp is definitely accessible.

Start in the village of Langar, a pretty but very underdeveloped village by the river. We came in late summer, at harvest time, and donkeys were being used to thresh the wheat, kept in check by small children wielding sticks. The donkeys were often bigger than the kids were.

The path starts by the bridge next to the MSDSP office. Follow it past the sign for the petroglyphs. If you haven't already seen these, you do want to take a short diversion: the petroglyphs start just 500m from the track and there are more than 6,000 of them, dating right back to the Stone Age (pages 168–9).

Pick one of the numerous goat trails which wind up the hillside: they are narrow but easy enough to spot. All these trails ultimately join up with the irrigation channel and parallel path 600m above the village. You will see the channel well before you reach it because the water (which inevitably leaks) means the plant life growing alongside it forms a green streak against the otherwise dry brown earth. Getting to this point should take no more than 2 hours. Reward yourself with a rest and admire the views of the Hindu Kush which unfurl before you across the Wakhan Corridor. Warning: this may inspire a future journey across the border into Afghanistan. The distinct, pyramid-shaped peak is Baba Tangi (6,513m) in Afghanistan, a mountain which has only recently been climbed.

The trail stays almost level, then turns left into the gorge. It's a little uneven under foot, so you'll want to be wearing good footwear, but it certainly is not overly strenuous.

For the next 2km you walk alongside the irrigation channel with Peak Engels in sight. When you reach the small dam (which should take around 30 minutes), the riverbank is somewhat rocky, so pick your way through carefully. You won't actually be able to see the path due to the rocks, but if you look down at the plain then it does become clear again, zigzagging into the meadow. Fix your eyes on the start of the path there, and pick your own route over there through the rocks.

This is a great short trek which can easily be completed in a day and a half by someone of moderate fitness. Make your way there on one day, then pitch camp for the night. You will need to sleep in a tent in the meadow as there's no settlement, but what a place to camp! It's incredibly peaceful and without a glimmer of manmade light, so the stars are exceptionally clear. We saw the edge of the Milky Way with the naked eye. Waking in the morning, the mountains all around you, the views aren't half bad, either!

Aidar Malikmadov, will proudly show off his instruments and also the solar calendar he used for determining the date of Nowruz (Iranian New Year). If the museum appears closed, ask around and someone will appear to open up. The building is as interesting as its collection: it's a predominantly wooden structure built in the traditional Wakhani style, the walls are beautifully painted, and there are animal horns above the entrance-way as a good omen.

with thanks to Helen Watson

The closest encounter you are likely to have with a Marco Polo sheep is with a pair of its vast curly horns set atop a Pamiri roadside shrine. Their horns are thought to be a symbol of purity associated with pre-Islamic Aryan and Zoroastrian traditions (the straighter ibex horns are also used on shrines). The Marco Polo sheep (or argali), is the world's largest sheep and the horns of the male, which sweep back from the top of the skull and curl forward and outward in a double spiral, can measure up to 190cm in length. Weighing up to 20kg, they also account for around 10% of the sheep's body weight – no trivial accessory to carry around in the harsh winters of the Pamirs. During the breeding season (October–January), incredibly, these mighty beasts raise themselves upright on to their stocky back legs and clash horns repeatedly in a bid to gain control over the gathered herds of (the much smaller) females. The reward to a male of expending all this energy is the opportunity to father a large proportion of the lambs – that's if he's not already totally exhausted!

Marco Polo sheep are found across the eastern Pamirs of Tajikistan. Population census is difficult to obtain in this unforgiving terrain and best estimates range from 10,000 to 40,000 individuals. As the animals are desirable, both for their majestic horns and for meat, uncontrolled hunting by trophy hunters and locals has the potential to be a great threat to the animal.

After Russian withdrawal in 1991, the collapse in social services resulted in many pastoralists having to sell off some of their livestock to buy food. This reduction in grazing pressure on the sparse grasslands of the higher Pamirs is thought to have benefited the Marco Polo, although poaching by the pastoralists, border guards and military has also increased in this time.

It is illegal to hunt Marco Polo sheep unless you are in possession of one of the 20–40 trophy permits that are issued every year. A hunting trip will cost in excess of US$42,000. This money has the potential to benefit both conservation and the needs of local communities, but it is currently unclear to what extent it actually trickles down. If you are planning to hunt, then make sure you will be doing so legally.

Vrang Prior to the Arab invasion, the Wakhan had a thriving Buddhist population as well as Zoroastrians, as evidenced by the **Buddhist stupa** in Vrang. The centre of what was once a substantial religious complex, the stupa probably dates from the 6th century, and on its top rests a stone which is said to have an imprint of the Buddha's footprint on it. The complex was protected from attackers by an adobe wall and watchtowers. The Buddhist monks lived in simple mud-brick dwellings and retreated into surrounding **caves** to pray. The 11 caves are not natural, but cut by hand into the terraced slope.

Vrang also had what a 10th-century Persian visitor described as a 'Tibetan fortress', though whether it was actually Tibetan is arguable. In any case, little of it remains. The village also has a **shrine** and **museum** dedicated to the 11th-century Sufi mystic and poet Abdullo Ansori, who came from Herat and was renowned for his oratory skills. He travelled across central Asia, preaching about jurisprudence, and is buried in an impressive Timurid-era mausoleum in his home town in Afghanistan.

Langar The Wakhan's other gem is Langar, at the confluence of the Wakhan and Pamir rivers. An hour's hike above the village are more than 6,000 **petroglyphs**, the largest such site in the Pamirs. The earliest depictions likely date from the Stone Age, and you can clearly see ibex, hunters, men on horseback and stickmen running. Much later additions include Islamic symbols and calligraphy, and even a small amount of 21st-century graffiti added by local children. If you see them defacing the site, chastise them strongly. You will need to get a guide from the village to take you up to the site. Budget US$5 for half a day of their time.

At Langar there is also an important **shrine to Shoh Kambari Oftab**, the 'Master of the Sun'. He is credited with bringing Ismaili Islam to the town, thus 'enlightening' the people, but the name may also be a reference to pre-Islamic traditions of fire- and sun-worship in the valley.

Around 5km west of Langar is the **Vishim Qala** or Silk Fortress, just above the village of Zong. Dating from the Medieval period, the fort was constructed to protect the valley's traders and monks from marauding Afghan and Chinese forces.

A similar distance east of the town is another fortress, the **Ratm (or First) Qala**. The earliest parts date from the 3rd–2nd century BC and it is thought to have been used by the 8th-century Chinese general Kao Hsien Chih to drive the Tibetans from the Wakhan.

There is a footbridge across the river to Afghanistan, but it is currently only open for local traffic.

UPDATES WEBSITE

You can post your comments and recommendations, and read feedback and updates from other readers online at **w** bradtupdates.com/tajikistan.

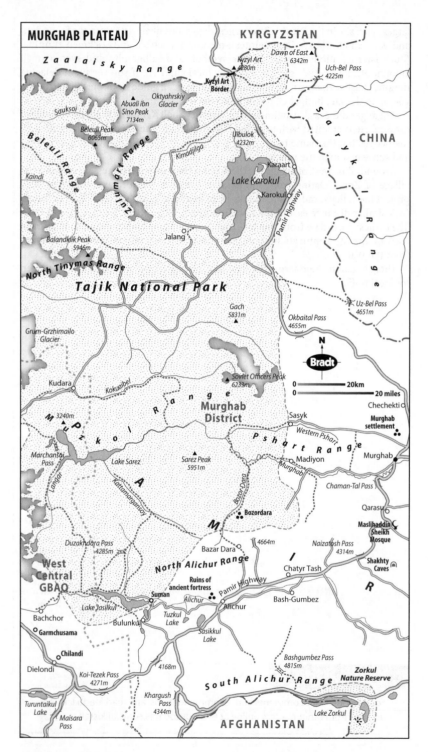

MURGHAB PLATEAU

KYRGYZSTAN

Z a a l a i s k y   R a n g e

Dawn of East ▲
6342m

Uch-Bel Pass
4225m

Kyzyl Art ▲
4280m

Kyzyl Art Border

Sauksoi

Oktyahrskiy
Glacier

Abuali ibn
Sino Peak
7134m

Beleuli Peak
6065m

B e l e u l i   R a n g e

T u m u n Z   R a n g e

Kimadjilga

Ulbulok
4232m

CHINA

S a r y k o l   R a n g e

Kaindi

Karaart ○

Lake Karokul

Karokul ○

Balandklik Peak
5946m

Jalang

North Tinymas Range

T a j i k   N a t i o n a l   P a r k

Gach
5831m

Grum-Grzhimailo
Glacier

Okbaital Pass
4655m

Uz-Bel Pass
4651m

N

Bradt

0   20km
0   20 miles

Kudara ○

Kokuibel

Soviet Officers Peak
6233m

U z k o l   R a n g e

**Murghab
District**

Chechekti ○

**Murghab
settlement**

Sasyk ○

Western Pshart

P s h a r t   R a n g e

▲ 3240m

M u

Marchansai
Pass

Langar

Lake Sarez

Sarez Peak
5951m

Madiyon ○

Murghab

Murghab ●

Chaman-Tal Pass

A

Kattamarganboj

Bartar-Dara

Bozordara

Qarasu ○

**Maslihaddin
Sheikh
Mosque**

Duzakhdara Pass
4285m

Bazar Dara ○

M

4664m

Naizatosh Pass
4314m

**West
Central
GBAO**

North Alichur Range

I

Chatyr Tash ○

**Shakhty
Caves**

**Ruins of
ancient fortress**

Suman ○

Alichur

Pamir Highway

Bash-Gumbez ○

R

Bachchor ○

○ **Garmchusama**

Lake Jasilkul

Bulunkul ○

Tuzkul
Lake

Alichur ○

Sasikkul
Lake

○ **Chilandi**

Dielondi ○

Koi-Tezek Pass
4271m

4168m

Bashgumbez Pass
4815m

**Zorkul
Nature Reserve**

S o u t h   A l i c h u r   R a n g e

*Turuntaikul
Lake*

*Maisara
Pass*

Khargush
Pass
4344m

Lake Zorkul

AFGHANISTAN

9

Murghab Plateau

The Murghab Plateau is the most remote and underpopulated part of Tajikistan, a vast expanse of land which is virtually barren due to the altitude and lack of rain. In the heart of the Pamir and cut off for much of the year by snow, the few communities who do live here – many of them nomadic – eke out a living in virtual isolation. Overlanders celebrate the Pamir Highway (Highway M41) as one of the world's greatest drives, however, and if you are prepared to take on the physical challenges of reaching this stunning wilderness, it also provides access to yurt camps and treks, Neolithic cave paintings and unspoilt mountain lakes.

THE PAMIR HIGHWAY: KHOROG TO MURGHAB

The eastern section of the Pamir Highway between Khorog and Osh, Kyrgyzstan, was built by Soviet military engineers in the early 1930s. Its construction was a phenomenal achievement. It is the second-highest international road in the world (after the Khujerab Pass between Pakistan and China), and primary construction took just three years. It was, however, significantly upgraded to allow improved military access for the Soviet invasion of Afghanistan in 1979, as this was one of the most important routes for the ill-fated campaign.

 WHERE TO STAY AND EAT Accommodation is scarce along the road as the long-distance truck drivers tend to drive the 310km between Khorog and Murghab in one go or, failing that, to sleep in their cabs. If you do need to break your journey *en route*, there is a **sanatorium** at Dielondi (**$**). **Murghab Ecotourism Association (META)** (page 175) can also arrange homestays in Bulunkul (**$**), 16km off the main road, between Dielondi and Alichur. **PECTA** (page 157) has four homestay options (**$**) in Alichur itself.

You will need to bring all your food with you for this leg of the journey. The only place you may get a meal is at Alichur, where fishermen throw their catch on a grill (**$**).

WHAT TO SEE AND DO The first part of the drive is described in *Khorog: Getting there and away* (pages 156–7). It brings you as far as the village of Dielondi, shortly after which a diversion from the main road takes you up to the scenic **Turuntaikul Lake** and the site of human settlements since ancient times. On the lake's northern side, where the river joins the lake, are curious **stone circles** and, a little further on, Scythian **burial mounds**. To the east are the ruins of what was probably a simple **caravanserai**, and also a **geyser** at Bekbulat, where it is possible to swim.

The Alichur Plain serves as a summer pasture for nomads grazing their livestock. Legend has it that the area was cursed by Ali and that this accounts for the inhospitable climate. There are several lakes here: **Tuzkul** (Salt Lake) and **Sasikkul** (Stinky Lake), which has earned its unfortunate moniker by virtue of the

Murghab Plateau   THE PAMIR HIGHWAY: KHOROG TO MURGHAB   9

TREKKING TO LAKE ZORKUL

Lake Zorkul (Sir-i Kol in Tajik) is a sapphire-blue body of water 20km long and situated at 4,125m above sea level. The Afghan–Tajik border runs east to west through the centre of the lake, and the first European certainly known to have travelled here (there being some doubt as to Marco Polo's journey along the valley), John Wood, approached from the Afghan side of the corridor in 1836. He believed Zorkul to be a source of the Pamir River, though this has subsequently been disproven.

Treks to Zorkul typically begin at Khargush, 45km past Langar along the Pamir River, and, although it's preferable to travel up by car, you could theoretically walk the distance in two days. The main trek starts from Korgush's military checkpoint, where it's customary to have a cup of tea with the guards in addition to going through paperwork formalities.

For the moderately fit, it's a two-day trek east from Korgush to the summer pastures of Bashgumbez (not to be confused with Bash-Gumbez near Alichur), where your guide will be able to arrange an informal yurt stay with the nomads grazing their sheep. The distance is only 40km but the terrain is steep and there is some risk of altitude sickness if you ascend too quickly.

From Bashgumbez it is just 4km to the lake, from where you turn east and follow the lakeshore into the Zorkul Nature Reserve. The trekking here is far easier, and it's worth taking your time to look out for wildlife: the reserve is known for its Indian mountain geese, red wolves and even the occasional snow leopard and Marco Polo sheep. Unless you have an Afghan visa and Wakhan permit to continue on to the Afghan side of the lake (highly recommended), you will then need to retrace your steps.

Note that you will need to get permission from the Tajik Border Force in Khorog to travel to Zorkul, and the permission letter will be checked at the border checkpoint between Langar and Korgush. PECTA (page 157) can help you with this, but be sure to apply at least one week in advance. Make sure you have detailed trekking maps (the best ones were produced by the Soviet military and are available to download from Mapstor, w *mapstor.com*) and the services of a reputable local trekking guide. Again, PECTA can advise.

sulphurous gases it releases. A little past Alichur village is a third lake called **Ak Balik** (White Fish). It is a holy place for the Kyrgyz. When they're here, the local population live in traditional yurts. You may be invited to stay the night with them, though this is an informal arrangement.

There are two sites of **petroglyphs** (ancient rock carvings) around Alichur: the small, Bronze Age collections at Ak Jilga and Madian. They are less impressive than those in the caves at **Shakhty** (page 179), but no special permission is required to visit them. The figures riding chariots are particularly fine.

The last site on the plain is the imposing **Chatyr Tash** (House of Rock) which, as the name suggests, is a huge lump of rock that was most probably dumped here during the last Ice Age. There are a few graves on top of the rock, and some rather more impressive views.

At Bulunkul, **Jasilkul** (also written as Yashil Kul on some maps) is a jade-green lake. The local area is criss-crossed with rivers, and as such it is an unusually fertile part of the plateau. Since ancient times, nomads have come here to graze their flocks, and they also established small settlements and even artisanal mines.

The lake's southern shore is accessible from the reasonable dirt road from Alichur (pages 171–2), but if you want to reach the northern shore, you will need to ford the Alichur River at the lake's eastern end. There is a track, which also extends along the riverbank to Bekbulat and Bolshoi Marjonai (page 174), but it is exceptionally rough. You will need a 4x4 if you intend to travel this far.

The **Mausoleum of Bekbulat** lies at the point where the Alichur River runs into Jasilkul. A square-based, mud-brick structure on an otherwise flat plain, it's the largest of three mausoleums on the site. There would originally have been a cupola atop the walls, though it has now largely collapsed. This architectural style dates back to the Sassanid period in the early centuries AD, though archaeologists who have examined this site tend to date it somewhat later, perhaps to the Medieval

HISTORY OF THE PAMIRS

The history of Tajikistan was covered in Chapter 1 (pages 9–15). However, that history largely ignored the Pamirs, because it was a remote and inhospitable landscape which people avoided if at all possible, and certainly did not settle. Traders passed through in the short months of summer when the mountain passes were not closed by snow, and the nomads grazed their flocks there, again in summer, but no-one thought it possible, or desirable, to build a town or city so high. That said, people have come and gone through the Pamirs for millennia, and so it is fitting to give their history here.

The oldest archaeological remains in the Pamirs date back some 20,000 years, to the Stone Age. Early people in the eastern Pamirs left cave paintings and rock carvings, including at Langar (pages 168–9), and at Shakhty (page 179). There is also evidence of solar calendars and fire temples. Travellers along the Silk Road left their monumental and artistic marks in the form of stupas, shrines and petroglyphs, which indicate both their religious beliefs and the sort of activities they were undertaking. In order to keep the trade routes open, it was essential to defend the mercantile caravans from attack, and so imposing fortresses were built, including along the Wakhan Corridor (pages 165–9).

The importance of the Pamirs was renewed in the 19th century during what is known as the Great Game (see box, pages 12–13). Along with parts of Afghanistan and northern Pakistan, these sparsely populated mountain regions were the buffer zone between the Russian and British empires, and hence they were of great strategic importance. Writing in *Tajikistan and the High Pamirs* (2012), Robert Middleton and Huw Thomas list numerous military officers, spies, geographers and diplomats who ventured here, including Lord Curzon and the Earl of Dunmore.

The Pamirs were important because they were seen to be empty territory: scarcely anyone lived here, and the region was under no-one's direct control. If either the Russians or the British could bring it under their influence, however, it would consolidate their position in the region, and infuriate the opposition.

It was the Russians who would prevail, largely because by the 1880s they controlled much of the surrounding territory in central Asia, and thus could more easily move troops, equipment and supplies through the mountains. They founded a military outpost at Murghab in 1893, and then built a garrison at Khorog following the signing of the 1896 Anglo–Russian–Afghan Border Treaty. In this period the Russians began the construction of the Pamir Highway, though it would be decades before it was completed.

period. Regardless of its true age, it remains a dramatic structure, and its surviving arches are testament to the engineering skills of its builders.

Past the mausoleum, the track moves away from the shore and crosses into the Bolshoi Marjonai Valley. There are three great **stone circles** overlooking the Bolshoi Marjonai river mouth, thought to date from the Bronze Age. The stone walls are positioned around 250m apart from one another and, despite archaeological excavations, their use remains completely unknown. It's a Megalithic mystery! Chinese coins and ceramics were discovered here, but they are much later in date than the stone circles themselves. It is probable that they were left by Silk Road merchants who used the site as a rudimentary caravanserai in the 18th century.

The heart of the Bolshoi Marjonai Valley is dotted with **Saka-era** *kurgans* (tombs), and there are also the ruins of two Medieval settlements. The first of these is on the Karademur riverbank, close to the Gozen Gorge, and it includes more than a dozen clay- and stone-built houses. Further along the valley, 11km past the confluence of the Karademur and Tshangil rivers, is a second site, which was probably a mining settlement. There are various small dwellings here, but the exciting structure is a 28-room structure of unknown use. Both settlements are thought to date from the 11th century.

MURGHAB   *Telephone code: 03554*

At 3,618m above sea level, Murghab is officially the highest town in Tajikistan. It celebrated its 80th birthday in 2012; before the arrival of the Pamir Highway there was insufficient traffic to support a permanent settlement here. There was previously a Russian garrison in the town, but now it's tourism that sustains the town's economy. Though there's nothing to see in Murghab itself, it is the starting and finishing point for many adventures in the Pamirs, and hence you'll find a ragtag band of cyclists, overlanders and mountaineers in the guesthouses and homestays in the short summer season.

GETTING THERE, AROUND AND AWAY Though just a distance of 310km from Khorog, getting to Murghab is a full day's drive. The road rises and falls, often for hundreds of feet in a short distance, and climaxes at the Koi-Tezek Pass (4,271m). The road surface is frequently poor, and at the higher points you can be struck by unexpected blizzards, even in summertime. The village of **Bulunkul**, which you pass through *en route*, is officially the coldest place in Tajikistan.

If you take the **minibus** to Khorog, it takes 9 hours and costs TJS80. Minibuses depart early in the morning and tend to fill up quickly, assuming they run that day. If you arrive late, you'll have to wait until the following day to leave. If you prefer to hire a car and driver, **Pamir Highway Adventure in Murghab** (m *090 409 1752;* e *tours@pamirhighwayadventure.com;* w *pamirhighwayadventure.com*) and the **Safar Drivers' Association in Khorog** (page 158) are the most reliable options. Expect to pay US$0.75 per kilometre.

> **WHAT IS A PAMIR?**
>
> 'Pamir' is a geological term for a flat plateau or U-shaped valley surrounded by mountains. It forms when a glacier or ice field melts away, leaving behind a rocky plain. This is typical of the valleys seen in the east of Gorno-Badakhshan, and in the northern part of the Wakhan Corridor. The climate is cold and dry year-round, with strong winds in the valleys.

The same organisations can also arrange onward travel to Osh, which at the time of going to print cost in the region of US$400 per vehicle. It's a distance of 420km and takes approximately 12 hours. If you plan to travel extensively within Kyrgyzstan, it is worth arranging a car and driver from the Kyrgyz side of the border. We particularly recommend contacting **CBT Kyrgyzstan** (\ +996 312 44 3331; e *cbtnetkg@gmail.com*; w *cbtkyrgyzstan.kg*) for travel and tour arrangements there.

If car hire is not within your budget, shared jeeps leave Murghab for Osh most days and cost TJS150 per person. They will not leave until full, so you may have to wait a while. It is also possible to hitch (see page 49 for advice). For more information on the border crossing, see page 37.

Murghab itself is small enough to explore on foot, and it is also possible to hire bikes from **Pamir Bikes** (*Syemdiesat Let Murghab*), who charge US$8 for a full day's hire. If you intend to travel around Murghab to nearby sites, you will require a car and driver. Book through **Pamir Highway Adventure** (see below), or approach one of the private drivers outside the bazaar. Expect to pay around US$0.75 per kilometre.

TOURIST INFORMATION, TOURS AND GUIDES Murghab is home to the well-organised and justifiably respected **Murghab Eco-Tourism Association (META)** (*102 Osh*; m *093 518 1808*; w *meta.tj*). META is responsible for tourism development in the region and is an excellent source of information.

To actually arrange your trip, you'll need one of the commercial offshoots META has dutifully spawned. **Pamir Highway Adventure** (*70 Solagi Murghab*; m *090 409 1752*; e *tours@pamirhighwayadventure.com*; w *pamirhighwayadventure.com*) arranges all manner of treks (including horse and camel treks), cycle tours, rafting and wildlife safaris. Packages are individually tailored and can include drivers, guides and homestays should you so wish.

Saidali Gaibudaliev and Kuban Kozubekov, two Murghab-based guides, have also established Pamir Guides (*51 Ismanov*; m *093 538 2545*; e *info@pamirguides.org*; w *pamirguides.org*). Both men speak a small amount of English in addition to Tajik and Russian, and provide tours and treks to valleys across the Pamir. Sample itineraries are available on their website.

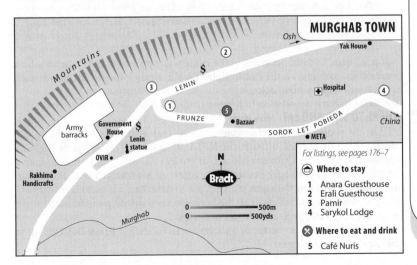

For listings, see pages 176–7

Where to stay
1 Anara Guesthouse
2 Erali Guesthouse
3 Pamir
4 Sarykol Lodge

Where to eat and drink
5 Café Nuris

Murghab Plateau MURGHAB 9

CYCLING THE PAMIR HIGHWAY   *Helen Watson*

We rounded a corner on the Pamir Highway and heard a squeal as three small figures rushed up the bank of the Panj River towards us. As we drew closer, there was another yelp, which this time can only have meant 'Woman!' because the smallest of the three boys, who was completely naked, dived behind his companions. We cycled on as they shoved each other, giggling and dripping river water on to the dust road.

It's certainly not a quick way to travel, but cycling is a great way to get a close-up experience of the Pamirs. Whether it's buying apricots and cherries from wayside sellers, slowing down to chat to women on their way home from working in the fields or discussing the hazards of transporting eggs with truck drivers at a water stop, taking to two wheels will allow the panorama of the Pamirs to bump by slowly enough for you to say your 'Salams' to the locals.

Cycling the Pamir Highway might, in fact, involve taking one of several route variations. Between Dushanbe and Kalaikhum, the more direct route via Darband climbs over the Saghirdasht Pass (3,252m). It is also possible to take a longer route via Kulob, which traverses the lower Shurabad Pass (2,200m) and then follows the Afghan border along the Panj river gorge. From Kalaikhum, the generally well-sealed M41 leads to Khorog, then over the Koi-Tezek Pass (4,271m) to the dusty outpost of Murghab and thence to Kyrgyzstan. The alternative is to continue along the Panj Valley with its vistas of Afghanistan and the snowy Hindu Kush and to rejoin the M41, 126km short of Murghab. You will want to leave at least three full weeks including rest days to do the route from Dushanbe to Murghab, and then there is the challenge of working out how to get back. If you cycle any section along the Afghan border you are likely to have numerous encounters with young border patrols in oversized khaki, carrying machine guns or bazookas. Be confident, unfailingly friendly and utterly ignorant of any insinuation that you might want to give a bribe and you will probably be pestered for little more than a flick through your passport and some conversation.

Whichever route you take, this trip will be a challenge. At a minimum, you need to be fit, have done your research and have a very hardy bicycle with plenty of spares. Stephen Lord's *The Adventure Cycle-Touring Handbook* (Trailblazer Publications) is a good guide for information about equipment.

Make sure you are kitted out for all weathers, especially the cold. At 3,000–4,000m of altitude, nights are freezing and winds are bitter. June–September are the months for cycling. Outside this period bad weather is likely to be a real hazard.

If you intend to climb seriously in the Pamir – as opposed to trek – then the best organisation to contact is the **Pamir Alpine Club** in Khorog (page 158), also known as the Pamir Guides Association.

 WHERE TO STAY AND EAT   *Map, page 175.*

META has supported the establishment of several **homestays ($)** in Murghab, which can all be booked through the **META office** (page 175) or **Pamir Highway Adventure** (page 175). Qalandar Milomirov (m *093 437 8573*) and Apal Doskuliva (m *093 547 3394*) both have homes in the centre of Murghab close to the bazaar, and if you want to stay the night in a yurt, ask to have Zarifa Ismailova (m *093 547 3957*) as your hostess. Toilets in all the homestays are squats, away from the main buildings, and water invariably comes in buckets.

Take meals at your homestay or guesthouse, in the café at **Pamir Hotel ($)**, or at **Café Nuris ($)** in the bazaar.

Food will inevitably occupy your thoughts for a great deal of the journey as the combination of altitude and exercise induces serious hunger. You will need to carry enough supplies for the stretch between Dushanbe to Khorog and then Khorog to Murghab. Many villages do have small shops but it is not advisable to rely on them entirely. You may have to survive much of the trip on mashed potato powder, super-noodles and semolina. If you are lucky enough to be invited into a Pamiri house you may be tempted to quaff all the sweets and biscuits on offer, but remember that food is not just short here for cyclists.

Dry, high-altitude air can also induce dehydration, so aside from food you will need to carry quite a lot of water each day (up to 5 litres). Along the Panj Valley water is not too hard to find, but in the High Pamirs you will have long stretches without, and be warned that a lot of the lakes are filled with salt water – don't make the mistake of boiling your pasta in it! The sun is fierce at this altitude, but if you cover up you will be doing yourself a favour in more ways than one: with all the kit you are carrying, long-sleeved shirts and trekking trousers will save on suncream and, more importantly, by not embarrassing local people with your exposed flesh and Lycra bulges, you may also have more opportunity to interact with them.

If you are serious about the challenge, then the chance to see things at your own pace and to meet Pamiris will be among the greatest rewards of cycling. It's not always hard work: at the end of a long day we approached the unsealed ascent out of the village of Langar with sinking hearts. Our tyres churned deep into the gravel, sending us skidding. We were just about to dismount, when there was a cry from a nearby house and a group of small girls ran out. Laying hands on our bikes, they started to run us up the hill, laughing all the way. Twenty minutes later, after we had thanked them repeatedly, we rested on our handlebars and watched them skip back down to the Panj Valley with its patchwork of green fields crammed underneath barren mountainsides. The peaks of Tajikistan, Afghanistan and Pakistan were turning pink in the soft light of evening.

Helen Watson, a finalist in Bradt's 2011 travel writing competition, cycled the Pamir Highway in June 2010 with her husband, Ed, as part of a 15,000km trip from Scotland to China (w blogspot.com).

🏠 **Anara Guesthouse** (3 rooms) Frunze; `21 324. When we first met Ibrahim & his family, we were looking a little worse for wear. Fortunately, they're now quite used to receiving tourists who haven't washed for a week, & probably assume foreigners naturally smell like that. The guesthouse's clean bathroom & plentiful hot water certainly come in handy & set the Anara apart from most other accommodation options in Murghab. **$$**

🏠 **Pamir Hotel** 2 Somoni; `21 762; w pamirhotel.com. Opened in summer 2013, this new hotel is basic but clean. It's on the western side of Murghab, close to the barracks. The café serves *shashlik* & salads. **$$**

🏠 **Sarykol Lodge** Sorok Let Pobieda; `21 789. Close to the bazaar, Sarykol is a small guesthouse with basic dorm accommodation & a clean-ish toilet. Evening meals cost US3 & are filling & tasty. **$–$$**

🏠 **Erali Guesthouse** (4 rooms) Pamir Highway. Just to the north of the town on the road to Karakol but still within walking distance of the bazaar, Erali falls somewhere between a guesthouse & a homestay. The family is charming & the bathroom is heated, which goes a long way to make up for showering under a bucket. **$**

Tajikistan's national sport is an adrenalin-fuelled battle on horseback. The name means 'pull the goat' and its origins are in the literal ram raiding of the past: horseback hordes would attack a neighbouring tribe, and seize their flocks, women and anything else of value that they could get their hands on. Nineteenth-century visitors Robert Shaw, Eugene Schuyler and Francis Henry Skrine all described the phenomenal horsemanship of the Tajik nomads in their accounts of their travels, and it seems that *buz kashi* in particular has changed very little since then.

Although we nickname *buz kashi* 'dead goat polo', and the origins of polo are the same, in fact this is more a game of horseback rugby, albeit one where the rugby ball has been replaced by a decapitated goat's carcass. Two teams of roughly equal size take to the pitch, and the aim of the game is to scoop the carcass off the floor and race with it to the end of the pitch, flinging it into a goal. The goat can easily weigh 40kg, and of course the opposite team is trying to grab it from you while you ride. Knifes and other sharp implements are banned from the pitch, but there's still a lot of damage you can do with elbows, knees and a well-timed turn to unbalance your opponent. Blood and teeth inevitably fly, and broken bones are not uncommon.

But team pride is at stake, so both teams battle on, either for an agreed time, or until a particular score is reached. The goat may not be in much of a state by the time they finish, having been flung about and frequently trampled underfoot by the horses. Whatever is left of it, however, will be cooked up into a celebratory feast for the victors, as well as the enthusiastic spectators.

SHOPPING On the eastern side of the town on the road to Osh, **Yak House** (*Murghab Hse;* ⊕ *09.00–18.00 Mon–Sat*) sells a selection of handicrafts made by local artisans. If you still haven't given in to the temptation of nice, warm, woolly Pamiri socks then you can get a pair (or three) here, and it also sells rugs and homeware. Many of the products show both Pamiri and Kyrgyz influences. The quality is high, and prices are fair. You can also buy a small selection of souvenirs from **Rakhima Handicrafts** (*Nr barracks, Jarbashy*).

Basic foodstuffs and some imported household goods (mostly Chinese) are available in the **bazaar** in the centre of the town. It is possible to stock up on dry goods, chocolate and other basic items here, but don't anticipate a wide choice.

OTHER PRACTICALITIES
Electricity Murghab suffers from extreme electricity shortages and blackouts are common. It is usual for only part of the town to have electricity at any one time, so charge up any batteries before leaving Khorog or Osh, and ideally carry spares. You will certainly need a torch.

Medical Murghab has one tiny **hospital** and **chemist** on Osh Street, almost opposite the META office. It goes without saying that you should carry your own medical kit with you, and use these facilities only in an emergency.

Money There are two **banks** on the main road (⊕ *08.00–17.00 Mon–Fri, 08.00– noon Sat*). They provide currency exchange and Western Union, but there's no ATM and currently no facility to withdraw funds with a card.

THE SOUND OF THE PAMIRS

Music and dance in the Pamirs are inextricably linked with Ismaili Islam. The performance of both vocal and instrumental genres is intended as an act of devotion, and many songs are linked with specific rituals or prayers.

Traditional Pamiri instruments loosely fit into three categories: wooden or ceramic drums, stringed lutes, and flutes. Drums known as *tavlak* and *daf* provide rhythmic accompaniment to both songs and instrumental pieces. The *rubob* (of which many variations exist), *sitor*, *komuz* and *tanbur* are all multi-stringed instruments that are plucked, while the strings of a *ghijak* are played with a bow. The *nay* is a wooden flute, not dissimilar in appearance to a recorder or penny whistle.

A strong singing voice is prized, and both men and women will sing solo or as part of a group. Melancholic songs in minor keys describe feelings of separation and loss, while the Persian *ghazal* genre explores the highs and lows of being in love.

The cultural wing of AKDN has made numerous recordings of Pamiri music, samples of which are available online at w iis.ac.uk.

AROUND MURGHAB A 9th-century centre for gold and silver mining, **Sasyk** is situated at the confluence of the Sasyk and Pshart rivers 60km northwest of Murghab. The site was still being exploited a thousand years later, and you can see the remains of two settlements and a small cemetery, as well evidence of the mines. *En route* to the mines you can also see Saka-period petroglyphs in the valley just before the Aktash Pass.

One of the Pamirs' most important ancient sites, **Shakhty**, lies 70km southwest of Murghab in the Kurteskei Valley. Discovered entirely by accident in 1958 by archaeologists working nearby, the Shakhty Caves contain some of the highest rock paintings in the world. The main area of decoration covers some 25m² of the cave wall. Figures are depicted in red pigment; it is possible to make out a hunting scene in which three bears are being shot at with arrows, and a figure that appears to be half man and half bird. Archaeologists have drawn similarities between these paintings and palaeolithic sites elsewhere, though these particular specimens cannot pre-date the arrival of people in the Pamirs after the end of the last Ice Age (8000–5000BC).

You will require permission from META to visit the caves, as the paintings are exceptionally fragile. Do not touch them. A guide will be required to help you to locate the caves.

About 3 hours' drive (120km) back towards Khorog, 30km off the Pamir Highway, is the Medieval silver-mining town of **Bazar Dara**. At 3,980m, the site overlooks the Ak Jilga River. It includes a **caravanserai** and almost a hundred domestic and administrative buildings. Public baths with a rudimentary heating system have also been excavated. At its peak, Bazar Dara would have had a population of 1,700 people; the cemeteries downstream contain more than 500 tombs.

THE PAMIR HIGHWAY: MURGHAB TO THE TAJIK–KYRGYZ BORDER

The final stretch of the Pamir Highway heads north from Murghab to Bor Dobo, just across the Tajik–Kyrgyz border, and thence to Sary Tash and Osh, Kyrgyzstan's second city. This northern part of the Pamirs is the remotest part of Tajikistan, and also home to some of the finest trekking routes (and rarest wildlife) in the country.

The Pamirs offer some of the world's most spectacular treks, but also some of the most physically challenging. The potential for avalanches, mudslides and blizzards, the guaranteed crevasses, and the significant risk of sunburn, dehydration, broken limbs and frostbite go a long way to suggest why even relatively benign trekking areas are largely uninhabited. You shouldn't be dissuaded by the hardships, but you should prepare yourself thoroughly in advance.

1 Research your planned route in detail before arrival in Tajikistan. Study maps of the region and take them with you so that in the event of something happening to your guide you are still able to navigate your way to safety.

   The best commercially available map of the Pamirs is *The Pamirs: A Tourist Map of Gorno-Badakhshan, Tajikistan, and Background Information on the Region*. The scale is 1:500,000 and it is distributed by Gekko Maps (w *geckomaps.com*). It includes trekking routes.

2 Trekking in the Pamirs is physically demanding and, due to the altitude, even fit individuals may find themselves struggling for breath. Make sure you are in good shape before you leave, and know where your physical limits lie. Stretch at the start of each day so that you reduce the risk of pulled muscles, and cool down properly before you go to bed.

KAROKUL Lake Karokul was formed by a meteor impact some ten million years ago. Its name, which means 'Black Lake' in Kyrgyz, aptly sums up the darkness of the deep waters in the winter months; at other times the water is a more attractive turquoise. The Chinese traveller Xuanzang visited the lake in the mid 7th century, long before there was a permanent settlement on the shore, and this was the first recorded reference to Karokul in historical texts. In the 19th century, the Great Game's cartographer dubbed it Lake Victoria, after Queen Victoria, but this name didn't last long: when the Soviet surveyors came, they replaced that name with Karokul.

Part of the Tajik National Park (see box, page 182), the lake is 25km across, though the impact crater is more than twice that size. It is higher in altitude than Lake Titicaca in South America, and since 2014 it has been the location of the Roof of the World Regatta, the highest sailing race in the world. The lake is also an extraordinary spot for kitesurfing, though you will need to bring all your own equipment with you as it is not possible to rent it locally.

Karokul is one of the best places in Tajikistan for **birdwatching**, so if birding is your thing, it's well worth making the journey here. The combination of ecosystems – marsh, peat bogs, water meadows, pebbly beaches and sands – support a wealth of birdlife, both resident and migrant, and the lake is recognised as an Important Bird Area (IBA). Look out for bar-headed geese, Tibetan sand grouse, yellow-billed chough, Caucasian great rose finch, white-winged snowfinch, ruddy shelduck, Himalayan vulture and saker falcon, among many others.

Getting there For transport, see *Murghab*, pages 174–5.

The Tajik–Kyrgyz border lies 60km north of Karokul at the Kyzyl Art Pass (4,280m). The Tajik and Kyrgyz immigration and customs posts are about 25km apart from each other on either side of the pass, so factor this into your journey time. Allow

3 Medevac insurance is a must. There is no proper medical care in the Pamirs, and no mountain rescue. If you become sick or have an accident, you will need to leave by helicopter. For this reason you will also need a GPS unit and a satellite phone (see box, page 59). Keep them turned off until you need them so you don't run out of batteries.

4 Consider taking a wilderness medicine or other advanced first aid course. This will prepare you to treat minor injuries and illnesses and also to stabilise a more severe casualty until expert help arrives. They will also teach you to recognise the signs of altitude sickness. The two wilderness medicine course providers we recommend are w expeditionmedicine.co.uk and w wildernessmedicaltraining.co.uk.

5 In addition to lightweight camping kit and multiple layers of clothing, pack snow goggles or UV protective sunglasses. The glare from the snow, particularly up on the glaciers, can cause snow blindness.

If in doubt, play it safe. The Pamirs are moving at a rate of just 20mm a year, so they'll be there next year and the year after, and probably the year after that too. If the weather's not right, you're not quite fit enough, or you simply don't feel confident, then wait. There will be another opportunity.

---

plenty of time for the crossing itself (if you get stuck behind a truck or minibus it'll take quite a while) and be sure to arrive by mid-afternoon at the latest as the border posts operate only during daylight hours. Check that you have been stamped out of one country and stamped into the next: this is particularly important when entering Kyrgyzstan, as many foreigners (including all EU nationals) no longer require a visa, and hence you will otherwise have no proof that you have entered the country via a permitted route.

Where to stay and eat There are two **homestays ($)** in Karokul, where you can get full board and lodging. Ask for Erkin Saidov (m *090 655 4831*) or Makhmatjon Yusupov (m *090 051 2462*). The latter has a yurt. You can also book in advance through META (page 175).

Outside Karokul, in the village of Jalang, are two more **META yurt stays ($)** belonging to Rainberde Kudaybergenov and Kanatali Pahyrov.

Other practicalities Karokul lies close to the Chinese border and so you will need to present your passport (including valid Tajik visa and GBAO permit) at the checkpoint just south of the village.

Around Karokul The village of Karaart is 8km north of Karokul. It is home to two **archaeological sites**: collections of geoglyphs and tombs. The first site, 1km from the village, has 16 geoglyphs, the largest of which is 30m long. They are marked out by black and white rocks, the darkest of which show the contours. There are four *kurgans* here also.

A few hundred metres away is Karaart's second site, which includes three more geoglyphs and a **necropolis** of 21 tombs. These were first properly excavated in

9

TAJIK NATIONAL PARK

At over 1.22 million hectares, the Tajik National Park (TNP) is the largest conservation area in central Asia. Most of the park is within GBAO, but it also stretches west towards Jirgatal in the Rasht Valley. From the geology to the biodiversity, it's a truly remarkable place.

Within the park are 40 peaks over 6,000m (19,684ft), of which three – Peak Somoni, Peak Lenin and Peak Korgenevskiy – are more than 7,000m (22,965ft). Trekkers and mountaineers are also attracted by several substantial glaciers (including the 77km-long Fedchenko and the 37km-long Grumm-Grzhimaylo glaciers) and the high-altitude lakes Sarez and Karakul.

The park has an exceptional level of biodiversity, in large part due to its isolation and the lack of human encroachment. There are more than 2,000 species of plant, about a hundred of which are endemic. Species such as the *Melandrium apetalum*, *Cerastium cerastoides* and *Sibbaldia tetandra* have evolved in such a way that they are able to survive the cold, even at altitudes above 4,800m.

Birdwatchers can spot more than 160 different species, most of which are migratory but a few live year-round in the park. Endemic species include the lesser Mongolian plover (*Charadrius mongolus pamiriensis*), the red-tailed wheatear (*Oenanthe xanthoprymna chrysopygia*) and the white-winged snowfinch (*Montifringilla nivalis alpicola*). It is also possible to see the mountain goose (*Ancer indicus*) and Himalayan griffon (*Gyps himalayensis*), two endangered species listed in Tajikistan's *Red Book*.

If you are hoping to see snow leopards (*Panthera uncia*), Tibetan lynx (*Felis lynx isabellina*), Pamiri brown bears (*Ursus arctos pamiriensis*) or Marco Polo sheep, the TNP offers one of the best opportunities, though they are still far from commonplace. You are more likely to catch sight of the endemic Pamirian vole (*Microtus juldaschi*) and Tolai hare (*Lepus tolai pamiriensis*), and the relatively widespread (and rather cute) red marmots (*Marmota caulata*), grey dwarf hamsters (*Cricetulus migratorius coerulescens*) and mountain weasels (*Mustela altaica*).

2003, and they date from the Saka period (the 8th to 3rd centuries BC). Bodies were laid to rest in an east–west orientation with grave goods such as china bowls, glassware, turquoise and lapis lazuli beads, hair pins and copper bracelets. There are differences between the male and female burials: women were buried with their jewellery and household items, while the male burial sites show remains of sheep skeletons, iron knife blades and copper-tipped arrow heads. The tombs were cased in schist plates, sometimes with the addition of a wooden roof. Circles of stones then covered the burial mound.

The **Shurali Valley**, carved out of the Pamir by the Kokulbel River, is the site of the best-preserved **geoglyphs** in Tajikistan, as well as a small, Saka-era necropolis. The road from Karokul (which is barely more than a track) follows the river east through a narrow passage and out on to an open plain. The road deteriorates further, but drive across the western part of the plain, then follow the track northwest into the Shurali Valley. The archaeological ensemble will be on your left. The village of Jalang is on the way, so you might want to spend a night in a yurt stay there (page 181).

Approaching the geoglyphs, you first pass by a small **necropolis** comprised of *kurgans*. Several of these have been excavated and attributed to the Saka period, though unlike the burial sites at Karaart, no significant grave goods were recovered. It is the 15 **geoglyphs** which are the real attraction, however: they vary from 6m to 13m in length, and are exceptionally intricate. Some of the geoglyphs are simple patterns, made up of triangles and rectangles, but there is also one phallic figure, and also the shape of an arrow head, in the group of geoglyphs closest to the river. Their creators clearly had a strong understanding of astronomy, because one of the figures points to the spring and autumn equinox, and another to the summer and winter solstice.

The geoglyphs are thought to be contemporary with the necropolis, so they are at least 2,500 years old. One of the reasons they have survived so well is their depth: the ground has been excavated to a depth of 25cm and filled in with small stones, which serves as a foundation. On top of this is a second layer, which reaches to about 10cm above ground, of dark rocks and white quartz, in colour blocks or alternating black and white.

There is no public transport available to reach either of these sites, due to the low population density, and hence lack of demand. You will need to get a **taxi and driver** from the bazaar in Murghab, or prearrange one with **META** (page 175).

Wanderlust
travel magazine

TRAVEL ADVENTURE CULTURE

Wanderlust

50 TOP TRIPS

Tokyo

Cayman Islands

South Africa

Since 1993, we've been helping travellers escape the crowds and seek out the most unique cultures, wildlife and activities around the globe.

Wanderlust offers a unique mix of inspiration and practical advice, making it the ultimate magazine for independent-minded, curious travellers.

For more about *Wanderlust* and for travel inspiration visit www.wanderlust.co.uk

9

Appendix 1

LANGUAGE

It pays to speak a few words of the local language; to rely entirely on English and charades leaves you open to serious misunderstanding and the sometimes warped sense of humour of the locals too. It's best summed up by recounting the unfortunate experience of John Newby, a seasoned traveller whom we met on our most recent trip to the 'Stans.

John ate something dodgy; it happens to us all. Short on Imodium, he visited the apteka and mimed his predicament, complete with a rendition of the relevant bowel movements. It was an Oscar-worthy performance. The pharmacist's assistant smiled pityingly and gave John his tablets. He took them, and spent the next three days in the bathroom. The tablets he was given were laxatives.

ALPHABET AND PRONUNCIATION

Cyrillic		Latin	Pronunciation
А	а	a	as in apple
Б	б	b	as in bed
В	в	v	as in vote
Г	г	g	as in goat
Ғ	ғ	gh	as in ghost
Д	д	d	as in dream
Е	е	e	as in end
Ё	ё	ye	as in yellow
Ж	ж	jh	as in pleasure
З	з	z	as in zoo
И	и	i	as in egg
Й	й	'i	as in milk
Й	й	yoo	as in new
К	к	k	as in kiss
Қ	қ	q	as in queen
Л	л	l	as in lip
М	м	m	as in man
Н	н	n	as in noon
О	о	o	as in old
П	п	p	as in pot
Р	р	r	as in room
С	с	s	as in small
Т	т	t	as in time
У	у	u	as in ultra
Ӯ	ӯ	oo	as in spoon

Ф	ф	f	as in fruit
Х	х	kh	as in khan
Ҳ	ҳ	h	as in home
Ч	ч	ch	as in chew
Ҷ	ҷ	j	as in job
Ш	ш	sh	as in show
ъ			no English equivalent
Э	э	e	as in egg
Ю	ю	you	as in youth
Я	я	ya	as in yard

HELPFUL TAJIK PHRASES

English	Tajik	Pronunciation
Hello	салом	*Sah-lohm*
How are you?	Шумо чи хел?	*Shoo-moh-chee-khel?*
Fine, thank you	Нағз, рахмат	*Naghz, rah-mat*
What is your name?	Номатон чист?	*No-ma-ton chist?*
My name is …	Номи ман …	*No-mi man …*
Nice to meet you	Аз вохуриамон шод ҳастам	*Az vo-khu-ri-amon shod has-tam*
Please	Лутфан	*Loot-fan*
Thank you	Рахмат	*Rah-mat*
You're welcome	Саломат бошед	*Salomat boshed*
Yes	Ҳа	*Ha*
No	Не	*Ne*
Sorry	Мебахшед	*Mebakhshed*
Excuse me (getting attention)	Мебахшед	*Mebakhshed*
Is there someone here who speaks English?	Оё касе дар инчо англиси гап мезанад?	*Oyo kase dar injo anglisi gap mezanad?*
I don't understand	Ман немефаҳмам/ ман нафаҳмидостам	*Man na-me-fah-mam/ Man na-fah-mi-dos-tam*
Where is …?	… кучо аст?	*… koojo ast?*
Where is the toilet?	Ҳочатхона кани?	*Ho-jat-kho-na kani?*
How much is this?	Ин чанд пул меистад?	*Jan čand pul mieistad?*
I am sick	ман касал хастам	*Man kasal hastam*
I have diarrhoea	у меня понос	*U menya ponos*
Help!	Ёри диҳед!	*Yori dihed!*

TAJIK NUMBERS

English	Tajik	Pronunciation
one	як	*yak*
two	ду	*doo*
three	се	*sye*
four	чаҳор	*chahor*
five	панҷ	*panç*
six	шаш	*shash*
seven	ҳафт	*haft*
eight	ҳашт	*hasht*
nine	нӯҳ	*nwh*

ten	дах̗	*dah*
20	бист	*bist*
100	сад	*sad*
1,000	як ҳазор	*yak hazor*
1,000,000	милён	*milyon*

HELPFUL RUSSIAN PHRASES

English	Russian	Pronunciation
Hello	Здравствуйте	*zdrahst-vooy-tyeh*
How are you?	Как дела?	*kahg dee-lah?*
Fine, thank you	Хорошо, спасибо	*khah-rah-shoh spah-see-buh*
What is your name?	Как Вас зовут?	*kahk vahs zah-voot?*
My name is …	Меня зовут …	*mee-nyah zah-voot …*
Nice to meet you	Очень приятно	*oh-cheen' pree-yaht-nuh*
Please	Пожалуйста	*pah-zhah-luh-stuh*
Thank you	Спасибо	*spuh-see-buh*
You're welcome	Не за что	*nyeh-zuh-shtoh*
Yes	Да	*dah*
No	Нет	*nyeh*
Sorry	Простите	*Prostite*
Excuse me (getting attention)	Извините	*eez-vee-neet-yeh*
Is there someone here who speaks English?	Кто-нибудь здесь говорит по-английски?	*ktoh-nee-bood' zdyehs guh-vah-reet pah an-glees-kee?*
I don't understand	Я не понимаю	*ya nee puh-nee-migh-yoo*
Please speak more slowly	Вы не могли бы говорить помедленнее?	*Vy ne mogli by govorit' pomedlennee?*
Where is …?	Где …?	*gde …?*
Where is the toilet?	Где туалет?	*gdyeh too-ah-lyeht?*
How much is this?	Сколько это стоит?	*Skol'ko èto stoit?*
I'm sick	Я болен (m) / Я больна (f)	*yah-boh-leen (m) / yah-bahl'-nah (f)*
I have diarrhoea	у меня понос	*u menya ponos*
Help!	Помогите!	*puh-mah-gee-tyeh!*

RUSSIAN NUMBERS

English	Russian	Pronunciation
one	один	*ahdeen*
two	два	*dvah*
three	три	*tree*
four	четыре	*cheetyhree*
five	пять	*pyaht'*
six	шесть	*shehst*
seven	семь	*syeem*
eight	восемь	*vohseem*
nine	девять	*dyeveet*
ten	десять	*dyesiht*
20	двадцать	*dvahdzuht*
100	сто	*stoh*
1,000	тысяча	*tyhseechuh*
1,000,000	миллион	*meeleeibn*

Appendix 2

GLOSSARY

Apteka	Pharmacy
ASSR	Autonomous Soviet Socialist Republic
Aviakassa	Airline ticket office
Avtobus	Bus
Avtostansiya	Bus stand
Babushka	Grandmother or older woman
Bagh	Garden
Basmachi	Muslim resistance fighters who fought the Bolsheviks
Buz kashi	Traditional sport played on horseback with a goat carcass in place of a ball
Caravanserai	Ancient hostelry for merchants and their animals
Chai	Tea
Chaykhona	Café or tea house
Chorsu	Crossroads
CIS	Commonwealth of Independent States
Dacha	Holiday home
Dariakhana	Pharmacy
Darya	River
Dom	Building or house
FSB	Current incarnation of the KGB
FSU	Former Soviet Union
GAI	Traffic police
Great Game	See box, pages 12–13
Hakimat	Municipal building
Ikat	Striped silk
IMU	Islamic Movement of Uzbekistan
IRP	Islamic Renaissance Party
Ismaili	Shiite sect; followers of the Aga Khan
Kala	Fortress

Kassa	Cashier
Khoja	Descendant of Arabian missionaries
Kino	Cinema
Koh	Mountain
Kupe	Locking railway compartment containing four bunks
Kurgan	Burial mound, typically of the Iron Age
Kurt	Salty, dried curd balls
Laghman	Noodle soup
LOI	Letter of Invitation
Madrasa	Islamic school
Manty	Meat-filled steamed dumplings
Marshrutka	Minibus
Maydoni	Square
Mazar	Mausoleum
Minor	Minaret
Non	Round, flat bread
Nowruz	Persian New Year
Oblast	Administrative region
OVIR	Office for visas and registration
Oxus	Greek name for the Amu Darya River
Piala	Handleless teacup
Platzkart	Economy-class train travel, featuring bunks in open compartments
Plov	Rice-based dish with meat and carrot
Prospekt	Avenue
Samsa	Meat-filled pastry
Shashlik	Skewered lumps of meat cooked over coals
Somoni	Tajikistan's currency
SSR	Soviet Socialist Republic
Sufi	Mystic Islamic tradition
Suzani	Embroidered fabric, usually used as a wall hanging or bedspread
Tepa	Fort
TsUM	Central department store
Turbaza	Soviet holiday camp
Ulitsa	Street
Viloyat	Province

Appendix 3

FURTHER INFORMATION

BOOKS
History and archaeology

Bergne, Paul *Birth of Tajikistan: National Identity and the Origins of the Republic* IB Tauris, 2007. Examination of Tajikistan as a nation state, from the time of the Bolshevik Revolution through the transformation of the khanates, and the creation of the Soviet Socialist Republic of Tajikistan.

Boulnois, Luce *Silk Road: Monks, Warriors and Merchants* Odyssey Illustrated Guides, 2012. Detailed history of the people and ideas that spread along the Silk Road. Also available in French.

Frankopan, Peter *The Silk Roads: A New History of the World* Bloomsbury, 2015. Vast and authoritative tome reassessing world history and exploring the importance of the Silk Roads – and central Asia in particular – as the cradles of civilisation.

Hiro, Dilip *Inside Central Asia: A Political and Cultural History of Uzbekistan, Turkmenistan, Kazakhstan, Kyrgyzstan, Tajikistan, Turkey, and Iran* Gerald Duckworth & Co Ltd, 2011. A straightforward introduction to the former Soviet republics of central Asia, and their immediate neighbours.

Hopkirk, Peter *The Great Game: On Secret Service in High Asia* John Murray, 2006. The seminal work on the Great Game. Lively, scholarly and full of all the excitement of a *Boy's Own* adventure.

Nourzhanov, Kirill, and Bleuer, Christian *Tajikistan: A Political and Social History* ANU Press, 2013. Authoritative study of state formation and identity from the ancient world to the modern nation state.

Soucek, Svat *A History of Inner Asia* Cambridge University Press, 2000. A scholarly account of the history of a complex region.

Whitfield, Susan *Aurel Stein on the Silk Road* British Museum Press, 2004. Beautifully illustrated account of Stein's exploration of central Asia and of his archaeological finds.

Wood, Michael *In the Footsteps of Alexander the Great: A Journey from Greece to India* BBC Books, 2004. A fascinating accompaniment to the television series of the same name.

Post-independence Tajikistan

Akiner, Shirin *Tajikistan: The Trials of Independence* Routledge, 2016. Eleven experts on central Asia provide their analysis of the political and social turmoil which characterised the first few years of independence in Tajikistan.

Bliss, Frank *Social and Economic Change in the Pamirs (Gorno-Badakhshan, Tajikistan)* Routledge, 2006.

Heathershaw, John *Post-Conflict Tajikistan: The politics of Peacebuilding and the Emergence of Legitimate Order* Routledge, 2011. Academic discourse on the nature of Tajikistan's civil war and the challenges of peace-building in an authoritarian state. Draws on personal fieldwork and observer reports.

Central Asian geopolitics

Jonson, Lena *Tajikistan in the New Central Asia: Geopolitics, Great Power Rivalry and Radical Islam* IB Tauris, 2009. Jonson explores Tajikistan's many internal contradictions and challenges, their impact on internal development and foreign policy, and potential paths for the future.

Müllerson, Rein *Central Asia: A Chessboard and Player in the New Great Game* Routledge, 2007. Looks at the geopolitics of the region, with the central Asian republics themselves as players (as against the 19th-century works about the Great Game which tended to regard the region as merely the chessboard across which the 'game' was played out by the great powers).

Whitlock, Monica *Beyond the Oxus: The Central Asians* John Murray, 2002. Vivid account of the last three decades of central Asia's history, including the civil war, by a former BBC correspondent to central Asia. This book is also published with the title *Land Beyond the River: The Untold Story of Central Asia*.

Travellers' accounts

Byron, Robert *The Road to Oxiana* OUP, 2007. The classic traveller's tale of the author's own exploration of central Asia in the 1930s.

Colegrave, Bill *Halfway House to Heaven: Unravelling the Mystery of the Majestic River Oxus* Bene Factum, 2010. Vivid account that incorporates both scholarship and exploration and is accompanied by fine photography.

Curzon, George Nathaniel *The Pamirs and the Source of the Oxus* Adamant Media Corporation, 2002. Lord Curzon's 1896 edition of his account of his search for the sources of the Oxus River has been republished for modern audiences.

Metcalfe, Daniel *Out of Steppe: The Lost Peoples of Central Asia* Hutchinson, 2009. Adventurous traveller Metcalfe traverses central Asia in pursuit of distinct ethnic communities disappearing as modernity impinges on their way of life. A finely written and often moving account.

Omrani, Bijan *Asia Overland: Tales of Travel on the Trans-Siberian and Silk Road* Odyssey Guides, 2010. Beautifully written and heavily illustrated historical travelogue drawing on accounts from Fa Xian to Anton Chekhov, and Marco Polo to Francis Younghusband. Full of humour, it is an entertaining and informative read for armchair travellers and modern-day explorers alike.

Paley, Matthieu and Mareile *Pamir* Knesebeck, 2012. Sublime photographic record of the travels of Paley and his wife in the Pamirs. The text is in German but the images speak for themselves.

Thubron, Colin *The Lost Heart of Asia* HarperCollins, 1994. The author travels through central Asia soon after the emergence of the independent republics. This is one of a spate of accounts of travels through the region written during this turbulent period. Elegantly written, though Uzbekistan grabs far more of the author's attention than does Tajikistan.

Wood, John *A Journey to the Source of the River Oxus* Adamant Media Corporation, 2001. Reprint of Wood's 1872 book of the same title. Interesting to compare his account with that of Curzon (see above).

Culture, traditions and language

Harvey, Janet *Traditional Textiles of Central Asia* Thames & Hudson, 1997. Good introduction to the textiles of the region.

Hunsberger, Alice *Nasir Khusraw – The Ruby of Badakhshan: A Portrait of the Persian Poet, Traveller and Philosopher* IB Tauris, 2002. Accessible biography of the 11th-century Tajik poet and thinker.

Knobloch, Edgar *Monuments of Central Asia: A Guide to the Archaeology, Art and Architecture of Turkestan* IB Tauris, 2000. Scholarly overview of artistic styles and influences.

Levin, Theodore *The Hundred Thousand Fools of God: Musical Travels in Central Asia* Indiana University Press, 1999. A rare and accessibly ethnomusicological study of central Asia which includes everything from Sufi chants to Uzbek pop stars! The books comes with an accompanying CD.

Middleton, Robert and Thomas, Huw *Tajikistan and the High Pamirs* Odyssey Publications, 2012. Beautifully illustrated guide focused on the history, culture and traditions of Tajikistan.

Sheppard, Katya *The Sandalwood Box* Scribner, 1976. To our knowledge, the only English translation of Tajik folk tales.

Other Bradt guides to nearby destinations

Brummell, Paul *Kazakhstan* Bradt Travel Guides, 2nd edition 2011 (forthcoming 3rd edition due in 2018)

Ibbotson, Sophie and Lovell-Hoare, Max *Uzbekistan*, Bradt Travel Guides, 2nd edition 2016

Mitchell, Laurence *Kyrgyzstan* Bradt Travel Guides, 3rd edition 2015

MAGAZINES

Open Central Asia Magazine Quarterly magazine, published in the UK, focused on the cultures, politics and events of central Asia and the Caucasus. It is distributed for free by the embassies, chambers of commerce, airlines, etc, and stories can also be read online at **w** ocamagazine.com.

MAPS
Tajikistan

Dushanbe 1:24,000 Tochikkoinot Maps, 2004. Large-scale city map available in Dushanbe. Russian only.

Northern Tajikistan 1:500,000 Gecko Maps, 2008. Topographical map focused on Sughd and the Pamir Mountains. Map and legend in English.

The Pamirs 1:500,000 Gecko Maps 2016. Produced with the assistance of the Swiss Agency for Development and Cooperation. Topographical map with information on cultural sites of particular interest.

Southern Tajikistan 1:500,000 Gecko Maps, 2008. Sister map to Northern Tajikistan, but covering the southern parts of the country.

Tajikistan Tourist Map 1:1,200,00 SUE Map Factory, 2009. Available in Dushanbe in both English and Russian editions.

Tourist map Zarafshan Valley 1:400,000 Yagnob Valley 1:100,000 SUE Map Factory, 2009. ZTDA map of trekking routes and key sites in the Zarafshan and Yagnob valleys. Available from the ZTDA office and the Bactria Centre in Dushanbe.

Maps.Me (**w** *maps.me*) has downloadable map apps, including of Tajikistan, which can be used completely offline. This is hugely helpful in areas with no 3G/4G, and on occasions when you don't want to be racking up international data charges.

Central Asia

Central Asia 1:1,750,000 Gizi Map, 2011. Large, predominantly topographic sheet map with a detailed index of places. Driving distances are given for major routes.

Central Asia 1:1,750,000 Nelles Map, 2014. Combined political and topographical map, including a small city plan of Dushanbe.

Zentralasien 1:1,500,000 Freytag and Berndt, 2010. Road map of central Asia with accompanying booklet of street plans and index arranged by country. In German.

WEBSITES
Tajik government sites
W parlament.tj/en Website of the parliament.
W mfa.tj Website of the Ministry of Foreign Affairs. Contains visa information.

Travel advice
W caravanistan.com Central Asia travel portal with excellent, regularly updated information on everything from bus routes to border closures. There are also plenty of feature stories to inspire you.

W fco.gov.uk/travel Foreign and Commonwealth Office travel advice.

W pamirs.org Pamirs-specific site including cultural information, suggested itineraries, maps, permits and practical advice.

W tajikistantourism.org Volunteer-led not-for-profit organisation aiming to develop tourism in southern Tajikistan, and to inform travellers about the opportunities the region offers.

W travel.state.gov US State Department travel advice.

W trekkinginthepamirs.com Trekking blog providing detailed information about routes in the Pamirs and Zarafshan Mountains. Includes some excellent photography. The blogger, Jan Bakker, also produces a trekking guide of the same name, downloadable as a PDF from the website. Jan is currently writing a new Tajikistan trekking guide that is due to be published by Cicerone in late 2018.

W ukintajikistan.fco.gov.uk Website of the British Embassy in Tajikistan.

News and political analysis
W bbc.co.uk/tajik Home of the BBC Tajik service.

W eurasianet.org News and analysis covering the central Asian region on a site run by the Open Society Institute.

W roberts-report.com Analysis of central Asian stories put together by US academic Sean Roberts, an expert on Kazakhstan.

W theconwaybulletin.com Weekly commentary on regional news stories by James Kilner, a former Reuters correspondent and central Asia correspondent for the *Daily Telegraph*.

W timesca.com The Bishkek-based *Times of Central Asia* reports in English on all five central Asian republics, plus Afghanistan.

Culture
W akdn.org/tajikistan_culture.asp Portal for the AKDN's cultural work in Tajikistan, including its preservation of traditional music.

W bactriacc.org Arts development and exhibition centre in Dushanbe.

NOTES

Index

Page numbers in **bold** indicate main entries; those in *italics* indicate maps.

INDEX OF ADVERTISERS